The Social Analysis of Class Structure

edited by

FRANK PARKIN

TAVISTOCK PUBLICATIONS

First published in 1974
by Tavistock Publications Limited
11 New Fetter Lane, London EC4
Printed in Great Britain in 10 on 12 pt Plantin
by Willmer Brothers Limited, Birkenhead

ISBN 0 422 74460 3 (hardbound)
ISBN 0 422 74470 0 (paperback)

A
/301.44

Distributed in the USA by
HARPER & ROW PUBLISHERS, INC.
BARNES & NOBLE IMPORT DIVISION

5

The Social Analysis of Class Structure

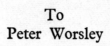

To
Peter Worsley

Contents

Contributors

SHEILA ALLEN, born 1930. Studied at London School of Economics, BA and post-graduate course in Anthropology. Research Assistant, L.S.E.; anthropological research in South East Asia; Senior Research Assistant, L.S.E.; has held various teaching posts in Birmingham, Leicester, and Bradford; Professor of Sociology at University of Bradford since 1972.

Author of *New Minorities, Old Conflicts*, 1971.

Since 1970, director of the Social Science Research Council financed project 'Youth and Work: A Study of Differential Ethnic Group Experience' at University of Bradford.

ZYGMUNT BAUMAN, born 1925, Poland. Studied at University of Warsaw, BA, 1950; MA, 1954; PhD, 1956. Lecturer in, then held Chair of General Sociology, Warsaw, 1953-68; Professor of Sociology at Universities of Tel-Aviv and Haifa, 1968-71; since 1971 Professor of Sociology at University of Leeds; Visiting Professor at the Universities of California, Yale, Manchester, and Sir George Williams; Chief Editor of the quarterly *Studia Socjologiczne*, 1960-68.

Author of *Outline of Sociology; Outline of the Marxist Theory of Society Culture and Society; Between Class and Elite; Culture as Praxis.*

FRANK BECHHOFER, born 1935, Germany. Studied at Cambridge University, BA (Mechanical Sciences); MA. Junior Research Officer, Department of Applied Economics, Cambridge University, 1962-5; Lecturer in Sociology, University of Edinburgh, 1965-71; Reader since 1971.

Co-author of the *Affluent Worker* studies, 1968-9; editor of *Population Growth and the Brain Drain*, 1969.

LESLIE BENSON, born 1941, Northumberland. Studied at Cambridge University, BA, 1964. 1964-6, school-teaching; Yugoslav Government Scholar, Belgrade, 1966-7; Research Student, Department of Sociology,

University of Kent, 1967, where he wrote a PhD thesis on stratification in Yugoslavia; in 1971 became Research Fellow at the Centre for Research in Social Sciences, at University of Kent; since 1974 Lecturer in Sociology at Massey University, New Zealand.

RICHARD BLAND, born 1944, Glasgow. Studied at University of Edinburgh, MA (Sociology and Social Anthropology). Research Associate, University of Edinburgh, 1969-72; since 1972, Lecturer in Sociology, University of Stirling.

J. M. COUSINS, born 1944, London. Studied at Oxford University, BA, and at London School of Economics. Research Assistant, University of Durham 1968-70; Research Officer, University of Bradford, 1970-71; Research Fellow, University of Durham, 1971-4.

R. L. DAVIS, born 1946, London, Studied at University of Sussex, BA, 1967; MA, 1969; Centre for Mass Communication Research, University of Leicester, 1969-71. Research Fellow, University of Durham, 1971-3; currently Research Fellow, Tynemouth Community Development Project, Newcastle upon Tyne Polytechnic.

BRIAN ELLIOTT, born 1941, London. Studied at University of Edinburgh, MA (Social Anthropology). Assistant Lecturer, University of Glasgow, 1963-5; since 1965, Lecturer, University of Edinburgh.

ROBERT Q. GRAY, born 1945, Glasgow. Studied at Cambridge University, BA; University of Edinburgh, PhD. Lecturer at Portsmouth Polytechnic since 1970.

Author of 'Styles of Life, the "Labour Aristocracy" and Class Relations' in *International Review of Social History* (1973); and 'Thrift and Working Class Mobility in Victorian Edinburgh', in A.A. MacLaren (ed.), *Essays in Class and Society* (forthcoming).

GAVIN MACKENZIE, born 1942, Bournemouth. Studied at University of Leicester, BA; Brown University, MA, PhD. Lecturer in Sociology,

Smith College, 1967-8; Lecturer in Sociology, University of Leicester, 1968-70; Fellow of Jesus College Cambridge and University Assistant Lecturer in Sociology, 1970-72; University Lecturer and fellow of Jesus College since 1973.

Author of *The Aristocracy of Labour: The Position of Skilled Craftsmen in the American Class Structure*, 1973; and *Class Theory and the Division of Labour* (forthcoming).

JANE MARCEAU, born 1943, Lincolnshire. Studied at London School of Economics, BA; Cambridge University, PhD. Lecturer in Sociology, University of Essex, 1967-72; currently Research Fellow, University of Essex.

Resident in France and engaged on Social Science Research Council financed study of a young French business elite.

Currently preparing a book on class and status in France.

CHRIS MIDDLETON, born 1946. Brighton. Studied at London School of Economics, BA (Sociology), 1971. Temporary Lecturer, University of Kent, 1971-2; Temporary Lecturer, University of Sheffield, 1972-4; from October 1974 will be Lecturer in Political Sociology at University of Sheffield.

Currently preparing book analysing the situation of women in Western capitalist societies.

FRANK PARKIN, born 1931, Aberdare, Glamorgan. Studied at London School of Economics, 1958-61; PhD, 1966. Assistant Lecturer in Sociology, University of Hull, 1964-5; currently Reader in Sociology, University of Kent.

Author of *Middle Class Radicalism*, 1968; *Class, Inequality and Political Order*, 1971.

W. G. RUNCIMAN, born 1934, London. Cambridge University Harkness Fellow, 1958-60; Fellow, Trinity College, Cambridge, 1959-63; Part-time Reader in Sociology, University of Sussex, 1967-9; Visiting Lecturer in Sociology, Harvard University, 1970; Fellow, Trinity College, Cambridge since 1971.

Author of *Social Science and Political Theory*, 1963; *Relative Deprivation and Social Justice*, 1966; *Sociology in its Place, and Other Essays*, 1970; *A Critique of Max Weber's Philosophy of Social Science*, 1972.

MONICA RUSHFORTH, born 1929, Lowestoft. Studied at University of Edinburgh, MA, 1951; MSc, 1968. Research Associate and subsequently Research Fellow, University of Edinburgh, 1964-72; Research Officer, Home Office Research Unit (Scottish Section), since 1972.

RICHARD SCASE. Studied at University of Leicester, BA (Soc.Sc.), MA. Senior Research Associate, University of East Anglia; Lecturer in Sociology, University of Kent at Canterbury; Chairman of Board of Studies for Sociology and Social Anthropology, 1973-4.

Currently engaged in research into aspects of social stratification in Sweden, with particular reference to the consequences of social democracy.

CHRISTOPHER SMITH, born 1947. Studied at Kingston Polytechnic, BSc Sociology (London); London School of Economics, MSc. Since 1971 Research Worker on the Social Science Research Council financed 'Youth and Work' project at University of Bradford.

Preface

With the exception of my contribution, all the papers brought together in this volume were originally presented at the British Sociological Association's Conference on Social Stratification, held at the University of Surrey in April 1973.

January 1974   Frank Parkin

Preface

Acknowledgements

The following bodies are thanked for their permission to reproduce material. Full details of sources are given in the text and references.

In connection with Jane Marceau's paper, 'Education and Social Mobility in France', *Table 1*: Librairie Armand Colin; *Table 2*: Institut National d'Études Démographiques; *Table 3*: Francois Maspero; *Table 4*: Ministère de L' Education Nationale; *Table 5*: Pierre Bourdieu, Directeur du Centre de Sociologie Européenne; *Table 6*: Institut National d'Études Démographiques; *Table 7*: L'Année Sociologique; *Table 10*: Professor H. C. de Bettignes, The European Institute of Business Administration; *Table 11*: *L'Expansion*.

In connection with Leslie Benson's paper, 'Market Socialism and Class Structure', *Tables 1* and *2*: Professor Josip Zupanov, University of Zagreb.

FRANK PARKIN

Strategies of Social Closure
in Class Formation

Although social relations both within and between classes or strata could be said to form part of a unitary stratification scheme they are conventionally treated as entirely different phenomena. For the most part, inter-class relations are viewed as an expression of certain generic features of the social system, whether conceived of in terms of property rights, authority relations, or the division of labour. Typically, classes are represented as paired, logically exhaustive categories – propertied and propertyless, superordinate and subordinate, manual and non-manual – dichotomies that seek to reveal the fundamental line of cleavage or structural 'fault' in the stratification order.

Divisions within classes on the other hand are not normally construed in terms of similar systemic principles, and least of all are such divisions represented as an extension of the same principles that govern inter-class relations. The intra-class distinctions commonly employed appear to take shape under the imprint of purely national conditions and lack those universal properties that characterize the relationship between class and class. Thus, in the sociology of the working class the terminology of affluent and traditional, new and old, rough and respectable, secular and deferential, and so forth, set up distinctions that appear to derive more from the British version of modern capitalism than from its universal, systematic features.[1] This capitalism-in-one-country approach serves perhaps as a more acceptable framework for the analysis of internal class relations than of the relations between classes because of the striking contrast in what is taken to be sociologically problematic in the two cases. Inter-class relations are conceived of as inherently antagonistic, a condition only to be comprehended through the idiom of dichotomy and conflict. At the intra-class level, however, the emphasis upon competitive struggle gives way to a rather blander concern with the niceties of social differentiation. The subject of investigation here becomes (among the working class) variations in

life-style and social consciousness or (among the middle class) variations
in the social composition and recruitment of elites. Sociological in-
genuity is directed to mapping out the social contours of a territory in
which a truce has been declared in the *omnium bellum contra omnes*.
Social differentiation within a given class, moreover, is analysed by
reference to conceptual categories that generally do not correspond to
existentially based groups with the capacity for mobilization; even less
could they be said to constitute social collectivities in mutal competition
for scarce resources. It is this contrast between the use of existentially
grounded social categories and purely formal or analytic categories that
demonstrates the extent to which inter-class and intra-class relations
are regarded as distinct phenomena requiring different conceptual
treatment.

The emphatic shift from conflict to social differentiation as the guiding
principle of intra-class analysis is largely attributable to the powerful
assumption that social action cannot be explained in terms of its
conflictual elements unless it is set within a framework of dichotomy.
Where class is defined by reference to dual, logically exhaustive
categories it follows that such antagonisms as occur *within* any given
category cannot properly be understood as manifestations of class
conflict in the accredited sense. A further difficulty stemming from the
definition of class as a procrustean dualism is encountered in the
analysis of the crucial middle levels of the stratification system. The
assignment of social groups to one of two inclusive categories is highly
productive of anomalies in the shape of those groups whose actions and
beliefs depart from the standards identified as typical for the class as a
whole. Thus, within the manual/non-manual definition of class the
inclusion of lower white-collar groups within the ranks of the professional middle class is not easily reconciled with those political and
economic activities that lend credence to the thesis of white-collar
proletarianization. This problem is of course even more acute for the
Marxist classificatory scheme in which the salaried bourgeoisie is
located on the propertyless side of the capital–labour divide. Such
anomalies necessarily arise from the use of a definitional framework
in which the complexities of class are squeezed into a simple zero-sum
model on the grounds that only this type of scheme is capable of
capturing the conflictual essence of class.

One final difficulty with current usages is that the vocabulary of class
does not readily lend itself to the analysis of stratification and cleavage
associated with membership in racial, ethnic, religious, and linguistic
communities. Communal divisions are normally seen as an outgrowth

of cultural diversity in which antagonisms between those of different colour, faith, or language are treated as the product of historically specific factors and not as inherent attributes of the social system.[2] The common properties of these diverse cleavages are not accorded the same theoretical weighting as the common properties of class; indeed, because class is characteristically held to be a systemic and universal feature of industrial society, and hence irreducible to specific cultural attributes, the temptation has been to treat communal antagonisms as a distorted version of class conflict or as residual, anachronistic features of an otherwise modern society.[3]

Alternatively, the acceptance of communal antagonisms as having a reality *sui generis* is generally accompanied by a theoretical recommendation to treat ascriptively based cleavages as fundamentally different in nature from the cleavages of class, such that the two phenomena need to be understood through the use of distinct sociological vocabularies.[4] The appeal of such a position could hardly fail to feed upon the inadequacies of current definitions and usages of class, given that communal conflict is not easily aligned with the prevalent treatment of intra-class relations as mere social differentiation.

In brief then, it may be suggested that the conceptualization of class in terms of dual, logically exhaustive categories (whatever particular form this classification takes) raises certain difficulties in the analysis of intermediate levels of the stratification system as well as of intra-class relations, particularly those of a communal nature. An alternative approach to class analysis which preserves the traditional and necessary focus on dichotomy without its constrictive zero-sum accompaniments, is contained in embryo form at least in Weber's concept of social closure.

By social closure Weber means the process by which social collectivities seek to maximize rewards by restricting access to rewards and opportunities to a limited circle of eligibles. This entails the singling out of certain identifiable social or physical attributes as the justificatory basis of exclusion. Weber suggests that virtually any group attribute – race, language, social origin, descent – may be seized upon provided it can be used for 'the monopolization of specific, usually economic opportunties' (Weber 1968: 342). 'This monopolization is directed against competitors who share some positive or negative characteristics; its purpose is always the closure of social and economic opportunities to *outsiders*' (Weber 1968). Social closure can be effected by groups located at any level in the stratification order, although the criteria adopted for exclusion purposes by any given group are likely to depend upon its general location in the distributive system.

Surprisingly, Weber's elaboration of the closure theme is not linked in any immediate way with his other main contributions to stratification theory despite the fact that techniques of inclusion and exclusion can properly be conceived of as an aspect of the distribution of power, which for Weber is practically synonymous with stratification. As a result, the usefulness of the concept for the study of class becomes conditional upon the acceptance of certain refinements and enlargements upon the original usage. An initial step in this direction is to extend the notion of closure to encompass other forms of competitive social action designed to maximize collective claims to rewards and opportunities. Strategies for laying claim to resources would thus include not only practices of social exclusion but also those adopted by the excluded themselves as a direct response to their status as outsiders. It is in any case hardly plausible to consider the effectiveness of exclusion practices without due reference to the countervailing actions of socially defined ineligibles. As Weber points out, 'such group action may provoke a corresponding reaction on the part of those against whom it is directed' (Weber 1968). In other words, collective efforts to resist a pattern of dominance governed by exclusion principles can properly be regarded as the other half of the social closure equation. This usage is in fact employed by Weber in his discussions of 'community closure' which, as Neuwirth (1969) has shown, bears directly upon those forms of collective action mounted by the excluded – i.e. 'negatively privileged status groups'. These brief remarks will have to suffice as ritual clearance for tampering with the original usage however unsatisfactory they are bound to seem to those who equate theoretical practice with textual exegesis.

The suggestion offered above to the effect that social closure refers to two distinct, reciprocal types of action can now be restated more formally as a distinction between two general strategies for staking claims to resources: those based upon the power of *exclusion* and those based upon the power of *solidarism*. These may be thought of as the two main generic forms of social closure, the former harbouring certain sub-types shortly to be identified.

Strategies of exclusion may be regarded as the predominant mode of closure in all stratification systems. The common element in these strategies is the attempt by a given social group to maintain or enhance its privileges by the process of subordination – i.e. the creation of another group or stratum of ineligibles beneath it. Where the latter in their turn also succeed in closing off access to remaining rewards and opportunities, so multiplying the number of sub-strata, the stratification order approaches that condition of political defusion that represents the furthest point of contrast to the Marxist model of class polarization. The traditional caste system and the stratification of ethnic communities in the United States provide the clearest illustrations of this type of closure pattern, though similar processes are easily detectable in societies in which class formation is paramount.

Strategies of closure referred to here by the generic term solidarism may be regarded as collective responses of excluded groups which are themselves unable to maximize resources by exclusion practices. The crucial distinction between these two modes of closure is that techniques of exclusion exert political pressure downwards, as it were, in that group advantages are secured at the expense of collectivities that can successfully be defined as inferior; whereas strategies of solidarism direct pressure upwards in so far as claims upon resources threaten to diminish the share of more privileged strata. Thus whereas exclusion is a form of closure that stabilizes the stratification order, solidarism is one that contains a potential challenge to the prevailing system of distribution through the threat of usurpation.

All this indicates the ease with which the language of closure can be translated into the language of power. Modes of closure can be thought of as a different means of mobilizing power for purposes of staking claims to resources and opportunities. To conceive of power as a built-in attribute of closure is at the very least to dispense with these fruitless searches for its 'location' inspired by Weber's more familiar but completely unhelpful definition in terms of the ubiquitous struggle between contending wills. Moreover, to speak of power in the light of closure principles encourages a reconceptualization of class along the lines of a dichotomy which, as will be made clear in due course, is not subject to the inflexibilities of current models. At this stage, however, all that needs to be said by way of illustration is that the division between bourgeoisie and proletariat, in its classic as well as its modern guise, may be understood as an expression of conflict between collectivities defined not specifically in relation to their place in the productive process but in relation to their prevalent modes of closure: exclusion and solidarism. From this angle, it is possible to visualize the fundamental cleavage in the stratification order as that point where one set of closure strategies gives way to a radically different set. To make the same point differently, the main structural fault in any stratification system falls along the line where power undergoes change in its organizing principles and its directional flow. This play with metaphor can now make way for a rather more concrete exposition of the argument.

SOCIAL CLOSURE AS EXCLUSION

As previously noted, strategies of exclusion are the predominant form of closure in all stratification systems. Historically, the rise and consolidation of ruling groups has been effected by the restriction of access to valued resources, such as land, esoteric knowledge, or arms, to a limited circle of eligibles marked out by certain social characteristics. Aristocratic domination and control of resources through the rules of descent is the obvious example from recent European history of this type of closure. Bourgeois forms of exclusion, by contrast, do not typically rest upon the restrictions of descent or similar group criteria for their effectiveness, but more upon what Weber calls the 'rational commitment to values'. Forms of exclusion based on such a commitment can be said to characterize those class or similar formations whose main political ingredient is the right to nominate successors rather than to ensure the transmission of statuses to lineal descendants. The medieval church and the Soviet communist party provide examples of ruling groups whose criteria of recruitment and exclusion are designed to ensure continuity through the nomination of suitable replacements and not by the simple transfer of positions to kith and kin.[5] 'Classes of nomination' are thus the product of exclusion rules that single out the specific attributes of individuals rather than the generalized attributes of social collectivities. By contrast, exclusion practices centred upon the collectively defined qualities of men are strategies of closure typically adopted by 'classes of reproduction', since the emphasis upon group as against individual characteristics is the most effective way of transmitting privileges to one's own, whether defined by lineage, colour, religion, language, or whatever.

This suggests that the contrast between classes of nomination and classes of reproduction is best thought of as expressive of a more general distinction: that between individualist and collectivist rules of exclusion.[6] Such a distinction refers not only to the processes underlying class recruitment and succession but also the means by which access to public goods and social resources in general is similarly monitored. It is not altogether sufficient to define class in terms of the denial of access to productive property, whether as ownership or control, since this form of exclusion is not necessarily coterminous with restricted access to political and civil rights, housing, education, and public resources external to the division of labour. At any rate, the actual extent to which the collectively derived status of 'worker', arising from property exclusion, operates to disqualify men and their families from access to other social resources and opportunities is an empirical question the answer to which is certainly open to historical and national variation. In many respects, changes in class conditions over the past century or more can be seen as representing a gradual shift from collectivist to individualist forms of exclusion, such that class stigmata are less consequential for social relations beyond the workplace. Changes in the rules of political exclusion and the gradual extension of citizenship rights are indicative of this transition towards forms of social closure based more upon individual than group attributes. Similarly, the protracted struggle of the bourgeoisie against the aristocracy may be seen as an attempt by the former to dismantle purely collectivist rules of exclusion in favour of individualist criteria – as for example in the replacement of the patronage system of recruitment by one of public examination.

Individualist rules of exclusion reach their apogee in that complex of social practices that Miller (1967) has dubbed 'credentialism' – i.e., the reliance upon examination certificates as a means of controlling entry to valued positions in the division of labour. The political rationale of these practices is the establishment of universal criteria of selection and exclusion on the basis of specific personal qualities and attributes, so conforming to the classic liberal preference for classes of nomination over classes of reproduction. Strategies of credentialism appear to correspond closely to this ideal in so far as the continuous raising of examination hurdles as a means of monitoring entry to the professional middle class results in definite risks for the progeny of its present incumbents. As Miller's work has shown, in most advanced societies attempts by established elites to ensure that their status is reproduced by their own children are only about fifty per cent successful, indicating that the well born 'have no firm perch in the upper tiers of society' (Miller 1960: 50). However, it is well understood that the full attainment of the ideal liberal condition of individualist exclusion and class nomination is only feasible to the extent that the 'means of credentialism' are not monopolized by any one social group. If the relationship between individual capacity and performance standards is distorted by the transmission of what Bourdieu (1973) calls 'cultural capital' along kinship lines, then class selection by examinations and certificates results, intentionally or otherwise, in *de facto* collectivist exclusion and class reproduction.[7] Individualist criteria of exclusion through the application of universal rules thus cannot guarantee the liberal conditions of justice as long as the state tolerates the intrusion of socially inherited handicaps and easements that directly affect the individual's capacity to perform. This situation bears close comparison with the condition of political exclusion in the nineteenth century. Admission to the franchise was similarly governed by ostensibly individualist rules of property and residential qualifications and not by the open presumption of class membership. Workers able to meet the registration requirements were admitted to the suffrage whilst men of bourgeois origin who could not were excluded. Political exclusion thus appeared wholly compatible with the bourgeois rejection of collectivist discrimination. However the justice of such an arrangement was dependent upon the tacit disregard of those inequalities of condition that ensured that only a predictable few would be able to meet the standards of political entry.[7a] This is not simply analagous to the modern case of educational exclusion through selective tests but an extension of the same principles. Involved in each case is an interpretation of distributive justice in which the rhetoric of individualism and the principles of class nomination obscure the processes of *de facto* collectivist exclusion and class reproduction.

Interestingly, the liberal critique of this situation has shown a similar consistency of principle. The essence of the liberal view is that the rules of exclusion conform to the standards of justice only in so far as they succeed in discriminating between individuals on the basis of those capacities and performances that are not attributable to the facts of social inheritance. The campaign by liberal reformers for the removal of the franchise qualification thus finds its modern equivalent in the various campaigns for 'compensatory education' to aid the disadvantaged young in the competition for certificates against their middle-class rivals. Both are inspired by the wish to ensure that exclusion practices are truly compatible with the tenets of bourgeois individualism by counteracting or negating those human endowments that are strictly social in character, so corresponding to that Durkheimian ideal in which 'social inequalities exactly express natural inequalities' (Durkheim 1964: 377).

In so far as exclusion practices vary along an individualist–collectivist dimension it should follow that the social character of excluded groups is related to the predominance of one or other of these tendencies. In ideal-typical terms, wholly collectivist rules of closure would produce a communal situation, characterized by a total negative status, of which the apartheid system is the clearest example, although the condition of all social groups whose exclusion rests largely on the peculiarities of colour, religion, or language will approximate the communal pole. The opposite extreme is represented by closure practices based wholly on individualist criteria, so giving rise to a condition of segmental statuses – a model implicit in representations of the classless society as one of differentiated status groups. In non-fictional societies individualist and collectivist modes of exclusion always co-exist, if in different combinations, so that the actual range of possible class situations varies historically and nationally between the limits set by the communal and status group polarity. Changes in the overall class situation of the proletariat during the past century could thus be portrayed as a shift away from the communal towards the status group pole; that is, a situation in which the collective category 'worker' becomes less encompassing in its negative social consequences.

Another way of putting this is to say that changes in the predominant mode of exclusion are equivalent to changes in the legal and political foundations of exploitation. Exploitation is the term here applied to those institutional practices by which social groups seek to maximize rewards by closing off resources and opportunities to others, on whatever basis. Whether the chosen criterion of exclusion is property ownership or control, or examination certificates, or pigmentation, or faith, the processes involved are generically of a kind that exhibits the defining hallmark of exploitation: namely, the exercise of power in a downward direction to produce a condition of group subordination. To define exploitation in this way, as an inherent feature of exclusion practices, is to draw the sharpest possible contrast with solidaristic strategies of closure, the general aim of which is usurpation.

SOCIAL CLOSURE AS SOLIDARISM

Solidarism is a generic term designating the closure attempts of excluded groups, whether of a class or communal nature. Because they generally lack legal or state support, solidaristic efforts are heavily dependent upon the capacity for social mobilization on the part of the excluded. As Olsen (1965) has argued, there are special difficulties in mobilizing individuals for common goals under conditions of purely voluntary association. Rational calculus always poses a threat to solidaristic actions, so that the effectiveness of this mode of closure is always dependent in the last resort upon the exercise of physical or other sanctions upon recalcitrants. The power of solidarism is thus perhaps more fragile than the power of exclusion in so far as it incurs heavy costs of organization and social control which the other does not, partly because the social costs of exclusion are borne mainly by the state and not directly by those who benefit from them. Exclusion practices in any case do not demand the same intensity of social collaboration because they do not generate the same degree of tension between individual and group interest; within excluding groups the problem of blacklegging is somewhat remote. This suggests the hypothesis that forms of closure based upon exclusion would generally be considered preferable to solidaristic practices, such that the adoption of the latter would be expected to result from an inability to maximize opportunities through exclusion strategies.

Solidaristic efforts are always directed at the usurpation of resources in the sense that claims to rewards, if successful, will normally result in some diminution of the share accruing to superordinate groups. The range of possibilities here extends of course from marginal redistribution to total dispossession. But whatever the intended scale of usurpation it is an aim that generally implies alternative standards of distributive justice to those solemnized by the rules of exclusion. For example, acts of social closure on the part of communal minorities generally contain a challenge to the monopoly of resources held by the majority group through an attempt to replace collectivist by individualist rules of exclusion. Civil rights movements by minority groups exemplify this form of action, in which the goal of social inclusion calls for the dismantling of the structure of privilege resulting from collective discrimination. Because these claims articulate well with the individualist tenets of liberalism, integrationist demands by the communally excluded tend to be regarded as completely legitimate, at least in principle, by influential sections of the dominant majority;[8] the phenomenon of 'white liberalism' has its analogue in all situations of collectivist exclusion, whatever its basis.

Under purely class situations, solidaristic closure tends to bifurcate along industrial and political lines. The formal political expression of solidarism is of course the mass party, a movement whose social programme is generally not dissimilar from classic liberal ideals of justice as enshrined in the slogan 'equality of opportunity'. Indeed, social democracy can without too much exaggeration be regarded as the inheritor of that political tradition which seeks to establish the preconditions for a proper system of class nomination – a goal not unrelated to the presence of a credentialist stratum within its ranks.

On the industrial front, solidarism is confined almost exclusively to the redistributive conflict between capital and labour and with the containment of managerial authority. It would appear that the long-term decline in the communal components of class is accompanied by a corresponding increase in the importance of industrial over political aspects of closure. The long-term shift away from purely collectivist rules of exclusion tends to produce a class situation in which the totalizing character of communal status, with all its potentiality for a wholly shared political identity, gives way to a somewhat more fragmented condition in which the inevitability sectional interests arising from the division of labour come to provide the main impetus for action. Partly in response to this situation, and partly as a result of those autonomous developments described by Michels, the ability of the mass political party to act as the *conscience collective* of the excluded class is thrown into question – a condition in which the industrial forms of solidarism are likely to become increasingly important as elementary forms of the political life. However, even though the incorporation of the mass party into the political apparatus and assumptions of the excluding class may increase the likelihood of the industrial front itself becoming politicized, there are definite limits to the extent to which industrial solidarism can fill the political vacuum. The main challenge from this quarter is not one of a constitutional kind but one that in effect questions the market system of distributive justice. Industrial solidarism relies increasingly for its effectiveness not simply upon the capacity for social mobilization but also upon the capacity for social and economic dislocation. Although the threatened withdrawal of labour has always been the main form of leverage available to organized workers, it seems likely that the increasing interdependence of functions under conditions of advanced technology has endowed certain groups with an unprecedented degree of bargaining power. Workers in a number of key industries now enjoy a form of leverage arising from their 'disruptive potential' which is quite distinct from the social facts of organizational unity. In other words, it is not merely the potential for collective action that governs the effectiveness or otherwise of solidaristic forms of closure but also the purely contingent features of production. Given the apparently increasing importance of system location over specifically social elements of organization, leadership, militancy, etc., there may well be a case for adding this as a fourth dimension to Lockwood's tripartite definition of class (Lockwood 1958). At least it does now seem necessary to highlight the distinction between claims to rewards based upon market criteria such as scarce skills, and those based upon disruptive potential. The two sets of claims entail sharply opposed principles of allocation as dramatized by the efforts of excluding groups to anathematize these

effective forms of solidarism as blackmail.[9] This is because usurpation
carried out under the threat of economic and social dislocation challen-
ges not only market principles of distribution but, indirectly, all the
various strategies of exclusion that both feed upon and reinforce these
principles. It is in this indirect challenge that the main political significance of industrial solidarism lies.

Interestingly, the lack of any formal articulation of this position
probably reflects the uncertainty among organized labour as to the
acceptability of disruptive potential as an alternative standard of allocation, if only because this would produce similar or possibly greater
disparities within the working class than those generated by the market.
It is the contrast between productively central and productively
marginal groups that underlies those analyses of the current situation
in terms of a radical cleavage within the working class – between those
able to effect social closure and the new 'pauper class' unable to exert
industrial leverage.[10] Whatever reservations may be felt about this type
of analysis it does serve to highlight the extent to which purely industrial forms of solidarism are not easily translated into political action
on behalf of an entire excluded class. Significantly, there are few signs
of any concerted attempt to use industrial leverage for any overt
assault upon the institutional apparatus of exclusion itself – as against
its mere distributive consequences – a fact which might be thought to
have some bearing on the stability of social inequality.

DISCUSSION

The argument advanced in this paper is that the basic line of cleavage
in the stratification system is that resulting from the opposition between
two contrasting modes of social closure, exclusion and solidarism. This
suggests that the distinction between, for example, bourgeoisie and
proletariat may be conceptualized in terms of contrary principles of
social action, rather than as differences in the formal attributes of
collectivities. The concept of closure refers to the *processual* features of
class, thereby directing attention to the principles underlying class
formation. This processual emphasis gives due acknowledgement to
the essential fluidity of class arrangements, something not readily
captured by standard dichotomies. The assignment of particular
groups to one of two categories creates anomalies in the shape of those
groups whose actions and beliefs deviate significantly from the general
pattern considered typical for the class as a whole. These anomalies
arise not only within the context of Marxist property categories but also

within the more conventional manual/non-manual schema, more especially in analyses of the middle levels of the stratification order. The dilemmas arising from this procrustean treatment are felt, perhaps, to be an acceptable price to pay for the theoretical benefits accruing from the use of dichotomous models in highlighting the conflictual elements of class. The abandonment of such models would seem to be equated with the virtual dissolution of the class concept and its replacement by one of mere status differentiation with all its overtones of integration and consensus.

The position adopted in this paper is that dichotomy is indeed a proper device for the analysis of class, but that the use of *logically exhaustive* categories is not an essential requirement of this procedure. To define classes by reference to the processes of social closure is in fact to adopt the necessary idiom of conflict without resorting to the rigidities of formal dichotomy. It should be recognized that social collectivities can, and commonly do, adopt *dual* strategies of closure in seeking to maximize claims to resources. Although the class character of any group is determined by its primary mode of closure this by no means precludes the possibility of its adopting supplementary strategies of the contrary type. Indeed, the apparent anomalies of class may be seen to arise precisely from this tendency for certain groups to resort to the practices of both solidarism and exclusion. For example, the special position of the labour aristocracy in the class structure results from the use of certain exclusion techniques, such as the apprenticeship system, designed to restrict entry to skilled trades, in combination with closure strategies of a purely solidaristic kind aimed at the reallocation of resources between capital and labour.[11]

The ambiguities in the class position of the 'white-collar proletariat' may similarly be understood in terms of their adoption of dual strategies. Here the reliance upon exclusion devices of a credentialist kind, epitomized by the efforts to attain professional status, is generally supplemented by the purely solidaristic tactics of organized labour. This resort to dual closure strategies is altogether characteristic of intermediate groups in the stratification order; moreover, certain of the political tensions within these groups arise from this very attempt to reconcile contrary modes of closure in the search for an optimal power strategy.[12]

An illustration of this same tendency is provided in the case of intra-class cleavages occuring along communal lines. Social closure on the part of white or Protestant workers against blacks or Catholics is a classic illustration of the use of exclusion techniques by social groups that are themselves denied access to resources and opportunities by bourgeois rules of property and credentialism. Solidaristic responses to this latter condition appear to be fully compatible with the employment of exclusion tactics against minority groups, despite the apparent confusion of conventional political symbols.[13] Although the exclusion of minority groups is based predominantly on collectivist criteria, whereas bourgeois forms of closure are typically weighted towards individualism, this should not obscure their essential comparability. Exclusion practices justified by reference to faith, pigmentation, or language are generically similar to those sanctified by property rights or credentials in so far as they represent exploitative forms of social action in the sense already defined.

The adoption of dual modes of closure is indicative of the fact that conflicts over the distribution of resources occurring within classes are not phenomena of a separate order from the struggles between classes. The objection to defining classes as logically exhaustive categories is that it seriously inhibits such an approach; if conflict is treated as an aspect of zero-sum relationships, such antagonisms as occur between groups *within* one of the diametrically opposed categories must have a different phenomenal status to that of 'pure' conflict. It is perhaps partly for this reason that the sociological treatment of intra-class affairs concerns itself largely with categorizing elements of social differentiation from which the conventional vocabulary of conflict is conspicuously absent.

The crux of the problem here is that the use of zero-sum categories precludes acknowledgement that the attributes by which one class is defined may also be possessed in lesser measure by the opposing class. Current usage requires us to treat collectivities as either manual *or* non-manual, propertied *or* propertyless, subordinate *or* superordinate; it is not logically possible to be partially manual, partially propertyless, or partially subordinate. And because classes are defined as logical opposites, relations within and relations between must refer to different orders of reality. Now it gives no affront to logic or common sense to state that a given social group may adopt strategies both of solidarism and exclusion; in other words that it possesses characteristics that are not merely typical of the opposing class but that are the very features distinguishing it as a class. Because it is entirely plausible to speak of primary and supplementary, or simply dual, closure practices it is possible to retain the necessary principle of dichotomy without the encumbrances of a zero-sum classification. Moreover, the emphasis upon modes of social action permits a definition of class that is sensitive to the possibilities of long-term changes in the position of different groups or strata. To treat, for example, the increasingly important lower white-collar groups as part of the 'non-manual' class does little to highlight the transformations that have taken place within this stratum over the past century; whereas the focus upon closure practices does point up the changing fortunes and character of these groups through time in which their non-manual status has remained constant.

In summary, Weber's concept of social closure recommends itself as a means of defining class in terms of those stratagems by which collectivities lay claim to and seek to justify rewards under changing material conditions. By focussing upon class as process it is somewhat better suited to capturing the elements of flux and ambiguity in class formation than are standard classifications. Finally, the vocabulary of closure is readily translatable into the language of power – not through the portrayal of power as a mysterious something extra whose uncertain location complicates the stratification system, but as a metaphor for describing the very operation of this system.

Notes

1 Giddens has pointed out for example that the notion of the 'new working class' appears to have different meanings in different national contexts. In French sociology it refers predominantly to qualified technical workers, whereas for American writers it is used to refer to the 'ethnic poor'. In British studies it appears to designate the 'non-traditional' segment of the working class.
  See Giddens (1973: 192–7; 215–222). Also Hörning (1971).
2 See the discussion of this point by Lockwood (1970.)
3 The view of racial and ethnic cleavages as anachronisms is of course an integral part of the convergence thesis:

> 'The differentiations among groups of workers that characterize the pre-industrial society – racial and ethnic groups, sex, residence and family – tend to be destroyed. A new set of priorities and differentiations is created based upon a wide range of occupations and job classifications, nationality or membership in labor organizations.' (Kerr, *et. al.* 1962: 250)

  For a critique of this position in the field of race relations see Blumer (1965).
4 The notion of 'plural society' is the obvious example of an alternative approach to class analysis. See again Lockwood (1970).

5 Orwell makes this point in his discussion of communist party oligarchy:

> 'The essence of oligarchial rule is not father-to-son inheritance, but the persistence of a certain world-view and a certain way of life, imposed by the dead upon the living. A ruling group is a ruling group so long as it can nominate its successors. The Party is not concerned with perpetuating its blood but with perpetuating itself.' Orwell (1949: 215)

6 This seems a preferable distinction to the more familiar contrast between ascription and achievement. 'Ascription' suggests exclusion on the basis of certain fixed social or physical attributes (colour, age, sex, etc.) whereas 'collectivist' carries a more general meaning of exclusion justified by reference to an individuals's assumed group membership of whatever kind.

The term 'achievement' is particularly unsatisfactory in so far as it implies a mode of social selection based on standards of justice which are 'non-discriminatory'. So much so that for many writers the shift from ascription to achievement values is tacitly understood as a mark of moral progress. This obscures the fact that what is actually involved in this shift is a change in the criteria employed for discriminatory purposes.

7 Bourdieu (1973) argues that in France, '. . . the academic market tends to sanction and to reproduce the distribution of cultural capital by proportioning academic success to the amount of cultural capital bequeathed by the family . . .' (86). The middle class monopoly of the educational system is 'concealed beneath the cloak of a perfectly democratic method of selection which takes into account only merit and talent . . .' (85). See also Jane Marceau's contribution to this volume, 'Education and Social Mobility in France'.

7a Moorhouse (1973) has drawn attention to the techniques by which a large section of the industrial working class was excluded from the franchise until 1918, despite the political rhetoric of universal male suffrage.

8 This is not of course the sole political response likely to occur among excluded communal groups; attempts at secession from the existing nation state are also a recurrent theme, as testified by separatist movements among minorities in Ulster, French Canada, Belgium, and the United States.

Interestingly, however, the main political effect of these movements appears to have been the granting of certain integrationist concessions on the part of the dominant group.

9 See for example Professor Roberts' recent condemnation of the 'crude exercise of power bargaining based upon the capricious ability to inflict damage on industry and the community' (Roberts 1972: 269).

'Under conditions of advanced technology involving high capital-labour ratios, low levels of intermediate stocks, and ever more closely integrated production and distributive processes, the balance of bargaining power has tipped in favour of groups who are prepared to exploit this critical strategic situation' (266). Hence 'The really critical question is can society stand the strain of the extension of uninhibited collective bargaining' (269). Interestingly, no similar concern is felt over the use of bargaining power deriving from credentialist or property closure.

10 For a clear statement of this view see in particular Jordan (1973).

11 Mackenzie describes the variety of exclusion practices used by in-digenous American craftsmen against the immigrant workers. These included the setting of examinations which large numbers would fail, prohibitive initiation fees, and formal citizenship requirements (Mackenzie 1973: 173). See also his contribution to this volume, 'The "Affluent Worker" Study: An Evaluation and Critique'.

12 The adoption of solidaristic tactics by white-collar groups appears to occur only after the inability to secure closure along purely creden-tialist lines has become acknowledged. This is well documented in the case of the technicians by Roberts, Loveridge, and Gennard (1972). It would seem exceptional for any occupational groups to give *priority* to solidaristic forms of closure over credentialism where the latter remains a feasible strategy.

13 Gray's work on the labour aristocracy shows similarly that those whose industrial strategies were highly exclusionist nevertheless played a crucial part in fostering solidarism at the political level in the creation of the Labour Party – a fact that appears to have had im-portant consequences for the aims and ideology of the party. See Gray's contribution to this volume, 'The Labour Aristocracy in the Victorian Class Structure'. Also Gray (1973).

References

BLUMER, H. 1965. Industrialization and Race Relations. In G. Hunter (ed.) *Industrialization and Race Realtions.* London: Oxford University Press.

BOURDIEU, P. 1973. Cultural Reproduction and Social Reproduction. In R. Brown (ed.) *Knowledge, Education, and Cultural Change.* London: Tavistock.

DURKHEIM, E. 1964. *The Division of Labour in Society.* New York: Free Press.

GIDDENS, A. 1973. *The Class Structure of the Advanced Societies.* London: Hutchinson.

GRAY, R. 1973. Styles of Life, the 'Labour Aristocracy' and Class Relations in Later Nineteenth Century Edinburgh. *International Review of Social History* **18,** Part 3: 428-452.

HÖRNING, K. H. (ed.) 1971. *Der 'neue' Arbeiter: zum Wandel sozialer Schichtstrukturen.* Frankfurt: Fischer.

JORDAN. B. 1973. *Paupers: The Making of the New Claiming Class.* London: Routledge & Kegan Paul.

KERR, C., DUNLOP, J. J., HARBISON, F. H., and MYERS, C. H. 1962. *Industrialism and Industrial Man.* London: Heinemann.

LOCKWOOD, D. 1958. *The Blackcoated Worker.* London: Allen & Unwin.

—— 1970. Race, Conflict and Plural Society. In S. Zubaida (ed.) *Race and Racialism.* London: Tavistock.

MACKENZIE, G. 1973. *The Aristocracy of Labour: The Position of Skilled Craftsmen in the American Class Structure.* Cambridge: Cambridge University Press.

MILLER, S. M. 1960. Comparative Social Mobility. *Current Sociology* **9** (1).

—— 1967. *Breaking the Credentials Barrier.* New York: Ford Foundation.

MOORHOUSE, H. F. 1973. The Political Incorporation of the British Working Class: An Interpretation. *Sociology* **7** (3), September: 341-359.

NEUWIRTH, G. 1969. A Weberian Outline of a Theory of Community: Its Application to the 'Dark Ghetto'. *British Journal of Sociology,* **20** (2), June: 148-163.

OLSEN, M. 1965. *The Logic of Collective Action.* Harvard: Harvard University Press.

ORWELL, G. 1949. *Nineteen Eighty-Four.* London: Secker & Warburg.

ROBERTS, B. C. 1972. Affluence and Disruption. In W. A. Robson (ed.) *Man and the Social Sciences.* London: Allen & Unwin.

ROBERTS, B. C., LOVERIDGE, R., and GENNARD, J. 1972. *Reluctant Militants.* London: Heinemann.

WEBER, M. 1968. *Economy and Society.* (eds. G. Roth and C. Wittich) New York: Bedminster Press.

ROBERT Q. GRAY

The Labour Aristocracy in the Victorian Class Structure

Discussions of the working class in western societies have drawn particular attention to recent economic, technological, occupational, and social development (see, e.g., Mann 1973). These changes must, however, be analysed in a wider historical context; their impact was felt, not by 'some nondescript undifferentiated raw material of humanity' (Thompson 1968: 213), but by working people who had, over a century and more of history, developed particular cultural patterns, institutions, modes of industrial and political action. Thus Goldthorpe and Lockwood (1963: 142) refer to 'a far-reaching adaptation and development of the traditional working-class way of life'. Yet the 'traditional working class' has been rather less thoroughly investigated than the various groups of the 'new working class'; too often, it seems, sociologists have been content with a 'sociological past . . . linked to the present not by carefully observed and temporally located social interaction but by inferentially necessary connections between concepts' (Abrams 1972: 20). In particular, it is important to realize that the accommodation of the working class to capitalist society is no recent phenomenon: 'The constriction of revolutionary perspectives in working-class ideology . . . is not simply the product of developments since 1945 but represents the working out of an historical tendency visible in the second half of the nineteenth century' (Birnbaum 1971: 104). Equally, the inhibiting effect on working-class consciousness of structural differentiation is, as social historians are well aware, a phenomenon visible throughout the history of industrial capitalism. Indeed, from even the most cursory examination of that history, it becomes apparent that the twentieth century has, if anything, seen an increase in the homogeneity and industrial and urban concentration of the proletariat.

The present paper addresses itself to this crucial historical dimension in the study of working-class consciousness. It will be argued that an analysis of stratification and cultural differences within the working class

in Victorian Britain can shed some light on the formation of a reformist
labour movement, and on the recurring tension in working-class life
between accommodative and oppositional responses to the capitalist
order. Many historians follow Victorian commentators in explaining
accommodative tendencies by the existence within the manual working
class of an upper stratum, or 'aristocracy of labour' (see Samuel 1959
for contemporary views). The best known statement of this view is
probably that of Hobsbawm (1964: 272-315) who describes the labour
aristocracy as composed of 'certain distinctive upper strata of the
working class, better paid, better treated and generally regarded as more
"respectable" and politically moderate than the mass of the proletariat'.
In a study of the working class in one city (Edinburgh), I have attempted
to show that such strata can in fact be identified, and to analyse the
nature and implications of their ideological perspectives and collective
action. In this paper I want, first, to summarize my findings – which
cannot, however, be at all adequately supported in the available space[1] –
and, second, to discuss some wider implications for the development
of the British working class.

An investigation of the labour aristocracy hypothesis must clearly
begin by analysing differences in the class situation of different groups
of manual workers. The first part of the present paper argues that there
were extremely wide differences in the life-chances of various sections
of the working population of Victorian Edinburgh. The existence of
such differences is, however, a necessary but not sufficient condition
for the formation of a distinctive upper stratum. To show the existence
of such a stratum it is necessary to consider styles of life and patterns of
behaviour. The second part of the paper argues that it is possible, from
an examination of cultural patterns in the urban community, to identify
a separate upper stratum, marked off from other working-class groups
by a particular style of life, and to some extent conscious of its distinctive
position. This means that we can in fact talk of a 'labour aristocracy'.
The remainder of the paper considers the relations of this stratum to
other social strata, and its historical significance for the more general
development of the labour movement.

CLASS SITUATION

Edinburgh was exceptional among cities of comparable size for the
proportion of its population engaged in non-manual occupations (for a
discussion of occupational structure see MacDougall 1968: xvi-xvii).
The large non-industrial sector made for diversity in the occupational

structure of the working class. Much employment depended on the small-scale traditional consumer crafts and 'luxury trades' serving the local middle-class market; the heavy industrial sector was of limited, though growing, extent. Most of the important local industries employed a high proportion of skilled labour. This situation facilitates a research strategy based upon a comparative occupational analysis of the range of skilled trades to be found in the city.

A diversity of economic experience characterized the local working class. Quantitative indicators, as well as documentary material, point to the wide material differences between artisans and labourers. But it is also essential to make two other sets of distinctions: between various skilled trades, and within certain trades. When we make these further distinctions, it becomes clear that the term 'aristocrat of labour' is by no means synonomous with 'skilled worker'. The wide differences in living conditions between skilled trades are usefully indicated by quoting data for the heights of schoolchildren (collected in 1904). The children of engineers – widely regarded as a working-class elite – were on average 0.93 inches shorter than the appropriate mean height for children of their sex and age at another school described as 'lower middle class' in social composition. The children of painters – a notoriously depressed skilled trade – were 2.40 inches shorter; and the children of unskilled workers were 3.29 inches shorter.[2] These occupational differences confirm the impression given by other non-quantitative sources.

But aggregate occupational comparisons have also to be seen in relation to intra-occupational variations. Every trade contained, on the one hand, an elite who would expect to be fully employed at all but the worst times; and, on the other hand, a varying proportion who could expect to be under-employed at all but the best times. These internal divisions were especially marked in those trades which were, on aggregate, economically disadvantaged. The extent of the casual labour market, and the capacity of the trade to limit it, were of critical importance. The recent study by Stedman Jones (1971), and the contemporary observations of Mayhew (Thompson and Yeo, eds. 1971) indicate the effects of casual labour in London. In Edinburgh too, *short-run* fluctuations in activity, casualization, and under-employment had a far more severe impact on living standards than the factors of cyclical unemployment and technical change so often discussed by economic historians. Thus, in tailoring in the 1850s, the average shop might take on thirty to forty men in the busy season, of whom only half a dozen regular employees were retained in the slack season; similarly, a report of 1869 gives a figure of 370 out of 600 painters being idle in winter.[3] Among compositors, 'you will find one section of the men continually kept setting the "rubbish" of the house, while others . . . are lolling in fat of all kinds'.[4]

This heterogeneity of certain trades means that the stratification within the working class is more complex than a simple division between skilled and unskilled, or even between 'prosperous' and 'deprived' skilled occupations. We must think of the upper stratum as composed of a large proportion of the men in those trades which were, on aggregate, well placed in the economic hierarchy of skilled labour; these trades include, in Edinburgh,[5] printing machinemen, bookbinders, masons, joiners, engineers, and furniture trades. But the advantaged stratum also included a smaller proportion of men from the other skilled trades. Every trade therefore contained a larger or smaller proportion of men who lived at the economic level of the upper stratum, and – at the other extreme – a larger or smaller proportion of casual workers whose economic conditions were little, if at all superior to those of unskilled labour.

A consideration of the work situation confirms the picture of wide differences in the experience of industrial employment. Nineteenth-century industry was heavily dependent – even in such capital-intensive sectors as engineering – on skills transmitted by apprenticeship and the expertise and initiative of the artisan (Pollard 1968). In a system of 'craft administration', to use Stinchcombe's term (Stinchcombe 1959), skilled workers performed tasks, including the direct supervision of semi and unskilled labour, that have subsequently become the specialized functions of managerial and technical employees. The artisan consequently had a considerable degree of autonomy within the workshop – an autonomy in many cases reinforced by the strength of traditional craft customs and practices.

There is, then, evidence of marked differences in the experience of industrial employment. The cumulative distribution of advantages and disadvantages enables us to talk of a well developed stratification within the manual working class – a stratification perhaps more pronounced during the third quarter of the nineteenth century than at any other period in history.

COMMUNITY AND CLASS CULTURE

It would also seem that social distinctions within the working class were widely recognized by contemporaries. It was said of engineers that they were 'generally the elite of the working men, and so far removed from the operatives and labourers at the lower end of the scale that they have not many sympathies in common, and not much intercourse with them'.[6] According to a writer in the local radical weekly (1870), 'the working classes are divided into upper, middle and lower ... The working man belonging to the upper class of his order is a member of the aristocracy of the working classes. He is a man of some culture, is well read in political and social history ... His self respect is also well developed'.[7]

Residential development in the city and the growth of certain leisure pursuits and voluntary organizations were important aspects of cultural differentiation. Improved dwellings built after the slum clearance of the 1860s 'were very eagerly looked after by artizans of a superior class, who acquired them with the little savings they had of their own, or with the assistance of loans from investment companies'.[8] Tenants in a later 'improved' block were a 'superior class of working men'; they included one baths superintendent, two butlers, a foreman baker, a foreman mason, a foreman painter, two joiners, a hairdresser, a compositor, and a van driver.[9] Of the families studied in the 1904 survey already cited, more than half the engineers and joiners lived in houses of three or more rooms, compared to 19 per cent of the painters and 15 per cent of the semi and unskilled workers.[10] Similarly, certain voluntary organizations seem to have catered especially for the 'superior artisan'; those for which records were found include committeemen of the Mechanics' Library (1840-58), members of a golf club (1869), and prizewinners at the Working Men's Flower Show (1870). Printers, bookbinders, engineers, smiths, masons, joiners and furniture trades were especially prominent in these organizations.[11] Certain sorts of leisure activity seem to have been bound up with an assertion of the distinctive status of the 'respectable artisan'. For example, at a gathering of printers: 'Here were a thousand men, nearly all in superfine black coats and spotless shirt-fronts; a thousand women in dresses and bonnets of the latest mode ... ; and in all this great mass of the "lower orders" not a word out of joint.'[12]

Housing and leisure patterns thus suggest the existence of distinctive styles of life within the working class, which marked off a separate upper stratum. Those trades already identified as economically advantaged were well represented in that upper stratum. Residential patterns and the development of 'respectable' formally organized leisure pursuits were bound up with the projection of a sense of cultural superiority. Asked by the Royal Commission on Housing whether slum-dwellers resented their poor conditions, the President of Edinburgh Trades Council (a joiner by trade) was quick to deny any knowledge of 'the Irish element, labourers and what not'. At the Royal Commission on Friendly Societies, the secretary of one local lodge similarly emphasized that his members were not to be confused with 'the poor', but 'are rather of a respectable class – what are called respectable artizans'.[13]

CLASS RELATIONS IN THE VICTORIAN CITY

It is thus possible to identify a distinct upper stratum in the manual working class of Victorian Edinburgh – a stratum distinguished not only by a relatively advantaged class situation, but also by a consciousness of social difference from the remainder of the working class. The rest of this paper examines the relationships between this aristocracy of labour and other strata. In this section, I consider first what Goldthorpe and Lockwood (1963: 136) call the 'relational' aspect of class – the social mixing or segregation of particular strata; and second the 'normative' aspect – value systems, norms of behaviour, social perspectives, etc. In the final section of the paper I examine the influence of the labour aristocracy on the emerging organization and ideology of the working class as a whole.

It is often remarked that, whereas the social boundary below the labour aristocrat was well defined, that above him was rather hazy, so that there was a 'shading over of the aristocracy of labour into other strata' (Hobsbawm 1964: 274). Some of my data lend support to this view. In the voluntary organizations mentioned above, business and white-collar groups account for as much as 53 per cent of the Mechanics' Library, 27 per cent of the golf club, and 23 per cent of the Flower Show. This is in striking contrast to the proportion of unskilled workers (respectively, 2 per cent, nil and 8 per cent). An analysis of marriage certificates for the years 1865-9 indicates a pattern broadly similar to that of voluntary organization membership. Certificates for all grooms in selected occupations were examined, with a view to comparing the social composition of brides' fathers for the various selected occupations.[14] In all the skilled trades, marriages to the daughters of other skilled workers account for the largest single category; more significantly perhaps, the printers, bookbinders, masons, joiners, engineers, and ironmoulders actually have more marriages to daughters of business and white-collar groups than to the daughters of unskilled workers.

The evidence of greater social contact with lower middle-class groups than with less skilled groups of manual workers is certainly striking. But its fuller implications depend on the relative position *within the middle class* of these business and white-collar strata. (My business category, in particular, is inevitably a hetrogeneous one.) It is worth noting here that a wide range of white-collar posts were, in the mid-nineteenth century, probably recruited from skilled workers or their children – the best documented example being the recruitment of elementary schoolteachers through the pupil-teacher system.[15] It is likely, then, that a considerable social gulf separated those school-teachers, minor officials, supervisory employees, white-collar workers, and small businessmen with whom the aristocracy of labour were likely to have had some contact, from what may be called the 'established' middle class. As the preface to the Mechanics' Library *Catalogue* put it, the officers 'have either been mechanics, or very slightly raised above them in the social scale'.[16] I would therefore argue that the social contacts of artisans were with a relatively unformed, fluid, and transi-tional lower middle class. Metaphors of a societal 'pyramid' of social statuses may well be misleading here; we should perhaps think instead of culturally differentiated social worlds within the stratified local society of the Victorian city. In this perspective, it is at least arguable that many small businessmen and white-collar employees inhabited the fringes of an upper artisan social world, rather than the lower reaches of a middle-class one.

Distinctive ideological perspectives characterized the upper artisan world. There is certainly no lack of evidence to support the view that the outlook of the aristocracy of labour reflects the diffusion of such dominant values in Victorian society as 'respectability', 'independence', and 'thrift' (see Best 1971: 256-64). But this view needs qualification, if we are to avoid oversimplifying a complex situation. Dominant values may have changed their meaning in becoming adapted to the con-ditions of artisan life. As Harrison (1968: 268-9) points out, 'self help' could take collective forms, quite alien to the perspective of the domi-nant middle class. The Victorian artisan might well have a perspective of relatively long-term improvement in his individual situation, achieved through the bourgeois virtues of industry and thrift. But this perspective must be seen in the context of the artisan's own economic and social experience. And here the intra-occupational economic differences considered above should be borne in mind. Thus, a man's chances of entering and remaining in the favoured section of his trade could depend on such factors as the quality of his tools (an important reason for saving in some trades), his efficiency and self-discipline, and his versatility and technical knowledge (which might well demand a certain level of basic education). All these factors were to some extent related to the economic circumstances of the worker, and the resources he had managed to accumulate. Above all, of course, saving was necessary to meet the periodic crises of working-class life without falling too far below the level of the 'superior artisan'.[17]

Therefore, although the labour aristocracy certainly behaved in ways congruent with middle-class norms of 'thrift', this behaviour should be interpreted in relation to the situation of the actors. It is also true that the values of 'respectability' and individualism co-existed with other, solidaristic values and modes of behaviour – most obviously in the formal and informal solidarity of the work situation. It was over the issue of combinations and strikes that the artisan was likely to dissent most sharply from the perspectives of the Victorian middle class; and it was precisely those trades with the strongest unions that were most heavily represented in the 'respectable' upper stratum of the working class.

The outlook of the Victorian labour aristocracy was thus an ambivalent one. Dominant values changed their meaning as they became adapted to the conditions of the artisan world and mediated through autonomous artisan institutions. The typical stress on the 'respectability' of the upper working-class stratum can often be seen as a claim to corporate social recognition. Thus the local radical newspaper commented on the 1866 reform demonstration: 'cabs and open carriages, with cynical or simply curious "swells", were driven slowly past to have, as they said, a view of "the great unwashed", who were, however, as was at once evident, not only washed but dressed – and that handsomely, too, for the occasion; and it will be unanimously allowed, even by those who habitually sneer at the working classes, that a better dressed procession of *working men* was never seen'.[18] The claim to political rights based on the 'growing virtue and intelligence of the working classes'[19] was indeed one of the great clichés of the age. This claim to social recognition was by no means resolved by the franchise extension of 1867; over a range of local issues and institutions it remained a source of class tension. Thus the pretensions of the middle-class Central Benevolent Association were attacked: 'The working men, who are the nearest to the "lapsed classes" in physical and social proximity, and therefore know all their bad habits, and how to cure and prevent them, and have also the deepest interest in the work for their wives' and children's sake, should not have been slighted so'; similarly, the arrangements for the 1871 Edinburgh meeting of the British Association allegedly reflected 'the great tendency in certain quarters of our city to confine all public arrangements to a small section of the community'.[20]

These community tensions must also be set beside the growth of trade unionism during the 1860s and '70s and the experience of industrial conflict, often on a far larger scale than ever before. Both in the employment situation and outside it, the labour aristocracy had a real, and growing sense of class identity (cf. Hobsbawm 1964: 323). It is therefore misleading to see the activities and attitudes of the stratum in terms simply of their commitment to middle-class norms and values – still less can they be seen in terms of a 'deferential' orientation to middle-class political and social leadership. As Parkin (1971: 88-96) has suggested, working-class ideology typically 'emphasizes various modes of adaptation, rather than either full endorsement of, or opposition to, the *status quo*' (Ibid: 88); to quote Parkin's apt phrase, a 'negotiated version' of dominant values is enacted and reproduced by the subordinate class. There is, then, a process of adaptation, manifested partly in the 'negotiated version' of dominant values and partly also in the containment of dissident institutions and values. The frequently noted ambivalence of the Victorian labour aristocracy must, in my view, be understood in this perspective. Thus, on one hand, the ideology of 'respectability' and 'self help' was adapted to the situation of the artisan, mediated by the distinctive institutions of his social world – trade unions, friendly societies, co-operative associations, working-men's clubs, and other recreational organizations. On the other hand, the articulation of class-interest and dissident radical ideologies was effectively contained, so as to maintain intact a social order based on the subordination of manual labour.

The accommodation of the aristocracy of labour to capitalist society was the result neither of a straightforward and direct ideological indoctrination made possible by the relative 'affluence' of the stratum, nor simply of the absence of class consciousness. The ideology of the stratum seems rather to exemplify the type of class consciousness defined by Gramsci (1971: 181) as 'corporate': 'the right is claimed to participate in legislation and administration, even to reform these – but within the existing fundamental structures'. The behaviour of the upper working-class stratum reflected, in certain contexts, a distinct sense of class identity; but this was still effectively contained within a social order dominated by the 'hegemonic' middle class. The working man articulated his aspirations for a better life for himself, his family, and his class[21] in a language 'adopted' from the dominant ideology, 'for reasons of submission and intellectual subordination' (Ibid: 327).

The fact that the containment of working-class opposition was mediated through a process of *negotiation* is, however, crucial to an understanding of the attitudes of the aristocracy of labour. The process of negotiation presupposes, precisely, strong and relatively autonomous class institutions; the sense of class pride and the ethic of class solidarity, associated with the defence of those institutions, is an important element in the perspectives of the upper working-class stratum. And the containment of working-class organizations and aspirations depended also on the readiness of middle-class groups to respect the autonomy of manual working-class institutions. Just as some employers were beginning to belive that unions might, in some respects, be a blessing in disguise, so the more intelligent middle-class intellectuals and philanthropists[22] stressed the importance of recognizing the working-man's claim to moral independence, expressed through the autonomy of his organizations. Thus the Reverend Dr Begg, writing about the housing problem, expressed the hope that, 'the whole problem, great as it is, may, by the Divine blessing, be entirely solved by the resources and power of the people themselves', and condemned 'the notion of treating working men as a kind of grown children'.[23] Similarly, in the political alignments that emerged after the franchise reform of 1867, working-class radicalism was a relatively autonomous component of the Gladstonian Liberal Party, within which it was nonetheless effectively contained (cf. Vincent 1966: esp. Ch. 2).

THE ARISTOCRACY OF LABOUR AND WORKING-CLASS MOVEMENTS

These patterns of class relationship and class consciousness have had important historical effects on the development of the working class as a whole. The mid-Victorian 'superior artisan' saw himself as in some sense the leader and instructor of less favoured working-class strata. As the Webbs (1920: 443) remarked, 'the Trade Unionists not only belong to the most highly-skilled and best-paid industries, but they include, as a general rule, the picked men in each trade. The moral and intellectual influence which they exercise on the rest of their class is, therefore, out of all proportion to their numbers'. This leadership often reflects an individualistic moral perspective, in some ways analogous to that of the middle-class 'social reformers'; the position of less fortunate strata of the working class was attributed to their moral failure in not adopting the modes of personal conduct typical of the 'respectable artisan'. Thus a leading co-operator in the city expressed the hope that, 'if the Co-operative element were to pervade society more generally than it did at the present time, a vast amount of the misery and crime, consequent upon intemperance and improvidence, would be altogether unknown'.[24] And the 'Radical-Liberal' politics that emerged after 1867 emphasized the attainment of formal political and legal equality, by further extension of citizenship rights, and determined opposition to aristocratic privilege and 'class legislation'.[25] 'A fair field and no favour is now all that is asked by average workmen in the struggle for existence; a right manly sentiment', the printers' union journal commented on the disappearance of testimonials from employers.[26] The mid-Victorian labour movement was pervaded by an interpretation of dominant values of individualism, which stressed the social and moral independence of the working man.

The response of other manual strata to the labour aristocracy's claim to exercise political and cultural leadership is hard to determine. The documentary record enables us to give some account, however tentative, of the activities and attitudes of the upper working-class stratum and their relations with middle-class groups. But the poorer sections of the working class have left less record; their institutions were certainly often of an informal kind, and their culture was in general a less 'literate' one than that of the 'superior artisan'. The earlier analysis of leisure activities and marriage certainly suggests considerable social distance within the manual working class; a similar pattern of relations at work is implied by the well attested existence of rigid work hierarchies – especially in those industries (such as building) whose organization was based on the traditional distinction between craftsman and labourer. The labour aristocracy's occasional pose as spokesmen of the 'working classes' (or even 'the poor') must often have presented a curious contrast to their cultural exclusiveness, the wide social gulf that separated them from the poorer sections of the working population. Thus the President of Edinburgh Trades Council, despite his denial of any association with 'the Irish element, labourers and what not', claimed to represent 'indirectly the working classes of Edinburgh generally'.[27]

The case of the mid-Victorian working class thus poses a general problem in the study of social stratification; it illustrates particularly well the fact that 'the relationship between classes is partly a function of the relationship of strata within classes' (Wolpe 1970: 172). The aristocracy of labour were clearly conscious of belonging to a manual working class, and of acting as a class; they created institutions (notably the unions) generally regarded as distinctive features of that class. This process institutionalized definitions of class identity and class interest essentially based on the position and outlook of the labour aristocracy, as an economically advantaged and culturally exclusive upper stratum. Historical definitions of 'class' have reflected the situation and outlook of those groups which have, at particular periods, been active and articulate; it is partly because of this that changes in class structure and class consciousness are complex and problematic phenomena.[28]

The labour aristocracy of the third quarter of the nineteenth century thus mediated particular ideological and institutional definitions of class identity. They have also had a considerable influence on the class formation of other manual strata in subsequent years. The last two decades of the nineteenth century were a critical period in the history of the British working class. Those decades saw attempts – far more determined and consistent than during the preceding years – to mobilize all strata of manual workers in a broad-based class movement. This was the period, industrially, of the growth of general and industrial unions, politically, of attempts to establish a more independent labour movement around programmes of 'collectivist' social reform. There was at the same time a limited, but none the less important propagation of socialist ideas in the working class. These developments must in my view be seen in relation to the changing position and attitude of the upper stratum, and not simply to the emergence of class organization and consciousness among other strata of the working class. There was a shift in the attitude and goals of the labour aristocracy itself, rather than an overthrow of its hegemony within the working class.

There is evidence that the position of the stratum was in various respects changing in the 1880s and '90s. Although it must be empha- sized that differences within the working class remained wide – and may have widened in some cases – the upper stratum were subjected to new pressures. The period was one of general improvement in real wages, partly because of falling food prices (Saul 1969: 30-2), and the advantaged sections of skilled labour maintained their relative position; but they nonetheless felt threatened by the more rapid mechnization that was also a feature of the period. Linked to this was a growth in the scale of industry, and possibly in the concentration of ownership and employers' organization. Changes in working practices and a tightening of supervision and work discipline impinged on valued traditions of workshop autonomy.[29] There are also some limited signs of a greater cultural homogeneity within the working class. The emergence of football as a 'mass' spectator sport may be one significant measure of changes in working-class life and attitudes (see Taylor 1971: 141-3). A comparison of patterns of marriage in the 1890s with those for the 1860s reveals in most of the skilled trades a higher rate of marriage to daughters of semi and unskilled workers, and a lower rate of marriage to daughters of business and white collar groups; perhaps most revealing, the two unskilled occupations analysed (building labourers and carters) both have an increased proportion of marriages to daughters of skilled workers.

These economic, industrial, and cultural trends may be related to shifts in political attitude. The early socialist movement in Edinburgh seems to have consisted mainly of artisans. The Socialist League were 'able to get our halls filled Sunday after Sunday by the very best class of workmen'; and a report in *Justice* noted that recruits to the Social Democratic Federation were 'certainly . . . not the occupants of the "one-roomed cells"'.[30] Although the immediate appeal of the socialist propaganda may have been limited, it undoubtedly helped form more diffuse class conscious, egalitarian, and 'collectivistic' attitudes – largely, I would suggest, because the socialist analysis provided for the artisan a way of understanding his changing social experience. The change in outlook is symbolized in the evidence to Royal Commissions of two Presidents of Edinburgh Trades Council (both joiners by trade). At the Royal Commission on Housing (1884), A. C. Telfer feared that publicly subsidized housing 'would strike at the industry and enterprise that lies at the very root of our national existence'. And at the Royal Commission on the Poor Laws (1910), Walter Bell attributed distress to the existence of 'a reserve army of unemployed', caused by mechanization, the employment of female and juvenile labour, etc., 'accentuated by the formation of syndicates and joint-stock companies', and asserted that this was best remedied by a legislative eight hour day.[31]

The developments of the 1880s and '90s predisposed artisans to mobilize wider strata of the working class around programes of 'collectivist' social reform (notably the eight-hour day). The interaction between the industrial[32] and community experience of skilled workers and the activities of the socialists (themselves largely artisans) explains the emergence of the Labour Party. It is interesting to note here that the constitution of the national Labour Representation Committee was anticipated in Edinburgh by a Workers' Municipal Committee, established in 1899, to which the socialist organizations, trade-union branches, co-operatives, etc. affiliated, with the aim of securing local labour representation independent of existing parties.[33] The labour aristocracy, then, adopted a role of leadership of a wider working-class movement. Crowley (1952) argues that the differences in the political attitudes of organized labour between the mid- and late-nineteenth century should not be exaggerated; as he points out, the rather diffuse eclectic character of the socialism of the Independent Labour Party (the largest and most influential of the socialist organizations) meant that the break with earlier traditions of labour ideology was a relatively gentle one. But the change in class experience and ideology should not be under-estimated. The upper stratum of the working class felt the need to create a separate Labour Party only because the socialist language – in however diffuse and modified a form – provided a meaningful interpretation of their experience. One of the features of the 'Lib-Labism' of the 1870s and '80s was the tendency to make the return of working men to representative bodies an end in itself, sought after as a mark of corporate status recognition. On the other hand, the distinctive feature of the 'labourism' that was emerging by the turn of the century was the attempt to unify the manual working class around local or national programmes of reform, which to some extent challenged the economic assumptions of Victorian liberalism. Whereas the typical demand of the 1870s was for the removal of 'class legislation' held to infringe the worker's rights as a citizen, that of the '90s was for the implementation, in his interest, of new legislative measures. It was only in the context of agitation around a positive programme of demands that the creation of a separate class-based party became possible.

I would thus argue that the aristocracy of labour played a key part in the emergence of a broadly based reformist-oriented labour movement. I want, finally, to make some rather speculative and tentative comments on the role of the stratum in the politics of 'labourism'. It is, in the first place, essential to distinguish the position of the labour aristocracy from that of professionalized labour leadership, with which it is sometimes conflated (e.g. Hobsbawn 1964: 324). The aristocrat of labour makes his living by manual work; on the other hand, the professionalized leadership described by Michels (1959: 276) consists of 'persons permanently and directly engaged in the service of the collectivity'. Despite the many defects of Michels' work, there can be no doubt that he identified an important tendency for such full-time officials and politicians to move in a bureaucratic or political world different from that of their followers and electorates. As an 'intermediary', a professional expert, the full-time labour leader works for an accommodation between the social and political order and the aspirations of organized workers, thereby channelling demands into 'constitutional' courses of action. The historical importance of the labour aristocracy lies partly in the similar role they played in the development of 'labourism' – but on a basis of *voluntary*, rather than professional activity in the labour movement. Through their roles as union and party activists, municipal representatives, etc., the labour aristocracy developed two sets of links with groups outside the local working-class world. The first set of links is with middle-class elites in the local society. In Edinburgh such links were well developed by the 1870s through the involvement in local politics of the upper working-class stratum, and their relationships with middle-class groups and individuals concerned to promote 'social reform' and 'self improvement' on the part of working men. Second, the aristocracy of labour linked particular working-class communities and cultures to national, professionalized labour leaderships – who may well themselves have been recruited predominantly from the upper stratum of the working class. Local political activists are of key importance in maintaining contacts between political elites and their followers. The aristocracy of labour could form such links on the one hand, because their conditions of life remained those of manual wage-labour – albeit at an economic level somewhat removed from that of the majority of the working population, and on the other hand, because their experience of participation in local affairs predisposed them perhaps to listen to 'accommodative' viewpoints.

The existence of an aristocratic upper stratum within the Victorian working class thus had important effects on the formation of a reformist labour movement. The institutions of that movement can, no doubt, be seen in two ways; from one point of view as institutions of adaptation to capitalist society, but from another as institutions of struggle created to serve the interests of sections of the subordinate class. The formation of a wider working-class movement in the late nineteenth century was partly a consequence of new attitudes on the part of members of the upper stratum, but the established attitudes and modes of action of that stratum also influenced the shape of the emerging labour movement, and the version of socialism to which parts of the movement became committed. A study of the complex patterns of internal stratification and cultural differentiation which characterized the Victorian working class may thus shed some light on the accommodation of the British working class to industrial capitalism and on the emergence of what Parkin (1971: 88-96) has called a 'subordinate value system'.

Notes

1 Fuller support for the argument will be found in my thesis (Gray

1972-3) which will not be cited in detail to avoid over-burdening the text with references. See also Gray (1973 and forthcoming) for fuller discussion of some of the issues raised in this paper.

2 The study quoted was made by the City of Edinburgh Charity Organization Society, and published in their *Report on the Physical Condition of Fourteen Hundred Schoolchildren in the City* (London 1906). This survey report separately tabulates information for each family, making possible re-analysis by occupation of household head. The survey population consists of all children at a school in central Edinburgh and their families; I have re-analysed information for all families headed by men in selected skilled occupations, and for a 10 per cent random sample of the remaining families, classified into skilled and semi and unskilled groups (households headed by widows, non-manual workers, and men of unclassifiable skill grade were dropped from this random sample). Because unduly small numbers make direct occupational comparisons of sex- and age-specific heights impossible, I use a measure based on the difference of each child's height from the appropriate mean height for his or her sex and age at another school studied by the C.O.S. and described as 'lower middle class'; the figures given in the text are occupational mean scores on this index. I am indebted to Dr R. Passmore of the Department of Physiology, Edinburgh University, for his expert advice on the relationships between living standards, nutrition, and the heights of children.

3 'The Condition of the Working Classes in Edinburgh and Leith', *Edinburgh News*, 12 March 1853; *The Reformer*, 6 March 1869.

4 *Scottish Typographical Circular*, January 1898. The terms 'rubbish' and 'fat' refer to the allocation of copy, which employers were often accused of manipulating to the detriment of piece-working compositors, thus accentuating fluctuations in employment and earnings and encouraging the growth of the casual labour market.

5 Local variations in economic and social structure must be borne in mind here; in so far as a similar upper stratum can be identified in other areas, its occupational composition may be somewhat different – the same occupations may have different *relative* positions in different areas. It is for this reason that local studies are essential to any analysis of stratification within the working class. It may, however, be worth noting that most of the advantaged trades in Edinburgh appear on the list of 'aristocratic' trades (based on national aggregate wage data) given by Hobsbawm (1964: 286).

6 *The Reformer*, 29 March 1873: review of *Our New Masters* by 'Journeyman Engineer' (Thomas Wright).

7 George Potter in *The Reformer*, 5 November 1870. Potter, a leader of the London joiners and prominent figure in working-class radical politics wrote a regular column in the *Reformer*, which was the organ of the Edinburgh 'Advanced Liberals' and trade unionists.

8 Evidence of Clerk to the City Improvement Trustees, *Royal Commission on the Housing of the Working Classes* (*Scotland*), Parliamentary Papers (PP) 1884-5, XXXI: Q 18738.

9 Ibid: Q 19161.

10 See above, note 2 for details of the data source. The definition of a 'room' is a notorious difficulty in measuring housing conditions, and my figures are based simply on the number of 'rooms' as stated by the compilers of the report; the data should not be regarded as at all precise.

11 Officers' occupations as listed in Edinburgh Mechanics' Library, *Laws and Catalogue* (1859: in National Library of Scotland); names and addresses, traced in census enumerators' books, from Minutes of Bruntsfield Links Allied Golf Club (in Edinburgh Public Library) list of members in 1869; and prize list of Workingmen's Flower Show in *The Reformer*, 13 August 1870. Seven out of forty-one golf club members, and nineteen out of ninety-seven Flower Show prize-winners could not be found in the census. Female and juvenile Flower Show prizewinners classified by occupation of household head; families with more than one prize, and Library officers serving for more than one year, or in more than one office, counted only once. I am indebted to the Registrar General for Scotland for allowing me to consult the enumerators' books.

12 D. Wilson, *William Nelson: a Memoir* (1889: privately printed: copy in the authors' possession): 82.

13 *Royal Commission on Housing*: Q 19273; *Royal Commission on Friendly Societies*, PP 1872, XXVI: Q 96159.

14 The selected occupations were printers, bookbinders, masons, joiners, painters, engineers, ironmoulders, brassfinishers, shoemakers, and two large unskilled occupations (building labourers and carters). I am indebted to the Registrar General for Scotland for permission to consult the certificates, and to Mr P. Morse for help with computing work.

15 See Sutherland (1971) for the recruitment and social position of elementary teachers; despite the important educational differences between England and Scotland, elementary schools in large cities and operation of the pupil-teacher system appear to have been similar (see Scotland 1969: Pt. III).

16 Mechanics' Library, *Laws* . . .: v. Officers during 1840-58 in white collar and business occupations include a clothier, a cheesemonger, a house agent, a corn merchant, a spirit merchant, a bookseller, eight clerks etc., four teachers, two reporters, a surveyor, and a collector; this list probably gives a fairly good picture of the composition of those non-manual strata with whom the labour aristocracy interacted.

17 I have discussed the significance of 'thrift' more fully elsewhere (Gray forthcoming). For the ubiquity in working-class life of various forms

of 'crisis' see Anderson (1971: Ch. 10). The economic superiority of
the labour aristocracy by no means freed them from the threat of such
crises; but their response to this threat was governed not simply by
physical survival, but also by the desire to retain their position of
relative advantage within the working class. Thus the impact on a
man's physical condition and industrial efficiency of a period of
sickness or unemployment – and hence his chances of regaining his
former earning-power – might well depend on the level of his savings.

18 *The North Briton*, 21 November 1866.

19 Speech by Alexander Fraser (blacksmith), printed in the *North Briton*,
16 March 1859.

20 *The North Briton*, 11 April 1868; 18 March 1871.

21 I use the term 'class' here regardless of the fact that the labour
aristocracy often defined their 'class' self-image in ways that excluded
other manual working-class groups; yet they certainly saw themselves
as comprising the 'working classes' and having specific class interests.
All references in this paper to 'class' institutions, ideologies, etc.
should be understood in this problematic sense.

22 Edinburgh, as a national centre of intellectual, legal, and religious
life, probably had an exceptional concentration of such individuals.

23 James Begg, DD, *Happy Homes for Working Men* (1866): 15, 17.
Begg was referring especially to the Co-operative Building Co., which
built houses for sale to 'the better class of working men' (*Royal Comm.
on Housing*: Q 19701). Cf. Price (1971) for a stimulating discussion of
the relation of middle-class 'social improvement' to working-class
cultures.

24 Speech (1864) by John Borrowman (joiner), quoted by W. Maxwell,
*First Fifty Years of St. Cuthbert's Co-operative Association Ltd.,
1859-1909* (1909): 47.

25 The condemnation of 'class legislation' – a recurrent theme in mid-
Victorian popular radicalism – referred to those statutes held to embody some principle of formal inequality and social discrimination
(for example the different treatment of workers and employers in the
law of contract, the land and game laws, etc.).

26 *Scottish Typo. Circular*, July 1872.

27 *Royal Commission on Housing*: Q 19167.

28 For a discussion of this problem see Mallet 1963; Mann 1973.

29 For a discussion of this otherwise somewhat neglected topic see
Crowley 1952: ch. 4.

30 *Commonweal*, February 1885; *Justice*, 22 February 1896. 'One-roomed
cells' is a reference to single roomed houses. A notable example of
unskilled political activism was, however, James Connolly (a carter by
occupation) who certainly played a leading part in the early socialist
movement in the city (see Greaves 1961).

31 *Royal Commission on Housing*: Q 19188; *Royal Commission on Poor*

Laws. Appendix vol. ix, PP 1910 XLVIII: appendix cxvii (statement by W. Bell, Edinburgh Trades Council).

32 The 1890s saw important disputes arising from mechanization in two large Edinburgh trades (compositors and shoemakers); the national lock-out of engineering workers (1897-8) also had a considerable local impact. These events undoubtedly helped widen the appeal of the socialist platform.

33 Minutes of Edinburgh and Leith Workers' Municipal Committee (among records of Edinburgh Trades Council). I wish to thank the secretary of the Council, Mr John Henry, for allowing me access to these minutes.

References

Note. Works listed here do not include nineteenth century source materials, for which full references are given in the notes.

ABRAMS, P. 1972. The Sense of the Past and the Origins of Sociology. *Past and Present* **55.**

ANDERSON, M. 1971. *Family Structure in Nineteenth Century Lancashire.* Cambridge: Cambridge University Press.

BEST, G. 1971. *Mid-Victorian Britain, 1851-75.* London: Weidenfeld and Nicolson.

BIRNBAUM, N. 1971. *Toward a Critical Sociology.* New York: Oxford University Press.

CROWLEY, D. W. 1952. The Origins of the Revolt of the British Labour Movement from Liberalism. University of London: Ph.D. thesis.

GOLDTHORPE, J. H., and LOCKWOOD, D. 1963. Affluence and the British Class Structure. *Sociological Review* **11** (2).

GRAMSCI, A. 1971. *Selections from the Prison Notebooks.* (Hoare, Q., and Nowell Smith, G., eds. and trans.) London: Lawrence and Wishart.

GRAY, R. Q. 1972-3. Class Structure and the Class Formation of Skilled Workers in Edinburgh, c. 1850-c. 1900. University of Edinburgh: Ph.D. thesis.

—— 1973. Styles of Life, the 'Labour Aristocracy' and Class Relations in later Nineteenth Century Edinburgh. *International Review of Social History* **8.**

—— (forthcoming). Thrift and Working Class Mobility in Victorian Edinburgh. In Maclaren, A. (ed.) *Essays in Class and Society.* London: Routledge & Kegan Paul.

GREAVES, C. D. 1961. *The Life and Times of James Connolly.* London: Lawrence and Wishart.

HARRISON, R. 1968. Afterword. In Smiles, S. *Self Help*. London: Sphere Books.

HOBSBAWM, E. J. 1964. *Labouring Men*. London: Weidenfeld and Nicolson.

JONES, G. S. 1971. *Outcast London*. Oxford: Oxford University Press.

MACDOUGALL, I. 1968. Introduction. In MacDougall, I. (ed.) *The Minutes of Edinburgh Trades Council, 1859-73*. Edinburgh: Scottish History Society.

MALLET, S. 1963. *La Nouvelle Classe Ouvrière*. Paris: Editions du Seuil.

MANN, M. 1973. *Consciousness and Action among the Western Working Class*. London: Macmillan.

MICHELS, R. 1959. *Political Parties*. New York: Dover Edition.

PARKIN, F. 1971. *Class Inequality and Political Order*. London: Mac-Gibbon and Kee.

POLLARD, S. 1968. *The Genesis of Modern Management*. Harmondsworth: Penguin.

PRICE, R. N. 1971. The Working Men's Club Movement and Victorian Social Reform Ideology. *Victorian Studies* **15** (2).

REID, F. 1968. Review article. *Bulletin of the Society for the Study of Labour History* **16**.

SAMUEL, R. 1959. Class and Classlessness. *Universities and Left Review* **6** (Spring).

SAUL, S. B. 1969. *The Myth of the Great Depression*. London: Macmillan.

SCOTLAND, J. S. 1969. *The History of Scottish Education*, Vol. I. London: London University Press.

STINCHCOMBE, A. L. 1959. Bureaucratic and Craft Administration of Production. *Administrative Science Quarterly* **4**.

SUTHERLAND, G. 1971. *Elementary Education in the Nineteenth Century*. London: Historical Association.

TAYLOR, I. R. 1971. Soccer Consciousness and Soccer Hooliganism. In Cohen, S. (ed.) *Images of Deviance*. Harmondsworth: Penguin.

THOMPSON, E. P. 1968. *The Making of the English Working Class*. Harmondsworth: Penguin.

THOMPSON, E. P. and YEO, E. (eds.) 1971. *The Unknown Mayhew*. London: Merlin Press.

VINCENT, J. 1966. *The Formation of the Liberal Party*. London: Constable.

WEBB, S. and WEBB, B. 1920. *The History of Trade Unionism* (Revised edition). London: Longmans.

WOLPE, H. 1970. Industrialism and Race in South Africa. In Zubaida, S. (ed.) *Race and Racialism*. London: Tavistock Publications.

SHEILA ALLEN and CHRISTOPHER SMITH

Race and Ethnicity in Class Formation: A Comparison of Asian and West Indian Workers[1]

This paper is concerned with the relationship of class and race in Britain. The aim has been to consider major theoretical questions in relation to some of the relevant trends that appear to be developing in our society.[2] Despite the insistence over the last few years that sociologists of race relations locate their work within a framework of the general stratification system, there have been few systematic attempts to develop this approach or even to confront the problems that are theoretically prior to such an attempt.[3]

THEORETICAL PROBLEMS

At the risk of seeming to state the obvious, it must be emphasized at the outset that we consider class and race not as things or categories, but as relationships. They are neither static nor descriptive and it follows therefore that our focus is on processes of becoming, developing, and transforming within situations that are always located within complex socio-historical formations. The working class is thus not, in our view, understandable in any sense without reference to the bourgeoise, nor is the present white population understandable without consideration of its relationship to the black population, and vice versa. Class experience and class consciousness, race experience and race consciousness, race conflict and class struggle must all involve aspects of relationships. Without them they would be bereft of meaning.

However, the question which faces those who would relate their explanations of race relations to the system of class domination is how these relationships are ordered. It has been argued, for instance, that

' . . . once they (racialist ideologies) are *institutionalised* into governmental, legal and economic practices, they become primary factors in the stratification system of which they form a part . . . the race relations situation is not just stratification plus racialist ideology and ascription, but the very dynamics of the stratification system become profoundly influenced by its racial elements.' (Zubaida 1970: 7)

Such statements raise important questions: What are 'primary factors' and 'the very dynamics of stratification', and what does 'profoundly influenced by racial elements' mean, particularly if such elements are themselves considered primary?

To specify these propositions more clearly, we should need a model that integrates class and race relations and further propositions about the condition under which one or other may be primary, or simply influential. Such a model would, for instance, clarify the meaning of the notion of 'underclass' or 'sub-proletariat', which is increasingly being used to describe, although not explain, the class position of black people in Britain and immigrant workers in western Europe. The thesis put forward by Andre Gorz maintains that the permanent presence of a migrant labour force, representing overall some twenty per cent of industrial labour power, not only confers tangible political and economic advantages on the bourgeoisie, but that its absence would modify the whole set of historical conditions on which labour power and the wage structure are determined, and would not simply provoke an increase in wages and in the political weight of the 'national' working class. The presence of migrant labour is indicative of a major contradiction since 'The maintenance of the social hierarchy, and scale of values on which capitalist civilisation rests, and thereby the survival of bourgeois society and its mode of domination, depend on the possibility of *excluding* from this civilisation and its labour market a decisive fraction of the working class' (Gorz 1970: 30-31). In so far as the position of black workers in Britain is conceptualized as that of an underclass, then if we are to go beyond simple description, a model of the type put forward by Gorz is necessary.

In other words, the thesis would be that black workers and foreign workers in Britain not only produce more surplus value than the 'national' working class; are effectively, if not legally, excluded from political power; provide the bourgeoisie, on the basis of racist and chauvinistic 'interests', with ideological allies from the national working class; but that they are integrated into the system in such a way that without them the stucture of existing class relationships would be critically affected. Such a model does not fit easily into our sociological perspectives. It is at once too stark, too speculative and perhaps too disturbing. It is however, the structural bones of the weakly developed flesh of the underclass notion.

It appears to underlie Zubaida's contention that 'It is clear . . . that immigrant workers in this country do not share similar market positions with native workers'. Their relationships to the trade unions, political parties, local government, and the State are also clearly different from those of native workers. But he goes on to argue that '*These differences are the main components of "race relations"* and a consideration of such differences is essential for the understanding of other aspects of the relationships between the groups' (Zubaida 1970:8, our italics). But he does not pursue the question of how these integrate with the overall structuring of class relationships.

To do so involves re-thinking mainstream sociology which, in general terms, provides for the analysis of class systems in terms of societal, if not national, entities conceptualized as ethnically homogeneous. This problem is well recognized: for instance, as both Lockwood and Zubaida agree, 'stratification situations in which race is an important element are different in certain respects from stratification situations not involving such elements' (Zubaida 1970: 7).

The problem is, however, dealt with by Lockwood in terms of indigenous class society versus plural society and so the emphasis moves away from re-conceptualizing class systems to the problems of pluralism or plural society.[4] He maintains that the focus of conflict is necessarily different in a plural society (i.e. a racially mixed and stratified society) from that in an indigenous class society. We would maintain that those bases of social differentiation that give rise to corporate groupings, at least in so far as they are systematically treated differentially, are as much a part of the indigenous class system as those factors that have been considered explanatory in mainstream sociology. In this sense, class systems conceptualized as indigenous obscure more than they reveal.

If we return to Gorz's thesis, we can see that he does not regard immigrants as factors exogenous to the class system but essentially part of it as it is developing in metropolitan centres in post-colonial capitalism. The fact that capitalism cannot be regarded as a collection of national capitalisms, but is essentially an international system, has been argued elsewhere (Cox 1964: Ch. 14), and the questions of class formation involving West Indian and Asian workers in Britain necessitates this as a central focus. The large-scale transfers of labour within and between societies in the British Empire and Commonwealth still await such an analysis. 'Indigenous' or 'national' class systems are not to be regarded as separate entities but are integrally related in their development to all aspects of the economic and policical structures of which they are a part. The experience of imperialism, economically, politically and culturally, presently and historically, is integral to the understanding and explanation of class in Britain.

Much present analysis of substantive systems encounters theoretical difficulties because the integration of ethnic and racial differentiation with class analysis is still lacking, and some of the elements which are central to the understanding of class relationships as they have developed in western Europe are still defined as exogenous factors. There are important similarities between the black workers in Britain and the immigrant workers in Europe. These similarities are closer since the enactment of the 1971 legislation in Britain.[5] The deprivation of a section of the working class (i.e. immigrant workers) of political, civil, and effectively of trade-union rights by this legislation carries serious implications for the social and political structure of the indigenous population. The disadvantages relate, strictly, to those governed by this legislation and not to the majority of black workers who came before the Act.[6]

This paper is therefore mainly concerned with those whose class position entails no denial of the basic protection of citizen status. It will attempt to deal with the structural determinants of class position and the social processes of class formation among the major groups coming from Britain's ex-colonies in Asia and the West Indies. The cultural, social, and economic exploitation of neo-imperialism is obvious and pervasive. It is our contention that to treat the groups as though they inevitably filled the role of an underclass is to obscure the nature of the relationships between metropolis and colonies and to assume that the colour dimension oblitereates the class dimension of this relationship.

In comparing the Asian with the West Indian experience in Britain, we must distinguish the economic, political, and cultural differences between the two groups and the processes whereby these are experienced and given meaning.

We shall obviously not attempt to do this in a comprehensive way. This would be beyond our competence and, we would maintain, beyond the evidence as it is so far available in Britain. Nor can we possibly try to do justice to the wide variety of groupings that are represented in the migration to Britain from India, Pakistan, Bangladesh, and the many West Indian societies. Our analysis is concerned only to point to some of the crucial differences that appear to us to be relevant to the discussion of class and race.

For all the groups the correlation between migration and the demand for labour in certain sectors of the British economy is relevant. The demand for labour has been discussed sufficiently for us now to take it for granted.[7] Briefly, black workers fulfilled two sorts of manpower requirements. During the period 1952 to 1965, the need for a mobile labour force to fill jobs at low levels of skill, status, and rewards in particular industries was partially met by the use of migrants from Asia and the Caribbean. Throughout this period and continuing to the present, highly skilled and professional workers in certain categories have come from Asia and the West Indies to meet specific shortfalls in manpower.[8] There has been an increasing class bias in the immigration legislation, not only in its content, but in its administration. Those wanting to work, and their dependants, are confronted by numerous bureaucratic hurdles. The necessary social skills in coping with immigration officials are possessed to a much lesser degree by a working-class migrant or dependent than by a middle-class entrant.

These groups compete within different labour markets and their occupational levels are not directly associated with skin colour. To some extent their occupations afford different life-styles and differential life-chances.

MIDDLE-CLASS MIGRANTS

The West Indians coming into middle-class occupations are exceptions. The infra-structure at home produce few such migrants. They figure most prominently in nursing and, to a much lesser extent, are found in a variety of non-manual jobs including teaching.[9] In nursing, they are concentrated in non-teaching hospitals and many are training at S.E.N. level, a qualification not recognized outside Britain, which ties them permanently to the bottom of the nursing hierarchy.[10] In life-chances and life-style, there are important potential differences between those with an S.R.N. qualification and those who have an S.E.N. qualification. The second group are firmly within the working class, but in politico–cultural terms, as with their white counterparts, their allegiance is likely to be to the lower middle class, except in so far as the spread of black consciousness produces a working-class perspective. The S.R.N. qualification carries middle-class career potential, but as yet there is little evidence to indicate any movement into the better paid and more attractive levels. As with the teaching profession, the presence of a few black individuals functions as a form of tokenism, and has little relevance for class formation.

The Asian migration presents a number of obvious contrasts. The middle-class element is weightier relative to the West Indians, not only in numbers but in potential development. They have entered a range of professions (for example medicine, law, teaching) as well as business and commercial occupations. The evidence on their position is most detailed with regard to the N.H.S. while in other spheres only scanty information exists.[11]

The racist processes present in the professional occupations in which Asians are to be found are such that Asian doctors, for instance, are clustered at the lower ends of the various medical hierarchies. The conditions that give rise to their employment ensure that they are unlikely to move out of these and the attempts of the professional associations to rationalize and confirm the situation have grown markedly in recent years. Nearly all are to be found in the least prestigious hospitals and in 'unfashionable' specialities such as geriatrics (See Gish and Robertson, 1969). Notwithstanding these processes, however, the Asian doctors relate to the class system as middle-class individuals, exhibiting towards White, Asian, and West Indian workers, the class character of their occupation. In life-style and, to a large extent, in life-chances, they are within the middle class: vis-à-vis other Asians and West Indians they constitute an elite. Their training and therefore their class position here derive not from the indigenous British definitions and structural constraints on 'Asians' but from the situation in the homelands. Since doctors have virtually free entry, this group will be constantly replaced or augmented from the same sources.

The experience of other professionals is more checkered. One survey showed a wide discrepancy at the age of thirty between white indigenous holders of bachelor degrees or diplomas in business studies and 'foreigners' (mostly Indians) with postgraduate qualifications in commerce and economics. The Indians on average earned less than half the income of the indigenous man. Similarly, a comparison of those qualified in chemistry (the foreign born holding masters or bachelors degrees and the native-born being of H.N.C. standard) showed the indigenous earnings to be one third higher. The discrepancies appeared to rise with age and experience. (*Sunday Times*: 1968).

Those with qualifications in teaching have met with a variety of experiences. Through a re-definition of skill, many with qualifications from their homelands were not given qualified teacher status here.[12] Those who succeeded in obtaining this were in many cases subjected through 'discretion' at local level to apparent discrimination (Allen: forthcoming). They had to find employment outside their profession.

Of those who succeeded in gaining entry to teaching, little is known except through local surveys.

Business and commercial activity has long been one aspect of the activity of Asian migrants to Britain. Little systematic research, however, is available. What is known relates largely to small-scale internally financed business activity. This is discussed later in the paper. The large-scale financing of business enterprise and the entrepreneurial role of Asians is obviously a question that has a direct bearing on class formation. But to say more than this in the present state of our knowledge would, however, be pure speculation.[13]

In general terms, the points made above indicate clear differences between the Asian and West Indians coming to Britain in the possession of those attributes necessary for entry into middle-class positions. We would conclude that despite the obvious factor of institutionalized racism these do not wholly remove class advantages in life-style and, more importantly, in life-chances for these sections of the minorities.

WORKING-CLASS MIGRANTS

West Indian migration into Britain has been almost totally into working-class jobs (IRR 1970: 22). Some of the migrants entered skilled occupations, but the majority of men and women are to be found in work designated as low-skilled.[14] Through the class mediating mechanisms operating in relation to their children, it is likely that a similar if not higher proportion of the second generation will be found at the lower levels of the occupational order. There is as yet only fragmentary evidence to indicate the level of access to any of the usual means of mobility, either through the educational system of further or higher education or the schemes of industrial training or apprenticeship. Our evidence indicates that semi-skilled work is most usual for both males and females, with the exception of a minority entering the lower levels of nursing and routine clerical/secretarial work. Relative to Asian workers the West Indians appear to be losing ground. For whereas a greater proportion of adult West Indians were classified as skilled in Bradford industry compared to Asians, the reverse is the case in apprenticeships (Allen, Bentley and Bornat: forthcoming).

The few West Indians who make it into the lower level white-collar jobs face immense obstacles. While a combination of white-collar unionism and black consciousness is likely to produce a politico-cultural thrust towards working-class allegiance, the isolation and racism experienced by recruits, together with their marginal advantages in social and economic terms, are just as likely to lead to withdrawal from any political commitment that would be regarded as endangering their status. A dynamic view of the clerical, routine, non-manual job situation demonstrates a clear trend towards the depression in status, career, and economic position of these groups. Mechanization and general reorganization of office work may provide niches for black women, for instance, as it has done in the United States, but these exhibit a process of proletarianization which so far is little analysed or understood (see Benet 1972).

Such possibilities are, however, likely to affect only a small minority and, generally, young West Indians seem destined for low paid, low status jobs. The evidence on education seems to indicate that they have twice the possibility compared to other immigrant children of gaining their education in E.S.N. schools[15] and many more are to be found in the lower streams. On leaving school, they form a pool of unskilled and semi-skilled labour which in times of economic restraint provides the core of those who are unemployed.[16]

In general terms, the West Indians are being allocated to the most menial working-class jobs, those that require little or no training, provide low economic rewards, possess no career structure. In addition, the evidence of unemployment indicates a greater likelihood of a casual working pattern. Moreover, the location of many of these jobs within the public and private service industries means that West Indians are competing in a housing market in which they are excluded from all except the most uneconomic properties, short leases, furnished lettings, and so on; i.e. within that sector of the urban *milieu* which is grossly under-privileged in terms of educational provision. These are some of the conditions historically related to the production of a lumpen-proletariat. Organization at work, at community level (e.g. tenants associations), claimants unions or black associations, all face enormous handicaps in their attempts to transform the situation. The Night-cleaners Campaign and the recent high level of organisation among black workers in the hospital service are clear indications that attempts to transform the material conditions receive much support; but such efforts are necessarily limited in what they can achieve. The resources available to the West Indian section of the lumpenproletariat are no greater and, in so far as racism is a factor, they are less than those available to the white section. The only resources open to the West Indians are combination with other minorities on a platform of racial identity and/or on a class basis. Both of these have so far proved difficult. Both involve directly the class and race consciousness of the white sections of the population. The responses of the white power-holders to attempts to engender black consciousness and organization have all been to deny the legitimacy of such efforts by all the means at their disposal. And this kind of response is not uncommon among liberal sections. So far they have successfully denied legitimacy. The question remains open whether a class basis can provide an alternative without the accompanying development of black consciousness and organization. The ideological collapse of black–white class solidarity, at least in its organizational forms such as the Labour Party and the labour movement generally, except in relatively isolated instances, is one of the more significant indications of racist influences operating within the stratification system. The explanation of the underlying conditions of this development has not so far been advanced by social scientists except in the most general terms. It is obviously an area needing very careful investigation.

The majority of Asians are, like the West Indians, to be found in working-class jobs. Semi-skilled and unskilled work in engineering, textiles, and transport is typical, while skilled work in building is a feature of some groups, notably Sikh carpenters. This pattern can be directly related to the heavy demand for labour, particularly where poor conditions or technological changes involve continuous working, so making the recruitment of local labour increasingly difficult. Foundry work in the Midlands and Yorkshire and textile work in Lancashire and West Yorkshire are characterized by the concentration of Asian workers, in some cases in regional–linguistic groupings.

The proportions in working-class jobs is not at issue, but what is problematic is how far organization within the Asian groups produces a potential for development different from that of the white or West Indian working class. Michael Lyon has suggested that the factor of ethnicity needs much greater consideration than has been given to it (Lyon 1972). Entering into a close analysis of the many insights contained in his papers is not possible here. Rather we shall point to the elements in the structural position of Asians in Britain and some of their activities that appear to confirm the significance of ethnic mobilization as a factor. We consider this whole area as problematic, given the paucity of empirical detail on the experiences of many of the Asian groups. However, there are sufficient doubts with regard to the notion of underclass, for instance, to justify a preliminary exploration.

The view of immigrant Asian workers as largely illiterate, non-English speaking peasants seriously underestimates the structural and cultural variations in their backgrounds. It also ignores the experience and skills of certain groups – for example the Sikhs, who have been most effective in reorganizing in migrant situations, not simply to preserve their traditional culture, but to deal effectively with the exigencies of the new situation.

Apart from the Mirpuris, many of whom came as a result of losing their land in the building of the Mangla Dam and subsequently of using the financial compensation to purchase charter flights, migrant Asians are not from landless families. They are typically younger sons of small or middle peasants, with above average education, coming from traditional areas of migration. Without the tightening of immigration control, it is quite likely that many of the Pakistanis would have continued as migrant workers, frequently working in British firms in segregated work groups, orientated firmly towards their homelands and continuing a pattern of sponsored male migration. The bringing over of wives and families, though it leads to a more permanent settlement, does not weaken the links of ethnicity either materially or ideologically.

The concentrations of Asian workers into 'ethnic' work groups may be considered as directly relevant to the question of class formation. Such groups are found in many industries employing Asians.

Typically, in the textile industry of West Yorkshire, permanent night-shift or multi-shift working in semi-skilled grades composed entirely of Asians characterizes the employment situation of Asian men. Asian women, mainly from India or Bangladesh, are similarly found at the semi-skilled level (See Allen, Bentley and Bornat forthcoming). The consequences of such concentrations are not, however, uniform from the point of view of industrial activity and organization. It has been argued that their position is weak in relation to the employer because of the privileged position of the English speaking 'go-betweens' appointed by the management. However, as Rimmer shows in his study of foundry workers, high levels of unionization and collective action can arise among such groups. He explains this in terms of traditional cultural ties and a lack of understanding of British industrial 'custom and practice' (Rimmer 1972). In our view, his material shows quite clearly the potential use of ethnicity as a mobilizing force, in the absence of other resources, for highly effective trade-union action, not in separate organizations, but within the British trade union movement. In the textile industry of West Yorkshire, ethnic concentrations have not produced these consequences, but attempts at separate organizations were also unsuccessful and non-unionism resulted from the experience of ineffective trade unions (See Zubaida 1970 : 106ff). The recent events in the hosiery industry appear to present another possible pattern.

What is clear is that these differences are not explicable by recourse to the dichotomous category 'coloured immigrants'/white working class. In each situation, racial labelling was evident as was the lack of under-standing, paternalism, and hostility from the unions, but the outcomes were markedly different. Cohesion through ethnicity is an important resource of some of the Asian groups, but by itself cannot explain why trade-union action is followed through successfully by some groups and not others. Part of such an explanation must lie in the differential experience and knowledge of the groups, but also must involve their overall position as workers within British industry and relate to such factors as working conditions and trade-union practices.

As yet, we know too little about the communal social organization of the groups concerned to establish the degree to which ethnicity can be considered as a resource for effective mobilization as workers.[17]

A further aspect of the role of ethnic social organization is the extent to which corporate groupings based on kin or village ties can, by providing support of an ideological and material kind, affect the life-chances of group members or even the position of the group as a whole. Two spheres appear to be particularly relevant. First, education, through which corporate support can enable children to stay on longer and achieve skills and qualifications which have market value as well as conferring prestige. Where necessary, use of the private sector can be made to overcome the disadvantages experienced by immigrant children in the State education system. Second, there is business activity, where the possibility of accumulating capital for small or medium sized business enterprise exists within the group. Fragmentary though the data are, there are evident differences between the possibilities open to some Asian groups and the West Indians or white working class in these respects.

It would not be reasonable at this point to assume that these differ-ences are sufficient to alter the overall life-chances of the succeeding generations. The factor of racial ordering may be such as to depress the position of Asians. But at present, both the structural position and the politico-cultural affiliations of Asian groups are not only more diverse, but more problematic in relation to class formation than those of the West Indians.

Notes

1 Part of this paper is derived from work currently being undertaken with financial support from the Social Science Research Council:

'Youth and Work: A study in differential group experience'. We should like to record at this point our indebtedness to the SSRC for all they have done in facilitating this research.

2 We are conscious that we have neglected certain factors, such as some dynamic features of ethnicity, migration, and so on, which either modify or complement our basic argument, but we are persuaded that the admittedly partial evidence points towards a conclusion such as we put forward.

3 See for instance Sami Zubaida's introduction and the contributions by John Rex and David Lockwood in Zubaida (1970.)

4 For a critical discussion of these concepts, see Allen (1972a), and Cross (1972). See, also, Kuper (1969).

5 This has recently come very much to the fore politically, see Grant and Pierce (1973). For a full analysis see Castles and Kosack (1973).

6 This is the legal position, but it cannot be assumed that black workers already here will know the position and be confident in exercising their rights. It has been argued, and there now appears some evidence to substantiate it, that all black people will be subject to increasing control and harassment because of the provisions of the Act. See, for instance, Tinker (1972).

7 For example, see Peach (1965) and Collard (1970). Collard states that between 1960-6 the male immigrant labour force responded positively to economic changes, although the level of significance is low, implying that other forces were at work also. (And Allen 1971a.) We are not implying that the demand for labour explains the motivations of the groups concerned but that they represented an available supply for meeting the existing demand.

8 The curtailing of immigration which has taken place over the last decade has been highly selective. It has kept out black workers though not white workers, but has allowed in and even encouraged black professionals, particularly doctors (see Allen 1972b). In 1968, 71 per cent of all category 'B' (i.e. skilled) work vouchers went to doctors (I.R.R. 1969: 26), and in 1969 had fallen to 57 per cent (I.R.R. 1970: 33). This downward trend was due to restrictions placed on the number of overseas doctors by the Secretary of State and changes in the Department of Employment regulations. However, these were clarified in 1971, and doctors again found themselves at a distinct advantage against other groups.

9 The high concentration of female West Indians in nursing can clearly be seen in the 1966 Census (Rose 1969: 157). The low proportion of West Indian males and females in professional occupations other than nursing can be seen in the 1961 Census (see Field and Haikin 1971: 44). For an analysis of the trends (Rose 1969: 163-166).

10 The level of ignorance on the part of potential nurses about different types of qualification when applying reveals a lack of any attempt on the part of the British Government to supply any detailed information to applications (Thomas and Williams 1972: 42-3). So, although applicants are attracted to Britain to gain a professional qualification often thought to be of value in gaining employment elsewhere, on arrival they may be channelled into a State Enrolled Course or offered a post as an auxiliary or assistant, and therefore do not gain an internationally recognized qualification. In such cases, the individual is precluded from returning to their country of origin as a nurse.

11 Something like 22 per cent of all doctors in Britain are from overseas, mostly fron the sub-continent of India. Only 12.4 per cent of consultancies are held by overseas doctors, whereas they constitute about 50 per cent of all junior hospital doctors (I.R.R. 1969: 26). For a full analysis see Gish (1971).

12 For a fuller discussion of the processes involved, see Allen (forthcoming).

13 An item in the local press is an indication of the possibilities. The Lord Mayor welcomed the Indian High Commissioner's proposal that Indian owned and financed manufacturing enterprises should be set up in Bradford (*Telegraph and Argus:* 1970). Something of this entrepreneurial zeal is also reflected in the 1966 figures, for those who were self-employed Asians, especially male Pakistanis in London, were the only non-European immigrant group to be well represented in this category (Rose: 154).

14 This should not be taken to imply that their occupational level in Britain was consistent with their actual skill level. Skill levels are rarely to be measured objectively and in the labour demand situation in Britain, the jobs available and the processes associating colour and low skill meant that the majority of West Indians found themselves in semi- or unskilled work. See Allen (1971 b: Ch. 4) for a fuller discussion of this point.

15 Although West Indian children represent only 39.6 per cent of the young immigrant population in compulsory education, they represent 78.4 per cent of immigrants in E.S.N. schools. These figures are calculated from tables 49(38), and 41(40) ii, H.M.S.O. (1972: 67 and 69). For a discussion of the factors involved in the situation, see Fethney (1972) and Neuk-Idem (1972).

16 For an analysis of the situation as reflected by the 1971 Census, see Smith (1973).

17 Subsequent analysis of the data gathered on Bradford industry shows marked differences between the degrees of unionization between Pakistanis on the one hand and Bangladeshis and Sikhs on the other.

References

ALLEN, S. 1971a. Race and Economy: Some Aspects of the Position of Non-Indigenous Labour. *Race* 13 (2): 170-174.

—— 1971b. *New Minorities, Old Conflicts*. New York: Random House.

—— 1972a. Plural Society and Conflict. *New Community*, 1 (5) Autumn 389-392.

—— 1972b. Black Workers in Great Britain. In Hans van Houte and Willy Melgert (eds.) *Foreigners in Our Community*. Amsterdam (N.D.): Keesing Publishers.

—— forthcoming. Minorities and Economic Institutions. In Robert Mast (ed.) *Institutional Response to Minority Demands: Britain and the United States Compared*. London: Oxford University Press.

ALLEN., BENTLEY, S., and BORNAT, J. forthcoming. *Colour and Work*. London: Institute of Race Relations.

BENET, M. K. 1972. *Secretary: An Enquiry into the Female Ghetto*, London: Sedgwick & Jackson.

COLLARD, D. 1970. Immigration and Discrimination: Some Economic Aspects. In C. Wilson, *et al. Economic Issues in Immigration*. London: Institute of Economic Affairs.

CASTLES, S. and KOSACK, G. 1973. *Immigrant Workers and the Class Structure in Western Europe*. London: I.R.R. and Oxford University Press.

CROMWELL COX, O. 1964. *Capitalism as a System*. New York: Monthly Review Press.

CROSS, M. 1972. Pluralism, Equality and Social Justice. *New Community* 1 (4).

FETHNEY, V. 1972. E.S.N. Children: What the Teachers Say. *Race Today* 4 (12) December: 400-401.

FIELD, F. and HAIKIN, P. 1917. *Black Britons*. London: Oxford University Press.

GISH, O. 1971. *Doctor Migration and World Health*. London: Bell & Son.

GISH, O. and ROBERTSON, A. 1969. Where Immigrant Doctors Go– and Why. *New Statesman* 14 March.

GORZ, A. 1970. Immigrant Labour. *New Left Review* No. 61, May-June.

GRANT, L. and PIERCE, G. 1973. Immigration: The Screw Tightens. *Race Today* 5 (3) March: 93-95.

H.M.S.O. 1972. *Statistics of Education: Schools* 1971, Vol. 1. London: H.M.S.O.

INSTITUTE OF RACE RELATIONS 1969. *Facts Paper*. London.

—— 1970. *Facts Paper*. 1970-71. London.

KUPER, L. 1969. Plural Societies: Perspectives and Problems. In L. Kuper and M. G. Smith (eds.) *Pluralism in Africa*. Berkeley, Calif: University of California Press.

LYON, M. 1972-3. Ethenicity and Gujerati Indians in Britain. *New Community* **2** (1) Winter.

NEUK-IDEM, M. 1972. A Schooling in Alienation. *Race Today* **4** (7) July: 244.

PEACH, C. 1965. West Indian Migration to Britain: The Economic Factors. *Race* 7 (2).

RIMMER, M. 1972. *Race and Industrial Conflict*. London: Heinemann.

ROSE, E. J. B. and associates 1969. *Colour and Citizenship*. London: I.R.R. and Oxford University Press.

SMITH, C. R. 1973. Unemployment – What the Census Shows. *Race Today* **5** (1) January: 7.

SUNDAY TIMES. 1968. 23 February, 1968. London.

TELEGRAPH & ARGUS. 1970. 30 January, 1970. Bradford.

THOMAS, M. and WILLIAMS, J. M. 1972. *Overseas Nurses in Britain*. P.E.P., Broad Sheet 539.

TINKER, H. 1972. Manifestations of Discrimination in Great Britain. In Hans van Houte and Willy Melgert (eds.) *Foreigners in Our Community*. Amsterdam (ND.): Keesing Publishers.

ZUBAIDA, S. (ed.) 1970. *Race and Racialism*. London: Tavistock Publications.

W. G. RUNCIMAN

Towards a Theory of Social Stratification*

The late Sir Cyril Hinshelwood, in a Presidential Address to the Royal Society, divided the progress of a science into three stages. The first stage is one of 'gross oversimplification', reflecting at once the need for workable rules to guide research and 'a too enthusiastic aspiration after elegance of form'. In the second stage, things become more and more untidy as 'recalcitrant facts increasingly rebel against uniformity'. In the third stage, if and when it is ever reached, 'a new order emerges, more intricately contrived, less obvious, and with its parts more subtly interwoven'. It may make the aim of this paper clearer if I begin by stating my conviction that the study of social stratification is now somewhere near the middle of the second stage. The first section of the paper will accordingly have to be devoted mainly to questions of method: it is no doubt a pity that it should, but at this stage in the progress of the subject discussion of method cannot be avoided without risk of retarding it yet further. The second section, however, will attempt to review some of our present knowledge about stratification and to arrange it in a perhaps less familiar way, and the third section will advance a number of hypotheses about contemporary industrial societies which if validated might help to bring Hinshelwood's third stage closer to realization.

I

The study of stratification has been claimed to be the central question of sociology (Lockwood 1971) in much the same way that the study of kinship has been claimed to be the central question of anthropology (Fox 1967: 10), since just as an understanding of the relations between consanguineal and/or affinal relatives in a small, pre-industrial society

*I am much indebted to Professor A. B. Cherns, Mr A. Giddens and Mr G. P. Hawthorn for their comments on the preliminary draft of this paper.

is likely to explain many other features of its organization, so will an understanding of the relations between the members of castes, estates, and/or classes in a larger and economically more developed one. But the contrast ought not be to pressed too far. Stratification, like kinship, is a cultural universal, however various its forms. Although the two may be more intimately connected in societies of the kind that anthropologists typically study, this does not alter the fact that all societies can be characterized in terms of the nature and degree of institutionalized differences of privilege among their members. The task of a theory of stratification (as of a theory of kinship) is to describe, classify, compare, and ultimately explain this aspect of social organization over the whole range of known and adequately documented cases. The substantive sections of this paper will be concerned almost wholly with industrialized or industrializing societies. But this is because that happens to be the direction of contemporary social evolution, not because the study of pre-industrial societies is in any way irrelevant to the development of stratification theory.

Some writers on stratification dispute that it is a cultural universal at all and wish instead to draw a specific distinction between 'stratified' and 'non-stratified' societies (Plotnicov and Tuden 1970; Littlejohn 1972). But it is in practice more useful to define 'stratification' in terms of any and all institutionalized differences of privilege among the adult members of society than to retain it in order to be able to mark off societies in which there is a clear hierarchical ranking of socially separated, externally visible categories of families or households. This is a verbal, not a substantive disagreement and all that matters is that the most convenient usage should be consistently followed. It is true that my own suggestion invites in turn a request for the definition of 'privilege'. But it is enough to have an approximate working definition which can be operationally modified in the course of research; in fact, I am not sure that we cannot still make do quite well, subject to one qualification, with the definition given in the *Encyclopédie*: 'Privilège signifie une distinction utile ou honorable dont jouissent certains membres de la société et dont les autres ne jouissent point'. The qualification is simply that privilege is normally a graded and not an all-or-nothing affair.

The more difficult question to which this broad definition leads is whether stratification consists in a ranking in three separate dimensions – the economic, the social (in the sense of social prestige), and the political. I have no wish to labour the controversy over this question in which I have already been a participant (Runciman 1968; Ingham 1970;

Runciman 1970). But it can, I hope, be agreed that some distinction along these lines is necessary, whether or not it is strictly appropriate to talk about separate 'dimensions', and whether or not all three should be subsumed under the heading of 'power'. Since the three are always connected in practice, there is no need to indulge in abstract speculation about whether a society is conceivable in which they would be quite separately explicable. But it is, on the other hand, central to the explanation of stratification to understand something about how the three do in fact relate to each other, and there is no reason why the relation should not to some degree at least be susceptible to empirical generalization.

An essential preliminary to any empirical generalization, however, let alone to a theory within which well-tested generalizations would be properly grounded at a more fundamental level, is an adequate framework for describing and categorizing stratification systems. Given the dangers, here as in any social science, of extrapolating such categories from one society to another in which they may not have an equivalent meaning, it might seem the prudent procedure to start from the purely formal properties of a rank-order (cf. again the example of kinship as discussed by Needham 1971). In practice, however, such an approach is likely to lead only to the worst of both worlds. On the one hand, there is the likelihood that derivation from the intuitive assumptions of transitivity, asymmetry, irreflexiveness, and chain-connection will suggest a picture of stratification not adequately matched by empirical observation, so that the benefits of axiomatization are gained only at the cost of realism (e.g. Fararo 1970). On the other hand, where only the simplest and most general notion of hierarchy is used to construct formal models of 'dominance', the number of theoretically possible structures quickly becomes unmanageable: for a three-person group the number of 'dominance structures' is two, but for an eight-person group it is already 6880 (Coleman 1960: 106). The practising sociologist has, for better or worse, no choice but to involve himself from the outset in substantive classification in terms of the criteria of ranking held, the nature of the relationship which obtains between the unequally privileged, and the cultural significance of the institutional context within which privilege is allocated.

It needs equally to be emphasized that even precise description and comparative generalization in purely static terms will be wholly inadequate as a basis for a theory of stratification. It may for some purposes be possible and, if so, convenient to construct a composite measure into which expectations for the future can be built: thus, to the extent that 'class' in the sense of economic *Lebenschancen* is expressed in monetary terms, future benefits which are a function of present position can be expressed as a capital sum discounted to net present value at the rate considered appropriate. But in general the adequate description, let alone the explanation, of any system of stratification requires not simply a specification of the relative position of all persons within it at some one given moment but also an account of the mechanisms which determine their position over the course of their lives, whether through individual mobility within the system as it now is or from changes in the degree of privilege attaching to the positions available to be occupied. Formally, therefore, each member of the system should be assigned a place in 'stratification space', whether three-dimensional (Runciman 1966: 26-27) or more complex (Hope 1972a: 3-4), and his/her movement along the several axes plotted over adult life from an initial position of parental or quasiparental origin.

Unfortunately, however, to say this still does not yield a check list of standard parameters whose value the researcher into any given society can in practice settle down to ascertain. First of all, differences in levels of culture and economic development are such that the list appropriate for one society may be altogether less appropriate for another. Second, many (perhaps most) aspects of stratification are not, or not yet, sufficiently amenable to precise definition and measurement. Third, the list which any researcher adopts in practice will be influenced, and rightly so, by his own particular concerns and by his view of the likelihood that one selection rather than another will generate the more powerful hypotheses about the relations either between stratification parameters or between one or more stratification parameters and some other independent variable or variables (a notable example is Andreski 1954). At the most general cross-cultural level, there are five questions which any researcher concerned with stratification will be bound to ask about any society he studies: first, who rules and who is ruled?; second, how are material goods and services allocated?; third, what degree of deference, or institutionalized respect, is accorded by who to whom?; fourth, among how many (if any) externally distinguishable, institutionally ranked groups or quasi-groups whose members acknowledge some common economic and/or social and/or political interest can the members of the society be said to be distributed?; fifth, what are the rates of social mobility between such groups or, in their absence, between vertically differentiated roles or positions? But the greater the detail in which the researcher tries to answer these questions the more likely he is to want to adopt not only techniques but also concepts which will differ widely according to the type of society in question.

The first stage, therefore, in the development of a theory of stratification must be the deliberately simplified description of a sample of societies (or communities – a point to which I shall return in a moment) in terms of a highly selected and perhaps quite loosely defined set of parameters, which relate more or less directly to these five fundamental questions.

It does not, however, follow from this that the most useful way to proceed at the following stage will be to try to establish inductive correlations between the values of the chosen parameters out of which presumptive laws might in the end be constructed. The approach for which I wish to argue in this paper calls rather for a specification of the range within which these values can be shown to vary and a demonstration of the way in which indentifiable constraints so act on stratification systems as to limit the values which might otherwise be observed. It is almost certainly unrewarding to try to generalize about stratification in terms of a direct correspondence between ecological or cultural variables on the one hand and the parameters of stratification on the other. No doubt such correspondences are somewhere implicit in any would-be theory of stratification. But to make them the initial goal of such a theory is to risk underemphasizing the dynamic, or if you prefer historical, aspect of stratification systems and the degree to which their evolution must be understood in terms of a continuing dialectic not only between the mode and the relations of production but between the conflicting goals being deliberately pursued by different groups, quasi-groups, and strata.

This, in a way, is merely a gloss on Marx's familiar dictum that men make their own history, but not as they please. But the approach that I am putting forward will involve more than simply a narrative account of the shifting patterns of class or quasi-group competition and/or conflict against the background of economic evolution. It goes without saying that each society chosen for study is in some respects unique, including in the awareness of its members of the history to date of other societies (Bendix 1970). But their systems of stratification can nonetheless all be validly described in terms of an interaction between the aims of the leaders of the currently dominant strata, the exogenous and/or endogenous constraints inhibiting the realization of those aims, and the more or less self-conscious reactions of the members of those strata which are for the moment, at any rate, subordinate (cf. Eisenstadt 1963: Ch. 5 for a similar approach in the case of pre-modern empires). This still sounds rather Marxian, and in one sense it is – but not in the sense that we can continue to operate in terms of the 'gross oversimplifications' of classical Marxism in which the scientific study of social stratification might be said to have reached the first, but only the first, of Hinshelwood's three stages. It is not so much that the predictions generated by classical Marxism have been falsified (or can be rescued only by highly selective manipulation of some of Marx's later views) as that we now understand, in a way that Marx could not conceivably have done, just how wide is the range of variation, even within the constraints imposed by the mode of production, open to the rulers of industrialized or industrializing societies. Britain has come to seem no longer the paradigm, but rather the deviant case (Moore 1966). The abolition of capitalism can no longer be plausibly seen as bringing about the transition to a classless society in which man ceases to be dominated (and/or 'exploited') by man but rather the replacement of one form of stratification by another (Djilas 1957; Ossowski 1963; Parkin 1969, 1971a; Lane 1971). Although class consciousness may be as significant as ever in bringing new groups into the political arena as organized competitors for privilege, this can in practice be brought about by consciousness of race or nationality as much as of class (Kuper 1971, 1972); and we can now begin to see more clearly in the experience of the Afro-Asian countries at once how much and how little option rests with the leaders of industrializing regimes ostensibly committed to reducing inequalities between rich and poor, high status groups and low, and rulers and ruled. The classical Marxian model is only one of the variations possible within the larger constraints of industrial society. Adequate cross-cultural comparison calls for an altogether wider range of ideal types.

From this perspective, Weber's advice (1956: I, 196) that 'for the purposes of theory it is useful to work with extreme cases' is particularly pertinent. Imprecise as our indicators may be, there is no doubt that the range of variation in human society does cover some very distant extremes; already at the stage of pre-industrial societies it stretches from the almost imperceptible degree of vertical differentiation in some hunting and gathering societies (e.g. L. Marshall 1960) to the almost total despotism of some of the traditional African Kingdoms (e.g. Herskovits 1938: Pt.V). But wide as the variation may be it is far from infinite; and it is quite clearly not random. There are discernible constraints within which patterns of stratification evolve, and under given ecological and demographic conditions they preclude the realization of the extreme values except at the unrealistic cost of drastic concomitant structural and/or cultural changes. Whatever the difficulties in predicting the emergence of hitherto unrealized, but conceivable, stratification systems, it is perfectly possible to account in retrospect for the observed emergence of a particular pattern of stratification parameters within a chosen sample of societies and to isolate those parameters which may be of significant influence on the subsequent evolution of systems of different types.

At this point, however, it will be as well to revert briefly to the difference between stratification in societies and in communities. The constraints operating on industrial or industrializing nation-states do not necessarily operate on local communities considered as autonomous stratification systems. Still less do they operate on self-recruiting communities deliberately organized to evade the anti-egalitarian pressures of the wider society. It is perfectly possible that in, for example, New Haven, Connecticut as studied by Dahl (1961) power is more widely dispersed and inequalities of wealth and status less marked than either in other American towns and cities or in the United States viewed as a whole; and there is no doubt whatever that, to take a still better example, the Israeli *Kibbutzim* exemplify a notably egalitarian social organization, even if not so wholly as their overt ideology implies. But it would be very misleading to regard either New Haven or the *Kibbutzim* as though they were entirely divorced from the nation-states of which they form a part. The most obvious omission in both cases would be the military. As Dahl's critics have not failed to point out, there is no Pentagon in New Haven, but there is in Washington D.C.; and in the same way, the *Kibbutzim* are no less involved than any other Israeli communities in their country's military organization and the network of political leadership and influence bound up with it. Indeed, Israel provides a particularly interesting example of the compromises imposed in the conflict between the ideological principles of the Zionist pioneers and the requirements of an industrializing Israeli state (Jonas 1965; Eisenstadt 1967: Ch.7). No doubt it is necessary always to remember the extent of local or regional differences within even quite highly industrialized nation-states (cf. eg. Dollard 1937, for the American South; Silverman 1970, for the case of Italy; or Germani 1971, for the case of Argentina). But in a world of nation-states such as ours has now become, this is the level at which stratification has primarily to be conceptualized and hypotheses about it put to empirical test.

How, therefore, are the systems of stratification evolved by industrial nation-states to be classified? An initial typology can be derived directly from the five questions which I earlier suggested that any researcher into the stratification system of any society is bound to ask. But the emphasis which I have placed on the interaction between dominant and subordinate strata and the constraints within which

TABLE 1

The distribution of power in six ideal types of industrial society

	A 'class' type	B. 'elite' type	C 'caste' type
1 basis	property-ownership	force and/or guile	ethnic group membership
2 degree of concentration	high ('ruling class')	high ('governing elite')	high
3 degree of cohesion among holders	very high (class interest)	medium (competitive power-struggle)	very high (status-group solidarity)
4 distance of holders from non-holders	large and increasing (until revolution)	large (and constant)	large (and impassable)
5 answerability of holders to non-holders	low (grudging concessions)	very low (skilful manipulation)	very low enforced (paternalism)
6 rate of elite turnover	very low (but long-range mobility not impossible)	violent and cyclical	nil (endogamous recruitment)
7 mode of elite recruitment	class inheritance	military/political skill/patronage	status-group inheritance
8 criterion of ritual status	wealth	office	ethnic purity
9 justifying ideology	bourgeois liberalism	any myth that works	historical and/or divine right
10 achilles heel	spread of proletarian class-consciousness	putschism leading to tyranny	implausibility of justifying ideology

both are required to act leads to a particular emphasis on those parameters which are most directly relevant to the first question – that is, to the mode of social control. It is notorious that the social sciences concerned with the concept of power are still without any adequate operational definition of it. But this does not preclude the elaboration of a range of ideal types of industrial society, of which England as depicted by Marx would be one, depicting patterns of access to and use of positions of political or quasi-political privilege. I do not imply that the chicken-and-egg debate on the primacy of economic class and political power is to be settled in favour of the latter, for the question

TABLE 1—*continued*

D *'pluralist' type*	E *'socialist' type*	F *'revolutionary' type*
technical expertise	position with bureau-cracy	role among leadership cadres
medium ('dispersed inequalities')	high	very high
medium ('free expression of alternative values')	medium (intra-party factionalism)	high (army/party antagonism latent)
medium	large (and constant)	large (but occasional attempts to diminish it)
medium (pressure groups)	low (iron law of oligarchy)	medium ('mass line')
medium (but steady)	low (but occasional purges)	medium (charismatic succession)
talent/professional education	professional education/ party antecedents	charismatic ('revolutionary') leadership
high-valued skills	party standing	ideological enthusiasm
'functional' social theory	'non-antagonistic classes'	'permanent revolution'
covert operation of 'power elite'	extra-party intellectual/ worker discontent	routinization leading to bureaucracy

in this form does not admit of this sort of answer. But in a different sense, political power has necessarily to have precedence since all actual property relations are subject to the tacit consent of those whose access to the means of physical coercion would enable them to disturb such relations if they so chose. As a starting point, therefore, the table set out above contrasts six ideal types, including Marx's, in terms of a partial list of parameters which may help to suggest both what range of variation is theoretically possible in industrial societies and what kinds of alternatives thus present themselves to those either holding or aspiring to hold political office. As Type A derives from Marx, so Type

B derives from Pareto, Type D from the writings of the American 'Functionalists' and Type F from Weber's notion of 'charismatic legitimacy'. But the point of the typology is not the respectability of its pedigree but its value as a preliminary to actual cross-national comparison.

In proferring an ideal typology defined in terms of modes of social control, I am not suggesting that a fully-fledged theory of stratification would rest exclusively, or even predominantly, on the specific parameters I have listed. But once industrialization is in train, size, complexity, and the need for social control go hand in hand. Allocation of privilege can no longer be regulated by ritual status and custom, even if in pre-industrial society this can furnish an adequate means (Southall 1970). It can be regulated only by the active exercise of institutional restraints: in capitalist society, the market functions as a state police, just as the party (or under certain conditions the army) functions as the capitalist class of socialist society. In either case – or in any admixture of ideal types – the first thing for the researcher to investigate is the kind of stratification system the governing elite wishes to maintain (which, of course, may not be at all the same as what its spokesmen say it wishes to maintain), and the second thing is the extent of its capacity to do it. It is in this sense that the complicated interrelations between stratification parameters characteristic of actual industrial or industrializing societies cannot be analysed adequately without reference to the particular system of social control and its concomitant ideology within which they work themselves out in the course of economic development.

The next step, however, in the development of a would-be theory of stratification must be the derivation from the ideal typology of an actual typology in terms of which existing nation-states can be classified. It is not necessary at this stage that the typology should be exhaustive, but only that there should be actual stratification systems which can be assigned to each type and compared by reference to the selected list of parameters, beginning with the mode of social control, on which they can be seen to differ. For this purpose, I propose a five-fold typology in which each type is composed of elements of two (or in one case, three) of the ideal types, as follows: (1) a 'neo-capitalist' type in which the mode of social control is a blend of the 'class' and 'pluralist' ideal types; (2) a 'social-democratic' type in which there is further added an element of the 'socialist' ideal type; (3) a 'state socialist' type in which the 'socialist' and 'elite' ideal types are blended; (4) a 'revolutionary socialist' type in which the 'revolutionary' and 'pluralist' ideal types are blended; and (5) an 'ethnocratic' type in which the 'caste' and 'elite' ideal types are blended. A current example of the first would be

Britain; of the second, Sweden; of the third, the Soviet Union; of the fourth, China; and of the fifth, South Africa. An actual society can, of course, move from one to another or even, as with Tito's Yugoslavia, hover between them (cf. Parkin 1971b). Likewise, there can be a society which has to be categorized in terms of a combination not covered by the five I have given: if, for example, it is true of pre-war Japan to say that 'With the introduction of the "Quasi-War-Order" at the beginning of the Shōwa era, almost all groups were reorganized *en masse* into control-bodies subordinated and subservient to a government which functioned primarily for the perpetuation and perfection of wartime state monopoly capitalism' (Taguchi 1968:468) then it might be appropriate to classify it as a 'fascist' type in which the 'elite' and 'socialist' ideal types were blended. Or again, some societies cut across the classification either because of regional differences or because a distinguishable minority of their members are treated on a different basis: thus, both present-day Japan and the United States are primarily 'neo-capitalist' but in both there is an ethnic minority subject to 'caste'-type forms of social control, so that they have strictly to be classified as blending ideal types A and D with an element of ideal type C. But the five actual examples which I have given do, I believe, fit sufficiently well for them to furnish a test, given certain specifiable conditions, of the hypotheses to be put forward in Section III.

To the different question how there come to be these actual types in the first place, the only proper answer that can be given is historical. There is not and never will be any general social theory in terms of which their emergence could be shown to have been inevitable. All that can be said is that in retrospect each nation-state chosen for comparison can be seen to have passed through a phase at the end of which it has a more or less established governing elite with a more or less coherent ideology which is able within limits to follow a consistent policy of progressive industrialization and to maintain the type of stratification system which has by this stage emerged. There is no single decisive event, or even set of conjoint conditions, common to all. It may possibly be meaningful to speak in each case of a 'revolution', if that dangerous term is sufficiently broadly defined. But the disparate causes which led up to the initial industrialization of Britain, the unification of Germany, the Meiji Restoration in Japan, the defeat of the Kuomintang in China, the emancipation of Yugoslavia from Soviet hegemony, the establishment and consolidation of social democracy in Sweden, the defeat by the Northern of the Southern United States, and all the rest cannot possibly be represented by a single common model. At most, there is a similar eventual replacement, but by very dissimilar means, of a governing elite whose position rested on the ownership of land and a strict monopoly of the most effective weapons, by a governing elite whose position rests rather on control not simply of weapons but of the commodity and labour markets within a much more specialized and complex division of labour. The change can still be meaningfully described in terms of a transformation in the mode and social relations of production. But the variety of forms which it can take is too wide for those terms taken by themselves to have more than limited explanatory value.

It follows from the fact of this variety that, once again, no standard checklist of parameters suggests itself as the obvious basis of comparison even between the five actual types of industrial society which I have put forward. We can say that classification in terms of mode of social control and the parameters related to it has to be supplemented by parameters belonging to the dimensions of economic class and social prestige, some of which are already implicit in *Table I*. But more needs to be done than simply to cite inequality in the distribution of goods and services on the one hand and inequality in the allocation of social prestige on the other. No doubt the same basic properties of a rank-order should be taken into account as far as they can, such as the distance between strata, the distribution of the population across them, the rate of upward and downward mobility from one to another, and so on. But this is in practice not wholly feasible even in the case of economic inequality, let alone of inequality of social prestige. As I remarked earlier, the researcher has no choice but to employ a set of parameters that embodies significant substantive assumptions about the nature of the system which it depicts. Measurement in detail of inequality of social prestige calls for (1) calculation of endogamy rates within subjectively chosen status-groups; (2) sample surveys of opinion on (a) the notional ranking of occupations and (b) the degree of contact held acceptable with occupational, ethnic, or other groups; (3) correlation of relations of friendship and commensalism with similarities in social origin and/or occupation; and (4) participant-observation and analysis of modes of social interaction symbolic of the acknowledgement of superior or inferior prestige. No purely formal model can possibly do justice to these. Measurement in detail of economic inequalities is, or should be, more straightforward since once beyond pre-monetary societies all the various components of income and wealth can in principle be assigned a cash value. But here, too, reliance on the validity of the measure used presupposes some quite strong assumptions about the intersubjective comparability of utilities and the perception of cultural significance on the part of the members of the society studied, and the selection to be made will be discretionary alike in the kinds of variables presumed to be important and in the way in which they are operationally defined.

Yet it would, despite all of this, be a mistake to exaggerate the difficulties of cross-cultural comparison of institutional inequalities, whether economic, social, or political. It is true that the detailed description of any particular stratification system is likely to make use of terms whose cross-cultural applicability is doubtful – 'slavery' is perhaps the most familiar example (cf. de Reuck and Knight 1967: Chs. 11-14). It is also true that even within the same culture the connotation of ostensibly unchanging role designations can shift widely – the most familiar example here is perhaps 'farmer' (cf. eg. Norbeck 1970 for the difficulties this raises in the case of Japan). But this is an obstacle to the development of stratification theory only if the changes or differences within or between cultures cannot be related even to an ordinal ranking of greater or lesser privilege, whether economic, social, or political. Stratification is sometimes discussed as though the difficulty to be resolved is whether or not it consists in inequality in income, levels of education, patterns of self-appraisal of status, objective differences in life-style, and so on. But this puts the question back to front. All these are relevant to stratification to the degree to which they can be shown to be valid indicators of institutionalized inequalities of wealth, prestige, or power. To say that any suggested parameter is relevant to stratification is to say that it can in principle be related to the distribution of privilege; and it is then a matter for empirical investigation to specify this relation both as accurately and as generally as can be done. The parameters discussed in the second section of the paper are not susceptible to accurate measurement (or at least, I make no claim to be able to measure them accurately). But this is for other reasons than that they cannot be cross-culturally applied.

One final point about method needs to be made. It is implicit in my argument that even a comprehensive typology supported by a theory much more advanced than we can now envisage would still have only a limited predictive value. This is in part because all social science, like all biological science, is evolutionary, and, even if we understood the underlying psychological mechanism of cultural evolution as well as we understand the underlying genetic mechanism of the evolution of species, sociologists could no more predict the emergence of as yet unrealized cultures than biologists can predict the emergence of as yet unrealized species. But more important, radical changes in stratification systems depend to a very considerable degree on exogenous causes which the stratification theorist has simply to accept as given. His hypotheses must, accordingly, be explicitly conditional on the non-occurrence of quite unpredictable events of a kind which he knows nonetheless to be bound sooner or later to occur, ranging from the decline of Rome and the adoption of the stirrup in western Europe to the defeat of the Tsarist armies and the arrival of Lenin at the Finland Station. There is, however, no formal objection to *ceteris paribus* clauses so long as their scope is made clear; and for as long as a sudden and drastic modification of the system is not imposed from outside by intimidation, subversion, or conquest (or, conversely, as a result of decolonization) the pattern of stratification in industrialized societies is likely to be not only further from the ideal type but at the same time more durable than the overall variation between systems might lead one to expect. It is true that the nation-states of the twentieth century are so linked as themselves to constitute a stratified system (Nettl and Robertson 1968) within which they influence each other not only politically but also economically through the operations of world-wide commodity markets. Moreover if, as some observers believe, there will be a serious world-wide shortage of natural resources by the end of the century, major changes both within and between them are likely to result. But the hypotheses advanced in Section III of this paper must be understood as conditional on a relative absence of exogenous disturbances. Unrealistic though this condition may be, the task of stratification theory is not to specify the future pattern of stratification for the nation-states of the world such that if it does not materialize the theory is invalidated. The theory, or would-be theory, will be invalidated only if the relations among the endogenous variables in a specified sample of nation-states turn out other than the theory postulated, even in the absence of any significant interference from outside of them.

II

Once given a suggested typology of actual nation-states, the next step is to set out the chosen list of parameters in terms of which they are to be compared and hypotheses about their future evolution framed, on the basis of such limited knowledge as we have. But at the same time it is important to remember what is constant rather than variable in the stratification systems of all industrial (or near-industrial) nation-states. Familiar and even obvious though they may be, we do have some well-validated generalizations which relate to each of the five initial questions and which, when taken together, serve quite drastically to limit the range of possibilities which would otherwise theoretically be open. In this section, accordingly, I begin by setting out some of what we can claim to know to be the constraints on the stratification systems of industrial or near-industrial nation-states, whatever may be the wishes of the governing elite and the relative strength of other groups or strata.

1. The universality of a discernible governing elite does not follow from the now discredited evolutionary hypothesis (Spencer 1876) that all political organization follows from military organization. But it does hold true that all societies above a minimal level of development, and certainly all those at the level where industrialization has become feasible, are organized to some degree both for internal control (or repression) and for territorial defence (or aggression). The role, influence, size, status, and policy of the military as distinct from the political arm of the governing elite vary widely (Andreski 1954; Janowitz 1964). Perhaps the only safe generalizations on this particular point are that the degree of privilege accorded to the military elite will vary inversely with the countervailing power of other elites (Aron 1960) and directly with the incidence of war (Stinchcombe 1963). But if the governing elite is considered as a whole, it is a further safe generalization that 'relatively the governing elite becomes increasingly exclusive with increasing size of the system' (Svalastoga 1965:150). This generalization cannot be given precise quantitative form. But simple arithmetic is enough to demonstrate that a constitution modelled on the methods of selection and tenure applied among the citizens of ancient Athens cannot conceivably be applied among the citizens of a large industrial nation-state even at the extreme theoretical rate of intra-generational mobility. Moreover the ethnographic literature on stratification seems to show that the almost total egalitarianism observed in some hunting and gathering societies becomes impossible already when population reaches somewhere between 10^2-10^3 (Murdock 1949; Steward 1955).

2. It is also universally true that stratification and size are correlated in the economic as well as the political dimension. Here, the impetus to stratification deriving from the division of labour may be a function not of size itself so much as 'level of activity' (Svalastoga 1964); and again, the relation cannot be expressed quantitatively. But the general proposition that hierarchial specialization of occupations is a joint function of increasing activity and exploitation of the environment can be usefully framed in terms of the notion of 'functional adjustment' as that term is used by Sahlins (1958). 'Functional' as so used implies neither adaptation for survival nor societal consensus on the criteria of stratification, but presupposes only that societies so organizing themselves as to increase rather than diminish productivity will have progressively to modify their organization in certain respects if they are to succeed.

Some degree of inequality of economic reward or equivalent amenities is then a function of the degree of specialization which an industrial society requires. In a market society, this holds for reasons which have been well understood since Adam Smith (1776: Bk I, Ch.10). In societies where the market is politically controlled and labour directed, there is obviously the possibility of imposing much greater economic equality. But cross-national comparison of the distribution of earnings in industrial societies strongly suggests that a discernible pattern persists even where deliberately egalitarian policies are in force and private property has been abolished (Lydall 1968; cf. Parkin 1969); and there is not yet any instance of an industrial society in which skill-cum-training differentials and productivity incentives have been abolished entirely.

3. Bound up in turn with the division of labour is the reinforcement of hierarchial differentiation by ascriptive grouping. This again is a generalization which has to be qualified at the level of social organization where stratification is intrafamilial (M. G. Smith 1965). But beyond this level of size and complexity, the combination of a specialized division of labour, overt competition for privilege, and a now necessarily sectional pattern of loyalty and affection within familial or other ascriptive groups renders it inevitable that differentiation in life-style between mutually visible groups should help both to engender and to perpetuate stratification in the dimension of status. It may not be unconditionally true that the institution of the family as such makes stratification unavoidable (Huaco 1966). But even where the influence of the family is deliberately countered by an alternative form of social organization, ascriptive groups will emerge whose members recognize them to be competitors for social prestige; the *Kibbutzim* again provide an obvious example (Spiro 1958: 404-5). In industrial societies where the allocation of adult occupational roles is effected principally through the joint agency of the family and the school, the process of status-differentiation is inevitably self-perpetuating. This will hold particularly if heads of families are free to operate in a market for residential and related amenities and the consequent tendency to endogamy within self-selecting status-groups is unchecked (Beshers 1962); but it applies also, if to a lesser degree, in socialist industrial society (Machonin 1970).

4. Any attempt to generalize about 'class-consciousness' is at first sight altogether more difficult. But if it is loosely defined as a common awareness of underprivilege and a willingness to act jointly to remedy it, there are a number of observable conditions under which it is known to be augmented or diminished in magnitude and/or degree. Mobility itself is one of the most important of them. It may not be strictly true –

or empirically testable – that 'individual competition and collective action are in principle mutually convertible' (Dahrendorf 1966: 19). But it is hard to dispute that the various channels of individual mobility open in industrial or near-industrial societies serve as 'powerful palliatives of inequality' (Casanova 1970: 114), and doubly so when combined with a high rate of emigration (*ibid;* and cf. e.g. Martins 1971: 84-5 for the case of Portugal). Conversely, the denial of expected mobility will serve at the same time to augment resentment and to recruit potential leaders for the under-privileged group or quasi-group to whom mobility is denied (ethnic barriers to mobility furnish the clearest example; but see e.g. Mann 1971: 65-6 on the militancy of scientific and technical workers in France). The consequential effects of varying levels of class-consciousness on the stratification system are not susceptible to generalization in these terms: they can only be understood by reference to both the cultural history of the society in question (cf. Runciman 1966, for the case of England and compare Scase 1974, for the case of Sweden), and the structural context of individual and/or collective mobility within it (contrast traditional India with Japan as described by Nakane 1970). But once a pattern of legitimate expectation has been disrupted, there will be bound to be generated a collective resentment which under suitable conditions will challenge the existing system of stratification and social control.

5. If we turn from static differences in political, economic, and social prestige to differences in rates of upward and/or downward mobility, then just as the maximum rate of intra-generational mobility into the elite is an arithmetical function of the ratio of elite to non-elite positions, so is the maximum rate of inter-generational mobility an arithmetical function of fertility, mortality, and migration as well as of changes in the number of potential vacancies for more or less privileged positions (Yasuda 1964; Duncan 1965; Fox and Miller 1967). It is also possible to generalize about the conditions under which a specified rate of 'modernization' defined in terms of (i) movement of labour from primary to secondary industry, (ii) bureaucratization and (iii) education will increase the rates of mobility theoretically attainable, which may, for example, increase relatively faster for long than short-range mobility where (ii) and (iii) proceed faster than (i) over the initial stage of economic development. To predict the combined effects of these structural constraints on mobility is of course very much more difficult (Soares 1967; Cutright 1968); but descriptive cross-cultural generalization within known theoretical limits is problematic only to the extent that the degree of privilege attaching to the occupational or analogous

positions chosen as the basis for mobility calculations may be different in different societies, particularly where elaborate occupational codings are used (cf. Carlsson 1958: 117-119; Svalastoga and Rishøj 1970: 523; Hope 1972b).

If these generalizations, however loosely framed, can be accepted as true it then becomes possible to put forward a list of related variables in such a way as to bring out the degree of difference to an existing stratification system which can still be made by overt political choice. I do not imply that other parameters which have been selected in national and/or cross-national research (such as rates of manual/non-manual mobility, scores on composite scales of 'socio-economic status', endogamy rates between occupational classes, etc.) are irrelevant. I mean only that those that follow are particularly relevant to the question how wide or how narrow a range of alternative stratification systems industrial society permits. The table below is accordingly followed by a short comment on the list of fifteen arbitrarily chosen variables, which again cites some of the established findings that may help in the framing of hypotheses about actual, and not merely ideal-typical, industrial societies.

1.1 'Decentralization' is a loose term, but it serves to bring together the second and fourth of the parameters from *Table 1* – degree of concentration of power and distance of holders from non-holders. Extreme cases might be Nazi Germany on the one hand and Yugoslavia on the other; in the first decentralization was limited to the deliberate, sometimes arbitrary playing-off of factions within the totalitarian elite against each other (Speer 1970 gives a vivid first-hand account); in the second, the institution of workers' councils seems to have been no less deliberately introduced in order to delegate the maximum autonomy to shop-floor workers compatible with the requirements of industrial production (Kolaja 1965; Blumberg 1968; Riddell 1968). There seems little doubt, however, in the Yugoslav case that workers' autonomy, whether or not it succeeds in reversing the relations of men to managers at the local factory level (Lukic 1965), is conditional on policies formulated at the level of central government. Just as in capitalist countries governmental 'neutrality' licences dissent within rather than about the institutions through which power is allocated, so in socialist societies, even those with a practical commitment to decentralization of authority, 'workers' autonomy' does not imply any weakening of party control; it implies only that party control will be used to equalize the distribution of power at a subordinate level.

1.2 'Rate' of in- or out-flow suggests a strictly quantifiable parameter. But the method of selection has also to be taken into account: an age-set

TABLE 2

Constants and selected variables of stratification in industrial society

constants	variables
1 presence of a governing elite	1.1 degree of decentralization
	1.2 rate of inflow/outflow
	1.3 degree of internal cohesion
2 differential remuneration of labour	2.1 scale of differentials allocated to skill/training
	2.2 rate of 'welfare' allowances
	2.3 degree of inequality of accumulated resources
3 prestige grading of occupational roles	3.1 extent of unanimity in grading
	3.2 ordering of intermediate grades
	3.3 degree of legitimacy accorded to status mobility
4 quasi-group consciousness of interests	4.1 degree of acceptance of under-privilege
	4.2 extent of structural/cultural pluralism
	4.3 degree of permissibility of inter-institutional conflict
5 incidence of vacancies for social mobility	5.1 extent of legal restriction
	5.2 role of education in intra-generational mobility
	5.3 ratio of individual to collective mobility

system in which tenure of privilege is automatic is very different from a tyranny in which turnover is brought about by successive purges within the governing elite and forced mobility into it. A traditional concern of stratification theorists is to identify the category of persons from among whom the elite is typically selected (see e.g. Duverger 1959: Bk I, Ch. 3; Lasswell and Lerner 1965). But the interesting question is not so much how far each category of citizen has an equal – that is, equally small – opportunity to hold office, as whether replacement, when it occurs, can ever involve more than a very limited inflow from strata previously quite unconnected with the existing governing elite. The most suggestive example here is probably China (see e.g. Oksenberg 1970 for the period up to the Cultural Revolution). It is still too soon, and the obstacles in the way of gathering reliable evidence are too numerous, for any conclusion drawn from it to be more than speculative. But if 'permanent revolution' remains the official policy of the regime, this implies a determination regularly to renew the composition of the elite from as previously disprivileged groups or classes as feasible. The dilemma to which this leads, however, concerns the elite within the elite; in practice, the policy has to be imposed on senior party and/or army functionaries by a central committee or its equivalent, and the capacity to force the rate of turnover, therefore, depends in turn on the degree of concentration of power at the very top.

1.3 The large literature on this topic is addressed mainly to the question of whether the 'power elite' of capitalist society is, despite appearances, highly cohesive (Mills 1965; Miliband 1969) or whether there is a genuine plurality of elites by comparison with the 'monolithic' centralism attributed to socialist society (Aron 1950; Keller 1963). But the difficulties both of comparing like with like and of collecting the evidence sufficient to test the comparison are such that no firm generalization in these terms is possible. All that can be said is that there is both more tacit agreement within the governing elites of capitalist societies and more factionalism within the governing elites of socialist societies than is suggested by pluralist theory in the one case or Marxist theory in the other. A more important comparison, however, from the standpoint of the society as a whole, is the relative openness of factions within the governing elite to pressures from outside it. Where there is a lack of cohesion, even if it does not extend to any willingness to question the political system as such, the outcome in terms of governmental policy may be more or less independent of the opinions and wishes of the governed. Thus, where the army is a contender for decision-making authority outside the purely military sphere, it may or may not wish or need to appeal for support among groups outside the governing elite. Again, precise comparison is impossible; but the range of variation can readily be seen by contrasting, say, Israel, China, and Greece.

2.1 Despite the broad similarity which has been observed in the distribution of the pre-tax incomes of full-time adult male non-farm workers in industrial societies, differentials between occupational categories can vary widely. In particular, the earnings of skilled manual relative to clerical workers may rise sufficiently to reverse the traditional differential, whether through vigorous trade unionism in capitalist societies or political direction in socialist ones. It is true that, as I remarked earlier, in all industrial societies for which data are available professional and senior technical workers earn substantially more than unskilled manual. Furthermore, when amenities other than earnings are taken into account also, the combined influence of education and income becomes clearly visible; in Poland, despite a government policy of equalization after 1945, Wesolowski and Slomczynski (1968) found a clear hierarchy in housing conditions and life-styles varying from professionals at the top to unskilled workers at the bottom, and similar inequalities have been documented in Czechoslovakia (Machonin 1970) and Hungary (sources cited by Lane 1971: 76-78). But the range of inequalities appears to be significantly less in China, even if here too, so far as newspaper reports suggest, some comparable differentials are permitted in the industrial sector.

2.2 Once given even minimal economic equality, there is an 'underprivileged' quasi-group by definition. But inequalities in wage, salary, or investment incomes need to be distinguished from inequalities between those in work (or in receipt of private profit) and those unable to work, past working, or otherwise qualifying for public or private maintenance benefit. Indeed, the establishment of an explicit political right to such benefit is one of the features of modern industrial society that stands in evident contrast to the limited and arbitrary provision characteristic of most pre-industrial societies (T. H. Marshall 1950). The allocation of such benefits tends, however, in socialist as well as capitalist society, to be linked to the overall stratification system (cf. Nove 1961 or Osborn 1970, for the case of the Soviet Union); and the range of variation extends to societies in which there is a category of the population denied full citizen rights and therewith restricted to an altogether lower scale of benefits than the dominant group (South Africa is the obvious case).

2.3 Relative equality of incomes after tax and net redistribution can co-exist with much greater inequality of wealth; reliable figures are available for few countries, but in Britain (Atkinson 1970), Canada (Porter 1965: Ch. 4) and the United States (Kolko 1962; Lampman 1962), large capital fortunes can be transmitted within families from one generation to another despite imposition of estate duties or inheritance taxes. This is evidently not possible in socialist societies; but if education is as important a determinant of future economic life-chances as is commonly claimed, and if chances of educational attainment are themselves much affected by family background, then analogous inequalities in 'human capital' will arise. No accurate comparative data can yet be offered; but to the degree that economic inequality extends to the accumulation of non-monetary resources and the possibility of their transmission, and not merely to allocation of income, the analogy is valid, and the possible range of variation in industrial societies curtailed.

3.1 Despite the well-known similarity in occupational prestige ratings discovered in a number of industrial societies (Inkeles and Rossi 1956; cf. Hodge *et al.* 1967), there is still in each case a deviant minority which rejects the majority's criteria, whether because of a generational difference or because of an 'egocentrism' of class (Young and Willmott 1955; Gerstl and Cohen 1964). It is true that the extent of deviance found in studies of this kind is remarkably small, even taking account of the difference between personal and public criteria (Svalastoga 1959: Sec. 2; cf. Siegel 1970, on American Negroes). But this is likely to be to some degree an artifact of the research technique (cf. Goldthorpe and Hope 1972) and in actual contact allocation of prestige may be much more fluid and contentious (Plowman *et al.* 1962). There is always the possibility of a cumulative rejection by the less privileged of the criteria by which their superiors rank them, even when an occupational hierarchy is supported by an explicit ideology of caste: to recognize an order of castes is not necessarily to accept it (Berreman 1972). Although all elites seek to disseminate and justify the criteria implicit in the rank-order which assigns them the highest place, this cannot always be achieved simply by the exercise of political control and/or economic dominance.

3.2 The most evident difference in the grading of occupations in industrial society which can be brought about by the exercise of political control concerns the relative position of clerical and skilled manual workers, which in socialist society can be done through the combination of changes in wage differentials and the dissemination of an officially proletarian ideology. The diametrically opposite tendency is evident in, for example, Puerto Rico or Jamaica where the historical conjunction of differences of colour with differences in occupational status serves to separate manual from white-collar workers more widely than the gap in income alone would suggest (R. T. Smith 1970: 64). But the traditional gap between artisans and unskilled labourers does not seem to be reversed even in socialist societies. A rough comparison (based on the comparison between Poland and Denmark drawn by Svalastoga 1965: 24 and that between Poland and Germany drawn by Sarapata 1966: 43) suggests that in both capitalist and socialist industrial societies an elite of the highly educated and/or qualified stands at the top of the hierarchy of occupational prestige and a stratum of unskilled manual workers at the bottom. In socialist countries, however, skilled manual workers will rank second only to the 'intelligentsia'; in capitalist countries, they will rank not only below intellectuals and the higher stratum of non-manual workers but also below small capitalists and self-employed artisans.

3.3 Variation is possible not only in the degree of prestige accorded to different occupations but also in the degree to which status mobility in this sense is publicly sanctioned; indeed it can be argued that illegitimacy of movement up the hierarchy of deference is the defining characteristic of so-called 'race relations' situations (Runciman 1972). It operates characteristically in caste-like forms of stratification where upward status mobility is denied to members of groups regarded as ritually unclean. But it may also be denied to members by ascription of a dispossessed elite (as exemplified in the reluctance to accord university places to the children of bourgeois parents in Eastern Europe after 1945). Castes proper may not be able to survive industrialization except in a modified form as 'building blocks in a different kind of system' (Bailey 1963: 123; cf. Srinivas 1967: 116). But 'racial' hierarchies of status undoubtedly can (Blumer 1965), whether or not associated with differences of colour (cf. de Vos and Wagatsuma 1966, for the Japanese *Burakumin*).

4.1 The influences which determine the feelings of the underprivileged about their relative position are so varied and complex that it would be absurd to subsume them under a single heading. What I have in mind here is simply the variation in degree of success with which different governing elites are able to justify the system of stratification in the eyes of the less privileged. Such justification does not necessarily depend on securing ideological commitment; it may depend merely on the conviction of the less privileged that they would be still worse off under any foreseeable alternative. No doubt a traditional and well-internalized 'deference' such has been attributed in various senses to the English (Kavanagh 1971) serves particularly well, or still better devotion to a charismatic leader (cf. Myrdal and Kessle 1970: 183, for a classic expression of 'deference' to Chairman Mao on the part of a young girl cadre). But acceptance of a stratification system may be secured by a wide variety of means, and indeed combination of means. In the United States (excepting always the Negroes), an ideology of free opportunity seems to have helped to reconcile many of the less privileged to the actual inequalities of the system (Lipset and Bendix 1959; but see further Blau and Duncan 1967: Ch.12). In Sweden, the combination of a stable Social Democratic government and a powerful trade-union movement seems to have led to a sense among working-class Swedes that the government is 'theirs' to a greater degree than in Britain (Scase 1972, 1974). In Israel, the contradiction between an egalitarian ideology and the inequalities generated by industrialization were mediated in part by elite affiliation of pioneer groups and allocation of symbolic status to the pioneer settlements (Eisenstadt 1967: Ch. 4).

4.2 By 'pluralism' I here mean not the multiplicity of elites or sub-elites of the ideal type of Section I of this paper, but the presence of socially separate, culturally homogenous, self-recruiting ethnic groups internally stratified in parallel with each other. Extent of pluralism in this sense and degree of stratification can of course vary independently (Van den Berghe 1970). But where such groups are so ranked within the overall distribution of privilege as to overlap in part, but only in part, with one another, their effect on the stratification system may be either to strengthen or to undermine it, depending chiefly on the policies which the governing elite chooses to adopt towards them. If mobility is denied them entirely, then the existing stratification system may be successfully preserved but only at the cost of increasing reliance on force (Benedict 1970: 36). But the market may already be enough to inhibit their mobility where low level of skill and education and cultural differences from the groups above serve by themselves to deny access to more privileged positions (Rex 1970: Ch. 4). Conversely, where such groups are permitted mobility in principle but denied it in practice, they may incline to a militant separatism which invites both a counter-reaction from the groups immediately above them and a recourse to coercive sanctions even by a governing elite which had hoped to avoid them: the *Gastarbeiter* of western Europe appear to serve the function of sustaining the existing stratification system at the cost of a perceptible but controlled increase in intra-societal tensions (Castles and Kosack 1973).

4.3 I have listed quasi-group consciousness of interests as a constant in the stratification system of industrial societies; and perhaps it goes without saying that these interests are bound not only to be seen but to be seen to conflict with each other, however powerful the ideology of the governing elite. But wide variation is possible in the degree to which different groups are allowed by the governing elite to resolve those conflicts of interest by direct confrontation among themselves. In this respect, the most obvious difference is between those regimes which allow more or less autonomous trade unions and those which do not. It is true that under the 'classical' capitalism of Marx and Engels British trade unions were denied recognition on the grounds of illegitimate interference in the workings of the market, and in not only the British but also the American case their struggle for recognition was long and often difficult. But they are now permitted within limits to engage in conflict with employers directly, even if with results in terms of governmental intervention intended by neither (Banks 1970). In the Soviet Union, by contrast, conflict of interest can be acted out only within the Party, which incorporates the representatives of the different occupational strata within it and tends to resolve conflict between them by summary replacement (Fainsod 1963). But a third alternative is suggested by the case of China, where although conflicts are not left to be resolved by the market, there is nonetheless an ideology of licensed opposition and the governing elite may deliberately mobilize one group or class against another, whether the army, the peasantry, or the intelligentsia (Schurmann 1968; Joffe 1972).

5.1 Wide variation in degree of restriction on mobility is compatible with the organization of industrial society, extending not merely to the denial in law of any possibility of upward mobility in wealth, prestige, or power to the members of disprivileged groups but even to expulsion and finally extermination (as in the case of Nazi Germany). Short of this, a governing elite may legislate to restrict the occupational mobility of subordinate ethnic groups as in the system of Job Reservation in South Africa (Doxey 1971) or merely act to debar members of specified groups from the elite itself, as in the central control of admission to party membership exercised in the Soviet Union (Matthews 1972: Ch. 8). In general, the proverbial trade-off between liberty and equality makes legal restrictions against mobility less likely the more the market is left to do the job of social control by itself. But South Africa furnishes a striking example of the way in which the market can be deliberately enlisted to reinforce the sanctions against mobility already imposed by legislation (Adam 1971).

5.2 The parameter commonly cited in historical and/or international comparisons of education is the proportion of children born into a designated stratum receiving a specified number of years' schooling. But it is as well to remember that this is relevant to individual mobility only if accompanied by an increased availability of more privileged positions to which the educated will gain preferential access. On the other hand, rising educational levels which follow on industrialization may, quite apart from this, generate collective mobility as 'automation builds on the rising levels of occupation of the population and markedly increases the opportunities and requirements for occupational self-direction' (Kohn 1969: 194). But to the extent that occupation is determined by education and education by social origin, chances of intra-generational individual mobility must be reduced (Goldthorpe 1964: 108; cf. Jencks 1972 on the United States), and this can in turn react back on patterns of parental upbringing in such a way that stratification will be further perpetuated unless there is a sufficient countervailing expansion in the requirement for higher levels of skill. The extreme case is again provided by South Africa, where by direct political control rigid educational stratification according to race is maintained even in the face of just such an expansion (Schlemmer 1972: Table V; for relative *per capita* expenditure on education, see Horrell 1972: 253, 267).

5.3 Taken together, the possible variations in mobility rates in industrial society (particularly if intra-generational manual/non-manual mobility is not given excessive emphasis) are such that both high individual but low collective and low individual but high collective mobility are alike possible. Either will tend to generate mounting strains within the stratification system if left unchecked. In the first case, the exclusion of the losers among the least favoured stratum from the economic benefits of advanced industrialization may generate an 'underclass' of those whose hopes of mobility are cumulatively foreclosed (Myrdal 1964: Ch. 3; Miller 1965). In the second, limitation of individual mobility for the best qualified and most ambitious members of a stratum whose expectations have been heightened by collective mobility may generate a more powerful sense of 'class'-consciousness than when both individual and collective mobility were low (Dunning 1972). Moreover, both can to some degree coincide within the same overall stratification system; in the case of the Negroes in the United States, the ratio of individual to collective mobility among the least privileged leaves a self-perpetuating underclass of unskilled and sometimes unemployable workers at the same time as the denial of individual mobility to members of an incipient 'black bourgeoisie', who have achieved substantial collective advancement, serves to reinforce the likelihood of a movement towards separatism. A possible example of the maximum of both individual and collective mobility is furnished by Northern Whites in the same system, who have not only benefited collectively from the mounting prosperity of the United States but have perhaps the best chances of long-range upward individual mobility of any industrialized society for which data are available (Blau and Duncan 1967).

It will be obvious that these fragmentary observations do not amount to a set of validated empirical generalizations either about how the fifteen variables chosen relate to each other or about their relative susceptibility to manipulation by the governing elite. But they do, I hope, serve to show within what broad limits – so far as our present knowledge allows us to say – they may vary, and how widely, therefore, the stratification systems of industrial societies may differ from each other. This approach deliberately leaves the 'convergence thesis' open. We may concede that there is a 'central core of traits common to all societies that are industrialized' (T. H. Marshall 1964: 144 citing Feldman and Moore), including some features of stratification, yet at the same time deny that their stratification systems will ever be such as all to be subsumable under a common rubric. Whether they will come to resemble each other more than they do at present does not simply depend on an inbuilt dialectic forcing either capitalist societies towards socialism or socialist societies towards capitalism; or to put it the other way round, there is nothing which necessarily prevents industrial nation-states from staying in the different categories of stratification systems to which they now belong until a sufficient further change in the mode of production impels them all into a new stage of evolution in which, once again, the differences between them may still be as apparent as the resemblances.

III

Before suggesting any hypotheses about actual stratification systems, I have still to enter three reservations without which the purpose of this final section might be misunderstood. First, I am not implying that industrial societies could not possibly become radically more egalitarian than any of those to which I refer. I imply only that this would require a drastic degree of de-industrialization. It is a perfectly reasonable request to put to the stratification theorist that he should be capable of specifying the conditions under which inequalities of economic, social, and/or political privilege will be at a minimum. The overwhelmingly plausible answer, however, is that such near-egalitarianism is attainable only in small, pre-(or non-) industrial societies. This is not a sufficient condition, as the ethnographic record shows. But it does seem to be a necessary one; and it follows from this that for the societies to which I refer to evolve in such a direction they would somehow have to reverse what for the moment is not merely an immensely powerful but also a world-wide trend. In a thoroughly decentralized, thoroughly deindustrialized society whose members were willing in addition to run the risk of dispensing with any form of standing army or police, social control would presumably be exercised through more sophisticated

D

variants of the devices observed among such peoples as the cognatic tropical forest tribes of South America – 'oaths, ordeals, duels, wrestling, sorcery and feuds' (Dole 1966: 85); differences in wealth and prestige would be minimal; and the notion of vertical social mobility would be virtually meaningless. Such an evolution seems to me so highly unlikely that it can be dismissed without further comment. But I do not deny that it is theoretically conceivable, and could even become conceivable in practice under such conditions as might, say, follow in the aftermath of thermonuclear war.

The second reservation concerns societies still only in the early stages of industrialization. There is a growing literature on the stratification systems of such societies. But they are so much more susceptible to the effects of exogenous influence than fully 'modernized' societies as to make prediction of how their stratification systems will evolve too difficult to be worth the attempt. Not only does their relative poverty and the concomitant weakness of their elites make them liable to rapid and sometimes drastic changes of government, but their subordinate position in the international political and economic system makes their governments exceptionally dependent, whatever their intentions, on factors beyond their control. The dependence of the Cuban economy on sugar and the consequent dependence of successive Cuban governments on outside powers, whether the United States before 1959 or the Soviet Union after, affords perhaps the most striking example (Dunn 1972: Ch. 8). It does not, of course, follow that the strength of governing elites and the consequent durability of the stratification systems over which they exercise control are simply a function of degree of industrialization. The Chinese governing elite appears able to dictate the form the country's stratification system is to take despite the overwhelming majority of its labour force which still remains employed on the land; the Czechoslovakian governing elite could not withstand Soviet influence even though Czechoslovakia was by this standard much more highly industrialized than the Soviet Union itself (*U.N. Economic Survey of Europe in 1969*, I, 18). But in general, the less industrial a nation-state the more uncertain what its system of stratification will be by the time that the process of industrialization is complete. No doubt adequate explanation may be possible in due course; but this paper make no claim whatever to forecast the future stratification systems of an industrialized Afro-Asian and Latin-American world.

The third reservation concerns the form of the hypotheses to be advanced. I make no attempt to specify any presumptively causal relations between the variables set out in Section II by which the stratification systems of the five contrasting societies are depicted. Indeed, any such attempt would be hopelessly premature. Instead, I merely offer a forecast of the future pattern of the stratification systems, so depicted, of the five countries which I have already cited as examples of the five suggested types. Since the forecast is based on the presumptions both that there are no significant pressures operating from outside the five systems and that all five fit clearly into the typology proposed, it should be read more as a derivation *a priori* than as an extrapolation of known present trends. Indeed, I should make clear that with the exception of the British system (and to a very limited degree the South African), any assumptions about the present state of the countries chosen are drawn entirely from a sketchy selection of secondary sources. But unless these sources are seriously misleading, and provided always that the assumption about exogenous pressures holds, I would hope that the history of the five countries over the next generation would furnish adequate evidence significantly to support or discredit the arguments I have advanced.

In one case out of the five – the Swedish – it could perhaps be objected that the classification itself is illegitimate. Sweden's economy is, after all, a market economy; wage rates are settled by collective bargaining; labour is not directed; the overwhelming proportion of industry is privately owned. Is not Sweden's stratification system, therefore, as much 'neo-capitalist' as Britain's? The answer, however, is that only if ownership of industry is made the decisive criterion by definition do Britain and Sweden belong together; and from this it would follow that South Africa is more 'social-democratic' than Sweden. In fact, there is no necessary connection between nationalization and equality, and stratification theory must explicitly recognize it. Depending on tax and company law, owners and/or managers of private businesses may be no better off financially than their public counterparts. The rapid recent expansion of state ownership in South Africa is egalitarian only in the sense of equalizing privilege as between Afrikaner and 'Anglo-Jewish' interests. Sweden, on the other hand, has a system of progressive taxation of wealth, gifts, inheritance, and capital gains (cf. Meade 1964: Preface) as well as a strong and by now longstanding commitment to the provision of welfare services for the relatively disprivileged (cf. the remarks of Miller and Roby 1970: 10-11, that in Sweden low income is not associated to anything like the same degree as in the United States with poor basic services), and a degree of institutionalized consultation with interested parties built into the legislative process which has been claimed to be unique among modern governments (Tomasson 1970: 23). Quantitative comparison with Britain is difficult and on some relevant topics impossible: for example, no Gini coefficient for the distribution of net personal wealth can be calculated for Sweden if only because of the lack of data below the exemption limit of the wealth tax. But figures for wealth-owners making returns compiled by the National Central Bureau of Statistics show a more equal distribution even despite the total omission of small wealth-owners (figures for 1964 supplied to me by Dr Richard Scase from an untranslated publication). Moreover, it is significant that the mobility data summarized by Blau and Duncan (1967: Table 12.1) show much higher mobility ratios, both manual class into elite and middle class into elite, for Sweden than Britain (.53 as against .30 for the first and 2.72 as against 1.15 for the second); and the qualitative difference by which all observers seem to be struck is the much greater and more pervasive influence of the trade unions which has been built up during the generation-long tenure of office by the Social Democrats. I conclude, from the admittedly limited evidence known to me, that the influence of the market on the Swedish stratification system is so far controlled by the strength of interest groups representing the less priveleged and by direct governmental action that it falls within the 'social-democratic' and not the 'neo-capitalist' category.

The five countries can now, therefore, be taken one by one. I deliberately refrain from citing any of the literature which bears on them at this point in my argument since, as I remarked above, I am concerned more to frame hypotheses of which the future experience of these countries may turn out to furnish a test than to extrapolate from such evidence as is at the present moment available.

1. *The British case*

The qualified label 'neo'-capitalist is evidently necessary because the degree of interference with the market now accepted by the governing elite, irrespective of party, goes well beyond anything compatible with classical capitalism as depicted by Marx. But the nature and degree of economic inequality is still determined initially by the market, and despite the imposition of a more or less progressive income tax and the provision of welfare benefits, the market still dictates the span and distribution of pre-tax incomes. This means, and will continue to mean, that although the net (i.e. post-tax) income span is much narrower than if the market were entirely unchecked, skill and training will command a premium, particularly if combined with restriction on entry. Welfare benefits will keep pace with rising earnings, but only in the sense that the ratio between them will be roughly constant; and wealth will remain much more unequally distributed than income even though the number of small property owners will increase. As the occupational distribution of the employed population changes with the ongoing course of economic development, the mean and mode of incomes will rise, but skill and training differentials will not be significantly affected. Upward collective mobility will thus be a function chiefly of overall growth, and the increasing importance of education in the allocation of intial position will keep individual intragenerational mobility rates low. Conversely, educational selection will help to generate individual downward intergenerational mobility; but collective downward intragenerational mobility (or 'proletarianization of the middle class') will be inhibited by the continuing automation of routine clerical tasks, expansion of vacancies in the tertiary sector, and the increasing use of short-term members of the labour force (principally women).

One consequence of this pattern will be the survival of the existing prestige ordering of non-manual as against manual occupations, at once symptomatized and strengthened by the traditional pattern of comparative and normative reference groups. Although routine clerical work will have lost its traditional prestige *vis-à-vis* skilled manual work, there will be fewer and fewer household heads whose lifelong occupation it is; and the increasing importance of education, together with the prospects of advancement traditionally associated with non-manual occupations, will serve to recreate in an analogous form the traditional divide between those who are lettered and/or numerate and those who are not, and to strengthen differences in life-style between them. On the other hand, consensus on the overall ranking of occupations will diminish, particularly in the tertiary sector where among the relatively skilled and well-rewarded increasing equality of status and feelings of relative deprivation of status will be mutually reinforcing.

There are not now, nor will there be, legal restrictions imposed on mobility, and the denial of legitimate status mobility to women and to members of subordinate ethnic groups may be expected to diminish. At the same time, however, the determination of occupational groups to secure and maintain their market position will continue to result in the successful imposition of restrictions on individual mobility by means of apprenticeship, formal qualifications, and sometimes ascriptive group membership as requirements for entry. In particular, the presence of immigrant groups within the occupational structure will serve to maintain a limited underclass whose ascribed status and weak market position will tend to reinforce each other. Intergenerational mobility rates, both upward and downward, will continue to increase at the middle levels of occupation, and therewith of privilege, but there will be no major increase in the rates of long distance intergenerational mobility.

In this situation, no radical change in the pattern of institutional conflict is to be expected, and talk of 'pluralism' in the sense used in Section II will be appropriate only where regionally based ethnic groups are concentrated in particular industries and occupations. (A sufficient influx of European and/or ex-colonial immigrants would, of course, change this.) There will, however, be a significant change at the middle level of white-collar occupations where unionization will increase at the same time as there will be a reduction in the number of existing (chiefly manual) unions. The result of this will be a gradual and partial redrawing of traditional boundaries to the point at which it will be appropriate to regard the adult full-time labour force as consisting broadly of three strata: an elite which will be relatively smaller than at present; a large middle stratum whose members will still be differentiated in earnings and life-style but will have in common that their interests will be well defended by organized pressure groups; and an underclass which will become relatively more disadvantaged even though improving its position by comparison with what it was. This pattern of stratification will command acceptance to the extent that each stratum will be concerned to better its market position rather than to press for adoption by the governing elite of a 'command' economy.

The small number of 'elite' positions – positions, that is, whose incumbents enjoy manifestly higher economic, social, and/or political privilege than the members of society at large – together with the increasing advantage of inheriting a predisposition to educational achievement instead of, or as well as, wealth will keep rates of both inflow and outflow low. There will be an element of decentralization to the extent that pressure groups of various kinds will become more powerful, and some of these will in turn afford opportunities for participation to people otherwise remote from influence. But no major decentralization of power will take place, and conflict within the elite, although it will of course occur, will not be such as to undermine its fundamental cohesiveness.

2. *The Swedish case*

Any forecast of the future pattern of the selected variables must evidently take account not merely of the present aims and policies of the Social Democratic governing elite but also of the already high levels of non-manual unionism, of union involvement in workers' education, and of working-class involvement in voluntary associations generally. Against this background, it seems reasonable to expect that existing inequalities of wealth and consumption will diminish somewhat further than they already have and welfare benefits to the least privileged will continue to increase: specifically, it may be predicted that the level of gross income at which the recipient pays more in tax than he receives in benefits will be consistently pitched to yield a more egalitarian distribution of net income than in Britain, and that whether or not public ownership is extended legislation will prevent the effective use of private stockholdings to maintain expensive life-styles on the scale possible in Britain. The constraint on economic equalization in Sweden will lie rather in the steadily increasing value of education coupled with the collective strength of the white-collar and professional unions. Although economic inequality will be less than in Britain there will nonetheless be the same tendency towards a division both between a highly-qualified elite and a broadened middle stratum and between the middle stratum and a smaller stratum of the still relatively underprivileged.

Consensus on prestige will, however, be greater than in Britain and social distance less. At present, there are still forms of speech dating back to the period of very marked distinctions of status which obtained into the present century. But these will disappear. The manual/non-manual distinction will cease to be significant even to the limited degree it now is, and legitimacy of status mobility, which at present is limited only by the residue of discrimination against women, will become total. There will be a distinguishable elite to whose members higher prestige will continue to be accorded, and educational qualifications will become progressively more highly valued; but within the elite, trade union leaders will rank (if they do not already) on a par with professional or managerial leaders. More generally, legitimacy will be more widely accorded to the stratification system as a whole than in any of the other four cases with the sole possible exception of China. Voters and unionists will no doubt continue to question whether their representatives are sufficiently combative and successful on their behalf: but this will be a reflection of inevitable conflicts of interest within the system rather than outright rejection of the system as such.

Cultural pluralism will not arise (unless, once again, there is a substantial inflow of immigrants from less developed countries), so that institutionalized conflict will continue to be 'class' conflict in the sense that occupation is the basic line of cleavage. Intergenerational mobility rates will, if anything, rise slightly (assuming no large interstratum differences in fertility, mortality, or migration), partly reflecting the narrowing of differences of privilege within the middle ranges of occupation. But the lower stratum will be characterized by relatively high individual and relatively low collective mobility, and it is here, therefore, that dissatisfaction will be greatest among those left behind.

The governing elite, although limited in size like that of any industrial society, will nonetheless remain relatively larger than the British, partly because of a much smaller size of population as a whole (just over eight million at the beginning of 1970) and partly because of a larger number of representatives of associations in a position to bring influence to bear on the government itself. The relatively greater integration of the trade unions into the political culture will help to promote higher rates of individual mobility into the elite, which will be marginally less cohesive than that of either neo-capitalist or state socialist society. Paradoxically, therefore, Sweden may come to exemplify a higher degree of high-level institutional conflict precisely because occupational associations, including the civil and military services, are better placed for the purpose than in either neo-capitalist or state socialist systems.

3. *The Soviet case*

Comparison of the future stratification system of the Soviet Union with that of any advanced neo-capitalist or social-democratic country is hampered not merely by the pervasive qualitative difference resulting from the institution of the Party but also by the high proportion of the population still on the land. I deliberately omit consideration of stratification within the rural sector, which both here and in China poses problems of its own. But any forecast of future mobility rates must start from the virtual certainty that the biggest single shift over the next generation will be the move into urban, industrial jobs by many millions of peasants and collective farm workers and their children. Only when this process is complete will it be possible to talk of mobility in terms which, if accurate statistics are made available, will permit meaningful international comparisons.

With this reservation, however, a rough forecast in terms of the listed variables can be made for the Soviet Union as for Sweden or Britain. Economic inequalities, which under Stalin were permitted to rise to levels in excess of those obtaining in the West, are now much less than they were. But there is no reason to suppose that they will be reduced substantially further. The premium assigned to skilled manual over non-skilled non-manual labour will not be reversed; but a pattern of reward according to skill and training will be preserved, and the level of welfare allowances will stand in roughly the same ratio to the level of earnings as in Britain. Inequalities in the distribution of 'human capital', however, will increase steadily with the increasing importance of education as a determinant of life-chances.

The prestige accorded to different occupations will continue roughly to correspond to the distribution of rewards (and thus may, paradoxically, vindicate the 'functionalist' account better than will neo-capitalist societies). But overshadowing this, as everything else, is and will be the significance of Party membership, whose importance to the distribution of privilege will increase at the same as its prestige will be less readily acknowledged by non-party members. Where social mobility is concerned, the most striking difference between state socialist and either neo-capitalist or social-democratic systems is the occurrence of 'forced' mobility, both long and short range. Purges on a Stalinist scale may by now be a thing of the past. But admission to party membership is, as I remarked earlier, subject to tight central control; educational opportunities are likewise tightly controlled in accordance with requirements laid down by central planning authorities; and those in possession of highly 'marketable' academic and professional skills are all subject to compulsory placement. It is, however, on the difficulties of managing an industrial society of the size of the Soviet Union that the 'convergence thesis' is most plausible. There is no reason to suppose that free bargaining between associations based on occupation will be permitted by the governing elite. But some degree of decentralization is virtually inevitable, even though it is not inevitable, and indeed highly unlikely, that the Party will be dissolved as the instrument of social control. It will merely expand in size from its present 10 per cent or so of adults and thus afford a channel of individual intragenerational mobility which, given the overriding importance of education, would not otherwise be present.

On the larger issues of legitimacy, pluralism, and conflict, however, the dominance of the party will make it increasingly the occasion as well as merely the context of conflict. Ethnic and regional pluralism is an important aspect of Soviet social structure, and although forced deportations, like party purges, may not be repeated it is plausible to expect that the relative exclusion of non-Russians from positions of privilege will be increasingly resented by them as a continuing general equalization of formal opportunities is not matched by substantive equalization. It may be that a policy of positive discrimination towards ethnic minorities, as towards women, will be implemented by the governing elite. But if it is true that continuing industrialization will impose an increasing strain on the central party bureaucracy, such a policy is unlikely to be sufficiently successful to maintain the legitimacy of the stratification system in the eyes of the disprivileged. (Migration may again be significant; but although members of some dissident minorities, such as the Jews, may be allowed to emigrate it seems unikely that such large numbers will be involved as to make a significant difference to the stratification system.) The conflicts of interest inevitably engendered between occupational groups, exacerbated to some degree by ethnic and regional imbalance, will be mediated by the Party, but acceptance of the stratification system will diminish (if, indeed, it is correct to suppose that acceptance as opposed to acquiescence is at the moment significantly higher than, or even as high as, in systems of other types).

The elite itself, however, will remain if anything more cohesive (partly for that very reason). In particular, the Army will continue to remain subordinate to the Party. Conflict within the Party will increase in terms of a widening difference of view between those in managerial and those in political roles, which will both promote and be promoted by limited formal decentralization of the 'command' economy. But this will not be conflict of a kind that will lead to any significant change in the system of stratification as such. Furthermore, the pattern of inflow and outflow to and from the elite will be relatively stable. Increased inflow will, as I have already suggested, result from expansion in the number of elite positions and the slight concomitant reduction of inequality of political privilege. But there is no reason to expect that either inter- or intragenerational outflow will significantly increase.

4. *The Chinese case*

Just as the most striking feature of social-democratic as compared to neo-capitalist society is the concern of the governing elite to avoid what it sees as the undesirable features of neo-capitalism, so the most striking feature of present-day Chinese society is the concern of its governing elite to avoid what it sees as the undesirable features of state socialism in the Soviet model. This makes China doubly interesting to the stratification theorist. In the first place, it automatically justifies the allocation of the Chinese system to a separate type. In the second, it suggests that the degree of inequality of privilege still remaining in Chinese society might in some respects, at least, exemplify the minimum compatible with the organization and control of a large industrial (or semi-industrial) society.

Although some differentials in earnings in the industrial sector are permitted, and therefore will presumably continue to be permitted, there is no reason to suppose that they will be widened to any significant degree. Further, to the extent that seniority as well as job qualification is among the criteria by which differentials may be awarded, the system of reward is egalitarian in age-set terms. Welfare allowances can be expected to remain at levels at least as high as under any other system, whether distributed in cash or through the provision of free services and goods, and accumulation of personal assets on any noticeable scale will remain impossible. Inequalities in 'human capital', however, will inevitably develop. It may be that positive discrimination against children of the intelligentsia will prevent the direct inheritance of privilege through the family. But there will nevertheless be a stratum of highly educated industrial and/or political administrators, managers, and technicians who will enjoy superior amenities and life-styles.

In the same way, despite the status ideologically accorded to workers and peasants, prestige will inevitably attach to elite occupations, particularly where there is an overlap between educational qualification and Party standing. The contradiction between 'red' and 'expert' carries with it an implicit divergence of consensus on the relative standing of industrial and political leaders, so that it may be predicted that the prestige accorded to managers will be less widely acknowledged than in any of the other four types of stratification system, while at the same time there will be a particular prestige accorded to status mobility from authentic worker/peasant origins into the Party elite. But there will nevertheless be a recognizable hierarchy of occupational prestige, with Army, Party, and (perhaps) managerial cadres at the top, technicians and skilled workers in the middle, and unskilled workers at the bottom.

Once the pre-Revolutionary bourgeoisie has entirely died out, the rate of long-range inter-generational mobility will fall. But if the governing elite remains determined to avoid the creation of a self-perpetuating bureaucracy in the higher echelons of the Party, relatively high rates of intragenerational mobility will be maintained by the deliberate selection of junior cadres to fill the vacancies created either by expansion or simply by retirement. Collective mobility on the other hand will be very low for the simple reason that there is no ideological incentive to alter the relative positions of quasi-groups or strata as they are now constituted. Whether the distribution of privilege will then continue to be regarded as legitimate by those outside the echelons of the Party and ineligible for any occupational promotion beyond seniority bonuses paid for routine industrial work will depend on the ability of the Party leadership to sustain an element of charismatic legitimacy under the ideology of permanent revolution. This will be helped, but not necessarily guaranteed, by the permissibility of institutional conflict between rival contenders for charismatic authority deriving from Chairman Mao (or, in due course, his memory). Not only will the intelligentsia and/or students sometimes challenge the policies of the Party bureacracy in the name of Mao, but also the Army will remain outside the control of the Party to a much greater degree than under the Soviet system.

Paradoxically, therefore, the Chinese system will permit a plurality of elites no further from, and possibly closer to, the ideal type of 'pluralism' in the sense of Section I than will the British system, subject only to the ultimate monopoly of political privilege in the hands of the central committee (or equivalent body) of the single Party. In this respect, no significant decentralization will take place. But at the lower levels, decentralization will be maintained to roughly its present degree and turnover in sub-elite positions at roughly its present level.

5. *The South African case*

Of the five actual cases, South Africa is the one where exogenous influence is likely to be most important. This is not because any significant change of its stratification system will be imposed by international sanctions, but because the disparity in numbers between Whites and Blacks in Southern Africa is so wide and the dependence of the White economy on Black labour is so great. The existing stratification system is, however, perfectly viable for the time being, and it is possible that under more favourable geographic and demographic conditions the 'ethnocratic' type might be no less stable than any of the other four.

The basis of the system, as I need hardly rehearse, is the retention of a virtual monopoly of economic, social, and political privilege alike by one self-defined ethnic group. Retention of such a monopoly depends, precisely as in the ideal-typical 'elite' model of social control, on both a willingness to use force, and a capacity successfully to manipulate public opinion. But beyond this it depends also on some genuine ideological commitment among the privileged group and some tacit recognition among the underprivileged groups that the system affords them economic benefits, however much smaller than those of the privileged group, which they would be reluctant to forego. In this situation, it is perhaps easier than in the other four cases for the governing elite to make political misjudgements which will in due course render the system unmaintainable. But if such misjudgements are not made, there is no intrinsic reason why an industrial society should not have a stratification system which is recognizably of the 'ethnocratic' type.

Assuming, therefore, a fair degree of skill on the part of the South

African governing elite in preserving the long-term interests of the White minority, the system may be predicted to develop on the following lines. Economic inequalities will, as at present, be governed by the market subject first, to ethnic restrictions on occupational entry and second, to the requirements for state investment and ownership on political and/or strategic grounds. Inequalities in wealth will therefore continue to increase; increases in Africans' earnings will be relatively smaller than in Whites' earnings; and welfare allowances, while becoming progressively more generous for Whites, will be increasingly ungenerous to Africans in relative (although not in absolute) terms. Differentials for skill and training will be determined by supply and demand within ethnic categories. But the shortage of White labour, together with the effective denial to Africans of the right to unionize, has already meant a degree of relative prosperity for skilled White manual workers unparallelled in systems of any other type. (Indeed, this aspect of ethnocratic stratification prompts the question in what sense a White manual worker taking home R8000 per annum at 1970 prices, owning his own home and swimming pool and employing a resident African domestic servant can be said *not* to be '*embourgeoisé*'.)

The prestige grading of occupational roles is in the same way overridden by the established hierarchy of ethnic prestige, so that the resulting pattern is of the type already familiar from parts of the United States where occupational roles are similarly ranked within but not between ethnic groups. There is, however, no reason to suppose that consensus exists on the ethnic grading. On the contrary: it can be predicted that as education is diffused among the African population not only will they still more strongly repudiate the rank assigned to them by Whites but will increasingly resent the denial of status mobility as well as equality of reward to those with high occupational qualifications.

Maintenance of the system will accordingly depend upon a degree of upward collective mobility within strictly held structural and cultural boundaries. A slow, even halting, but perceptible rise in real incomes among those dependent on White-owned industry for their employment, a continuing restriction on inter-institutional conflict, whether between political parties with African and White membership or between African trade unions and White employers, a delegation of carefully circumscribed powers to the quasi-governing elites of fragmented client territories, and a legally enforced ethnic segregation of professional as well as political roles will serve to channel quasi-group consciousness of interests among the African population into pragmatic accommodation to a system they would overturn if they could. (This may, however, cease to hold for the Coloured population, whose ambiguous position might lead the governing elite to make just the sort of political miscalculation they could not in the end afford.)

Within the governing elite itself, centralization will, if anything, increase in response to the increasing difficulty of carrying through the policy I have outlined against the wishes not only of the African population but also (for opposite reasons) of sections of the Whites. But cohesion will, for the same reason, diminish and factionalism within the highly centralized governing elite may be expected to increase. Inflow will increase in the short-term as a result of the deliberate creation of opportunities for specifically Afrikaner individual intra-generational mobility; but once this is complete the system will stabilize and rates of either in- or outflow will be very low.

IV

It hardly needs saying that none of these hypotheses comes anywhere near the degree of precision which a theory of stratification belonging to Hinshelwood's third stage would require. But they are at least falsifiable; and if they turn out to be falsified, it will at least be instructive to see why. If on the other hand they are vindicated, three general conclusions will, I think, suggest themselves. First, it will be still more clearly apparent than it is already that the debate over 'conflict' versus 'consensus' theories which has plagued the study of stratification for some thirty years is wholly factitious. Second, it will be conclusively shown that the variation between industrial stratification systems cannot be accounted for by reference to any one predominating variable, whether economic, social, or political, but only by reference to the working-out of an interrelation between all three dimensions determined initially by the policies of the governing elite during the course of modernization. Third, it will be confirmed that industrial societies can continue to be stratified in markedly divergent ways, even though at the same time constrained by a mutually exclusive choice between relative political and relative economic equality and the broadly similar processes of allocation to occupational roles common to them all.

If one then tries to look beyond this to the next major change in the mode of production, it is not implausible to envisage a thorough-going modification of the division and specialization of labour in their contemporary forms. But as I hinted at the end of Section II, this need not by itself constitute grounds for predicting 'convergence': the vision of

Marx and Engels in *The German Ideology* of a society in which the daily round has been transformed into a varying succession of part-time jobs could be as nearly realized in a highly prosperous, highly automated neo-capitalist society through self-employment and moonlighting as in a highly prosperous, highly automated revolutionary socialist society through programmed allocation of roles within production communes. This speculation invites in its turn the further question whether any one system of stratification is more likely than the others over the long term to maximize the welfare and happiness of its members. But I doubt if it falls within the competence of the stratification theorist to proffer an answer. All he can say is that whether for better or worse institutionalized competition for privilege will be universal among post-industrial as among industrial societies: or as Michels (1915: 408) concluded in a more limited context, the 'cruel game' is likely to continue without end.

References

ADAM, H. 1971. *Modernizing Racial Domination*. Berkeley, Calif: University of California Press.

ANDRESKI, S. 1954. *Military Organization and Society*. London: Routledge.

ARON, R. 1950. Social Structure and the Ruling Class. *British Journal of Sociology* 1.

—— 1960. Classe Sociale, Classe Politique, Classe Dirigeante. *Archives Européennes de Sociologie* 1.

ATKINSON, A. B. 1972. *Unequal Shares*. London: Allen Lane.

BAILEY, F. G. 1963. Closed Social Stratification in India. *Archives Européennes de Sociologie* 4.

BANKS, J. A. 1970. *Marxist Sociology in Action*. London: Faber.

BENEDICT, B. 1970. Pluralism and Stratification. In L. Plotnicov and A. Tuden (eds.) *Essays in Comparative Social Stratification*. Pittsburgh: University of Pittsburgh Press.

BENDIX, R. 1970. Tradition and Modernity Reconsidered. In L. Plotnicov and A. Tuden (ed.) *Essays in Comparative Social Stratification* op. cit.

BERREMAN, G. D. 1972. Race, Caste and Other Invidious Distinctions in Social Stratification. *Race* 13.

BESHERS, J. M. 1962. *Urban Social Structure*. New York: Free Press.

BLAU, P. M. and DUNCAN, O. D. 1967. *The American Occupational Structure*. New York: Wiley.

BLUMBERG, P. 1968. *Industrial Democracy*. London: Constable.

BLUMER, H. 1965. Industrialisation and Race Relations. In G. Hunter (ed.) *Industrialisation and Race Relations*. London: Oxford University Press.

CARLSSON, GØSTA 1958. *Social Mobility and Class Structure*. Lund: Gleerup.

CASANOVA, P. G. 1970. *Democracy in Mexico*. New York: Oxford University Press.

CASTLES, S. and KOSACK, G. 1973. *Immigrant Workers and Social Structure in Western Europe*. London: Oxford University Press.

COLEMAN, J. S. 1960. The Mathematical Study of Small Groups. In H. Solomon (ed.) *Mathematical Thinking in the Measurement of Behaviour*. Glencoe, Ill: The Free Press.

CUTRIGHT, P. 1968. Occupational Inheritance: a Cross-National Analysis. *American Journal of Sociology* 73.

DAHL, R. A. 1961. *Who Governs?* New Haven: Yale University Press.

DAHRENDORF, R. 1966. Conflict After Class. University of Essex (Noel Buxton Lecture).

DE REUCK, A. and KNIGHT, J. (ed.) 1967. *Caste and Race: Comparative Approaches*. London: Churchill (CIBA Foundation).

DE VOS, G. and WAGATSUMA, H. 1966. *Japan's Invisible Race*. Berkeley, Calif: University of California Press.

DJILAS, M. 1957. *The New Class*. London: Unwin.

DOLE, G. E. 1966. Anarchy Without Chaos: Alternatives to Political Authority among the Kuikuru. In M. J. Swartz, V. W. Turner and A. Tuden (eds.) *Political Anthropology*. Chicago: Aldine.

DOLLARD, J. 1937. *Caste and Class in a Southern Town*. New Haven: Yale University Press.

DOXEY, G. V. 1971. Enforced Racial Stratification in the South African Labour Market. In H. Adam (ed.) *South Africa: Sociological Perspectives*. London: Oxford University Press.

DUNCAN, O. D. 1965. Methodological Issues in the Analysis of Social Mobility. In N. J. Smelser and S. M. Lipset (eds.) *Social Structure and Mobility in Economic Development*. London: Routledge.

DUNN, J. 1972. *Modern Revolutions*. Cambridge: Cambridge University Press.

DUNNING, E. 1972. Dynamics of Racial Stratification: Some Preliminary Observations. *Race* 13.

DUVERGER, M. 1959. *Political Parties* (2nd Edition). London: Methuen.

EISENSTADT, S. N. 1963. *The Polical Systems of Empires*. New York: Free Press.

—— 1967. *Israeli Society*. London: Weidenfeld.

FAINSOD, M. 1963. *How Russia is Ruled* (2nd edition). Cambridge, Mass: Harvard University Press.

FARARO, T. J. 1970. Strictly Stratified Systems. *Sociology* 4.

FOX, R. 1967. *Kinship and Marriage*. Harmondsworth: Penguin.

FOX, T. and MILLER, S. M. 1967. Occupational Stratification and Mobility. In R. Bendix and S. M. Lipset (eds.) *Class, Status and Power* (2nd Edition). London: Routledge.

GERMANI, G. 1971. Stratificazione Sociale e Sua Evoluzione Storica in Argentina. *Sociologica* 5.

GERSTL, J. and COHEN, L. K. 1964. Dissensus, Situs and Egocentrism in Occupational Ranking. *British Journal of Sociology* 15.

GOLDTHORPE, J. H. 1964. Social Stratification in Industrial Society. In P. Halmos (ed.) *The Development of Industrial Societies. The Sociological Review:* Monograph No. 8.

GOLDTHORPE, J. H. and HOPE, K. 1972. Occupational Grading and Occupational Prestige. In K. Hope (ed.) *The Analysis of Social Mobility: Methods and Approaches*. Oxford: Clarendon Press.

HERSKOVITS, M. 1938. *Dahomey: an Ancient West African Kingdom*. Locust Valley: Augustin.

HODGE, R. W., TREIMAN, D. J., and ROSSI, P. H. 1967. A Comparative Study of Occupational Prestige. In R. Bendix and S. M. Lipset (ed.) *Class, Status and Power* op. cit.

HOPE, K. 1972a. Introduction: Taking the Metaphor Seriously. In K. Hope (ed.) *The Analysis of Social Mobility: Methods and Approaches* op. cit.

—— 1972b. Quantifying Constraints on Social Mobility. In K. Hope (ed.) *The Analysis of Social Mobility: Methods and Approaches* op. cit.

HORRELL, M. 1972. *A Survey of Race Relations in South Africa 1971*. Johannesburg: S. A. Institute of Race Relations.

HUACO, G. C. 1966. The Functionalist Theory of Stratification: Two Decades of Controversy. *Inquiry* 9.

INGHAM, G. K. 1970. Social Stratification: Individual Attributes and Social Relationships. *Sociology* 4.

INKELES, A. and ROSSI, P. H. 1956. National Comparisons of Occupational Prestige. *American Journal of Sociology* 61.

JANOWITZ, M. 1964. *The Military in the Political Development of New Nations*. Chicago: University of Chicago Press.

JENCKS, C. 1972. *Inequality: a Reassessment of the Effect of Family and Schooling in America*. New York: Basic Books.

JOFFE, E. 1972. The Chinese Army under Lin Piao: Prelude to Political Intervention. In J. M. H. Lindbeck (ed.) *China: Management of a Revolutionary Society*. London: Unwin.

JONAS, S. 1965. Les Classes Sociales en Israel. *Cahiers Internationaux de Sociologie* 38.

KAVANAGH, D. 1971. The Deferential English: a Comparative Critique. *Government and Opposition* 6.

KELLER, S. 1963. *Beyond the Ruling Class*. New York: Random House.

KOHN, M. L. 1969. *Class and Conformity*. Homewood: Dorsey.

KOLAJA, J. 1965. *Workers' Councils: The Yugoslav Experience*. London: Tavistock.

KOLKO, G. 1962. *Wealth and Power in America*. New York: Praeger.

KUPER, L. 1971. Theories of Revolution and Race Relations. *Comparative Studies in Society and History* **13.**

—— 1972. Race, Class and Power: Some Comments on Revolutionary Change. *Comparative Studies in Society and History* **14.**

LAMPMAN, R. J. 1962. *The Share of Top Wealth-Holders in National Wealth 1922-1956*. Princeton: Princeton University Press.

LANE, D. 1971. *The End of Inequality*? Harmondsworth: Penguin.

LASSWELL, H. and LERNER, D. (eds.) 1965. *World Revolutionary Elites*. Cambridge, Mass: M.I.T. Press.

LIPSET, S. M. and BENDIX, R. 1959. *Social Mobility in Industrial Society*. Berkeley, Calif: University of California Press.

LITTLEJOHN, J. 1972. *Social Stratification: an Introduction*. London: Unwin.

LOCKWOOD, D. 1971. Editorial Foreword to D. Lane *The End of Inequality?* op. cit.

LUKIC, R. V. 1965. L'influence de l'Autogestion Ouvrière sur la Structure de Classe de la Société Yugoslave. *Cahiers Internationaux de Sociologie* **38.**

LYDALL, H. 1968. *The Structure of Earnings*. Oxford: Clarendon Press.

MACHONIN, P. 1970. Social Stratification in Contemporary Czechoslovakia. *American Journal of Sociology* **75.**

MANN, M. 1971. *Consciousness and Action among the Western Working Class*. London: MacMillan.

MARSHALL, L. 1960. !Kung Bushmen Bands. *Africa* **30.**

MARSHALL, T. H. 1950. *Citizenship and Social Class*. Cambridge: Cambridge University Press.

—— 1964. A Summing Up. In P. Halmos (ed.) *The Development of Industrial Societies* op. cit.

MARTINS, H. 1971. Portugal. In M. Scotford Archer and S. Giner (eds.) *Contemporary Europe: Class, Status and Power*. London: Weidenfeld.

MATTHEWS, M. 1972. *Class and Society in Soviet Russia*. London: Allen Lane.

MEADE, J. E. 1964. *Efficiency, Equality and the Ownership of Property*. London: Unwin.

MICHELS, R. 1913. *Political Parties*. London: Peter Smith.

MILIBAND, R. 1969. *The State in Capitalist Society*. London: Weidenfeld.

MILLER, S. M. 1965. The New Working Class. In A. B. Shostak and W. Gomberg (eds.) *Blue-Collar World*. Englewood Cliffs: Prentice Hall.

MILLER, S. M. and ROBY, A. 1970. *The Future of Inequality.* New York: Basic Books.

MILLS, C. W. 1965. *The Power Elite.* New York: Oxford University Press.

MOORE, BARRINGTON Jr. 1966. *Social Origins of Dictatorship and Democracy.* Boston: Beacon Press.

MURDOCK, G. P. 1949. *Social Structure.* New York: Macmillan.

MYRDAL, G. 1964. *Challenge to Affluence.* London: Gollancz.

MYRDAL, J. and KESSLE, G. 1970. *China: The Revolution Continued.* London: Chatto.

NAKANE, C. 1970. *Japanese Society.* London: Weidenfeld.

NEEDHAM, R. 1971. Remarks on the Analysis of Kinship and Marriage. In R. Needham (ed.) *Rethinking Kinship and Marriage.* London: Tavistock.

NETTL, J. P. and ROBERTSON, R. 1968. *International Systems and the Modernisation of Societies.* London: Faber.

NORBECK, E. 1970. Continuities in Japanese Social Stratification. In L. Plotnicov and A. Tuden (ed.) *Essays in Comparative Social Stratification* op. cit.

NOVE, A. 1961. Is the Soviet Union a Welfare State? In A. Inkeles and K. Geiger (ed.) *Soviet Society.* London: Constable.

OKSENBERG, M. 1970. Getting Ahead and Along in Communist China: The Ladder of Success on the Eve of the Cultural Revolution. In J. W. Lewis (ed.) *Party Leadership and Revolutionary Power in China.* Cambridge: Cambridge University Press.

OSBORN, J. 1970. *Soviet Social Policies.* Homewood: Dorsey.

OSSOWSKI, S. 1963. *Class Structure in the Social Consciousness.* London: Routledge.

PARKIN, F. 1969. Class Stratification in Socialist Societies. *British Journal of Sociology* **20.**

—— 1971a. *Class, Inequality and Political Order.* London: MacGibbon and Kee.

——1971b. Yugoslavia. In M. Scotford Archer and S. Giner (ed.). *Contemporary Europe: Class, Status and Power.* London: Weidenfeld.

PLOTNICOV, L. and TUDEN, A. 1970. Introduction to L. Plotnicov and A. Tuden (eds.) *Essays in Comparative Social Stratification* op. cit.

PLOWMAN, D. E. G., MINCHINTON, W. E., and STACEY, M. 1962. Local Status Systems in England and Wales. *Sociological Review* **10.**

PORTER, J. 1965. *The Vertical Mosaic.* Toronto: University of Toronto Press.

REX, J. 1970. *Race Relations in Sociological Theory.* London: Weidenfeld.

RIDDELL, D. S. 1968. Social Self-government: the Background of Theory and Practice in Yugoslav Socialism. *British Journal of Sociology* **19.**

RUNCIMAN, W. G. 1966. *Relative Deprivation and Social Justice.* London: Routledge.

—— 1968. Class, Status and Power? In J. A. Jackson (ed.) *Social Stratification.* Cambridge: Cambridge University Press.

—— 1970. Social Stratification: a Rejoinder to Mr. Ingham. *Sociology* **4.**

—— 1972. Race and Social Stratification. *Race* **13.**

SAHLINS, M. D. 1958. *Social Stratification in Polynesia.* Washington: University of Washington Press.

SARPATA, A. 1966. Stratification and Social Mobility. In J. Szczepanski (ed.) *Empirical Sociology in Poland.* Warsaw: Polish Scientific Publishers.

SCASE, R. 1972. 'Industrial Man': A Reassessment with English and Swedish Data. *British Journal of Sociology* **23.**

—— 1974. Relative Deprivation: a Comparison of English and Swedish Manual Workers. In D. Wedderburn (ed.) *Poverty, Inequality and Class Structure.* Cambridge: Cambridge University Press.

SCHLEMMER, L. 1972. Employment Opportunity and Race in South Africa (paper presented at Serbelloni Conference, Lake Como).

SCHURMANN, F. 1968. *Ideology and Organization in Communist China* (2nd Edition). Berkeley, Calif: University of California Press.

SIEGEL, P. M. 1970. Occupational Prestige in the Negro Subculture. In E. O. Laumann (ed.) *Social Stratification: Research and Theory for the 1970's.* Indianapolis: Bobbs-Merrill.

SILVERMAN, S. 1970. Stratification in Italian Communities. In L. Plotnicov and A. Tuden (ed.) *Essays in Comparative Social Stratification* op. cit.

SMITH, A. 1776. *The Wealth of Nations.* London: Strahan and Cadell.

SMITH, M. G. 1965. Preindustrial Stratification Systems. In N. J. Smelser and S. M. Lipset (eds.) *Social Structure and Mobility in Economic Development.* London: Routledge.

SMITH, R. T. 1970. Social Stratification in the Caribbean. In L. Plotnicov and A. Tuden (ed.) *Essays in Comparative Social Stratification* op. cit.

SOARES, G. A. O. 1967. Economic Development and Class Structure. In R. Bendix and S. M. Lipset (ed.) *Class, Status and Power* op. cit.

SOUTHALL, A. W. 1970. Stratification in Africa. In L. Plotnicov and A. Tuden (ed.) *Essays in Comparative Social Stratification* op. cit.

SPEER, A. 1970. *Inside the Third Reich.* New York: Macmillan.

SPENCER, H. 1876. *Principles of Sociology.* London: Williams & Norgate.

SPIRO, M. E. 1958. *Children of the Kibbutz.* Cambridge, Mass: Harvard. University Press.

SRINIVAS, M. N. 1967. *Social Change in Modern India*. Berkeley, Calif: University of California Press.

STEWARD, J. 1955. *Theory of Culture Change*. University of Illinois Press.

STINCHCOMBE, A. L. 1963. Some Empirical Consequences of the Davis-Moore Theory of Stratification. *American Sociological Review* 28.

SVALASTOGA, K. 1959. *Prestige, Class and Mobility*. Copenhagen: Gyldendal.

—— 1964. Social Differentiation. In R.E.L. Faris (ed.) *Handbook of Sociology*. New York: Rand.

—— 1965. *Social Differentiation*. New York: MacKay.

SVALASTOGA, K. and RISHØJ, T. 1970. Western European Mobility. *American Journal of Sociology* 76.

TAGUCHI, F. 1968. Pressure Groups in Japanese Politics. In H. Shirohara (ed.). *The Developing Economies VI*. Tokyo: Institute of Asian Economic Affairs.

TOMASSON, R. F. 1970. *Sweden: Prototype of Modern Society*. New York: Random House.

VAN DEN BERGHE, P. L. 1970. Pluralism and the Polity: a Theoretical Exploration. In L. Kuper and M. G. Smith (ed.) *Pluralism in Africa*. Berkeley, Calif: University of California Press.

WEBER, M. 1956. *Wirtschaft und Gesellschaft* (4th edition). Tübingen: Mohr.

WESOLOWSKI, W. and SLOMCZYNSKI, K. 1968. Social Stratification in Polish Cities. In J. A. Jackson (ed.) *Social Stratification*. Cambridge: Cambridge University Press.

YASUDA, S. 1964. A Methodological Enquiry into Social Mobility. *American Sociological Review* 29.

YOUNG, M. and WILLMOTT, P. 1956. Social Grading of Manual Workers. *British Journal of Sociology* 7.

FRANK BECHHOFER, BRIAN ELLIOTT,
MONICA RUSHFORTH, and RICHARD BLAND

The Petits Bourgeois in the Class Structure: the Case of the Small Shopkeepers*

Five years ago we wrote a prolegomenon to our study of small shop-keepers in which we explored the major themes that were to inform our investigations. We discussed the class and status situations of this group in so far as we could assess them from the available literature and we made a number of guesses at the broad patterns of attitude and behaviour that we might expect to find in our sample (Bechhofer and Elliott 1968).

The empirical evidence for our assertions was generally rather poor for few detailed studies of small shopkeepers or other small business-men existed – a situation that has not shown any marked change. Indeed, in sociological writing on stratification the petit bourgeois figures as little more than a caricature. He is depicted as powerless, isolated, and alienated, struggling against hostile economic forces, enduring the psychological pressures of 'status incongruency', and caught between the battalions of big business and organized labour. The studies from which we draw even these crude impressions are scattered, diverse and

* The study began in October 1967 and was funded by the Social Science Research Council until September 1972. The sample was drawn entirely from Edinburgh; 398 shopkeepers and their spouses were interviewed between August 1969 and July 1970. The response rate at 64 per cent was low, but the persistent efforts of the research officers provided some small compensation in that we were able to gather a good deal of information about those who were not willing to take part in the survey. A 'small shopkeeper' was operationally defined as one with not more than three full-time (or as an equivalent, six part-time) assistants, a definition arrived at after consulting the *Census of Distribution* which showed that in 1961, 76.8 per cent of all retail establishments were of this size and according to unpublished data kindly made available by the Board of (Trade), 63.4 per cent were of this size in 1966.

fragmentary.[1] They have in common, however, two basic features. They are primarily concerned with the political activities and sentiments of this stratum and they seek to explain these largely in terms of 'marginality'. Whether the researches are focused on patterns of support for McCarthy in the USA. or Poujade in France, whether they relate to the inter-war years in Germany or the post-war period in Britain, there seems to be a general agreement that what distinguishes the stratum most is the fact that it sits uncomfortably between the mass of manual workers and the lower echelons of the middle class. In terms of occupational prestige the small independent businessmen, including shopkeepers, rank with the 'middle class' but it is clear that their position is by no means well established.

In our own paper we made a good deal of the 'marginality' idea and following a well-trodden path we argued that the shopkeepers' claim to be middle class rested upon peculiar features of their market and work situations. In particular, the ownership of modest amounts of capital and the element of autonomy at work seemed to provide the major reasons for distinguishing them from manual workers and placing them with the traditional bourgeois elements of our society. At the same time it was obvious that the self-same factors marked them off from most of the other groups conventionally labelled 'lower middle class'. The work situations of those with whom they might most obviously be compared, – the clerical and minor administrative workers – are radically different, for typically the latter are engaged in bureaucratically organized enterprises. For them the firm provides a degree of security, offers some kind of career, and allocates specific and narrow areas of responsibility. All this is in sharp contrast to the lot of the small retailer. He must fend for himself. He operates in a more or less free market and his poverty or prosperity, his survival as a businessman, depend upon his own efforts. Much of our interest then was directed to the implications of being your own boss and owning small amounts of capital. How did these factors influence the lives of our respondents? How did they affect their attitudes and values?

The idea of marginality implied that shopkeepers were 'in' but not 'of' the middle class, but it also suggested that there were similarities as well as differences between this group and some sectors of the working class. It is plain, for example, that shopkeepers and artisans have a good deal in common. Many of the latter enjoy considerable independence, owning their own businesses and occasionally maintaining a retail shop as well as practising their skill. These parallels between the artisans and the petits bourgeois have also attracted the attention of some historians in recent years. Nossiter (1972), exploring the involvement of shopkeepers in the radical politics of the nineteenth century, indicates some of the reasons why they shared the political interests of some of the working class. But he also points out that in the nineteenth century the British shopkeepers were a distinct class and that they were distinguished from the craftsmen by aspects of their work situation. Thus, 'firstly, the shopkeeper was primarily concerned with the sale rather than the making of goods; secondly, his job called for a range of skills rather than a specific one; and finally his orientation was to the customer not the craft'. It was considerations like these that led us to exclude artisans from our sample unless it could be shown that running a shop and selling goods was their primary activity and the source of most of their income.

As our study developed it became increasingly clear that this operational decision was right. The small traders really do deserve to be treated as a separate stratum, separate that is from both the so-called lower middle class and from skilled and independent manual workers. The Victorians used to talk of a 'shopocracy', and while the shopkeepers no longer enjoy the political influence which must have prompted that term, they do retain in their work and market situations much of the distinctiveness that it implies. In our view they are properly to be seen as petits bourgeois – as belonging to neither of the major classes in our current system of stratification. When we examine their values and attitudes we are reminded that systems of structured inequality emerge out of lengthy and complex historical processes; that change is uneven, affecting particular sectors of the social and economic system in widely divergent ways; that occupational structures display persistence as well as change. Thus, in some respects shopkeepers may be regarded as a stratum moulded by the economic forces of another era, and in their attitudes and values, their orientations to work and politics, we find echoes of an earlier age.

In this paper we shall look at the position of this group within the British social structure. Ours is an inegalitarian society in terms both of the distribution of scarce resources and also of the opportunities for self advancement or the transmission of privilege to one's children. We must ask how their social position affects the life-chances of the petits bourgeois and what part they play in the maintenance and transmission of patterned inequality. But to begin with we need to know how they fare in the struggle for economic rewards.

THE ECONOMIC DIMENSION

It is clear from the analysis (Bechhofer, Elliott, and Rushforth 1971) that we have already made of the Census of Distribution data that the economic position of the independent retailer is far from enviable and that the really small shopkeepers derive a very small reward for their labours. If we look at figures for turnover and profit margins we find that data gathered from our own respondents generally fit well with those obtained from the official sources (see *Table 1*).

TABLE 1

Turnover, gross profit margins—by kind of business *

(Figures in brackets are those from 1966 Census of Distribution data on Independents)

kind of business	N	mean turnover per establishment £	gross profit margin as a percentage of turnover, per establishment
entire Sample	330	15,664 (15,546)	19.9 (24.8)
grocers	79	16,240 (14,000)	14.2 (14.8)
butchers	31	18,653 (19,000)	21.4 (21.2)
confectioners, tobacconists and newsagents	78	20,580 (15,600)	15.3 (15.0)
women's and girls' wear	31	8,960 (12,200)	28.4 (30.6)
leather and jewellery	17	9,897 (12,100)	25.1 (31.8)

* Kinds of business with more than 15 respondents

Income data are, of course, subject to a good deal of error and the apparent consistency between our figures and those gathered by the Census of Distribution may simply indicate that our sample generally gave us the figure which they used for tax purposes. On the other hand we went to some lengths in the interviews to cross check the information and we were able to calculate a series of 'income' measures from information about turnover, profits, and outgoings. The results indicated that for our respondents the average income derived from the shop in 1969/70 was around £1300 and that the mean family income was about £1700. On these figures the small shopkeepers look to be little better off than a good many skilled and semi-skilled manual workers,[2] but such crude statistics conceal many subtle differences. Most of our retailers (74 per cent) paid themselves a weekly wage, generally a very modest figure of between £15 and £20, and when we began to explore their patterns of expenditure it became obvious that small capital sums must accumulate in the business and these were drawn upon from to time. Thus, unlike many manual workers, their whole income was not absorbed by the week to week demands of living. As we collated the information on consumption patterns we were surprised to find that a very large number of our sample owned a wide range of consumer goods. Given the average incomes how did so many manage to obtain these items? The answer lies partly in this dual method of taking money from the business and partly in the use made of income from other sources. In both cases it is possible for the small shopkeeper to accumulate sums large enough to purchase many of the major household   items.

TABLE 2
Consumer durables

	T.V.	'fridge'	percentages washing machine	telephone	N
own (did not use H.P.)	64	61	56	–	
own (did use H.P.)	10	9	13	–	
rent	15	–	–	78	387*

* 11 missing observations

TABLE 3
Housing – forms of tenure

	percentages	N
fully owned	51	197
mortgaged	28	108
rented (private sector)	8	31
rented (public housing)	8	32
living with parents or in lodgings	4	15
other	1	4
	100	387*

* 11 missing observations

TABLE 4
Car ownership

	percentages	*N*
own (used H.P., bought through business)	17	67
own (not H.P., bought through business)	42	160
own (used H.P., not through business)	3	11
own (not H.P., not business)	17	66
does not own	21	82
	100	386*

* 12 missing observations

Tables 2 – 4 present some of the information on consumption patterns and it is immediately apparent that the figures relating to housing are very unusual. Over half the sample own their houses outright and a further 28 per cent own them with the aid of a mortgage. Figures such as these would be high even for professional groups.[3] Taking a sceptical view we hypothesized that this finding was simply a reflection of the high average age of our sample (median age fifty-four) or that the properties owned were very modest ones.

The first hypothesis certainly is not substantiated. With the exception of the very small number in the lowest age category (under thirty) there was no relationship between age and ownership. The second hypothesis is hard to test with our data but analysis of ecological data referring to places of residence renders such a proposition implausible. We extended our analysis by age to all the data on consumer durables but found essentially the same thing. It was not the case that the propensity to own was related to age in any simple way.

More interesting and important than these crude ownership figures is the kind of attitude which underlies them. It is very noticeable that just as houses are owned outright, so the consumer durables are purchased for cash and the extent to which hire purchase is used is minimal. We should look here for two kinds of explanation. First, a structural interpretation might be that the weekly takings of many shops will vary quite widely and in consequence the owner will pay himself an amount low enough to be covered by a bad week's trading.[4] This produces a weekly income too low to cover hire-purchase commitments. However, provided trading over a year or some months is good there will be a lump sum available with which to purchase commodities such as refrigerators and television sets.

Second, we would argue that this pattern of outright ownership is related to a general constellation of beliefs and attitudes which we might label 'economic traditionalism'.[5] As we soon found when we asked about possible changes in the ways in which they ran their businesses, small shopkeepers are not remarkable for their innovative urges.[6] Time and again we were struck by their very cautious approach. Few had any desire to build up their businesses, to create large and prosperous concerns. Indeed, a sizeable majority (77 per cent) expressed no interest at all in changing the ways in which they carried on their trade. Rather, what was wanted was a 'comfortable' living and 'independence'. Now, the outright ownership of property confers a kind of independence. Tawney (1921) recognized this in his discussion of the symbolic meaning of private property when he talked of 'a limited form of sovereignty'. Owning your own house (and if possible your business premises),[7] paying 'on the nail' for consumer goods ensures that you are beholden to no one and gives you a measure of control over your own fate. To adopt this pattern of ownership may not be entirely 'rational' when rates of inflation are high and when extensive credit facilities exist, nor does it fit with an orientation in which the calculative seeking after ever renewed profit is paramount; but it is perfectly reconcilable with a view emphasizing 'traditional' levels of reward, stressing autonomy and security. Further evidence of their attitude to these matters is found when we look at the response to the question 'How did you come by the capital to get started in business?'. The vast majority gave 'personal savings' as the answer and few made use of any kind of credit facility when they established or bought their shops. The failure to use banks or insurance companies is not entirely to be explained in terms of 'constraints', of these institutions being unwilling to advance money on small retail businesses. It is at least in part a matter of attitude and deliberate choice.

Earlier writing has suggested that many shopkeepers survive in the market only by supplementing their shop income in various ways and the responses to our questions confirm this. No less than 40 per cent of the sample drew money from another source. Commonly this other source was capital or savings and thus our data tend to support the impression of small retailers eking out their existence by slowly eroding a small capital sum. The other most frequent source of income was, of course, other jobs and for 18 percent of the sample the employment of the owner or spouse in some other occupation provided additional funds. In a few cases the shopkeeper chose to leave his business in the hands of an assistant for a good deal of the time and earn money himself in another occupation. More often one found the wife running the shop while her husband pursued another occupation, and in a few instances it was obvious that the shop and the money derived from it were clearly regarded as of secondary importance. In most cases the supplement to the business income was, in absolute terms, quite small – a matter of three or four hundred pounds per year – but as a proportion of the family's total funds it was considerable and illustrated very clearly the inadequate rewards of small-scale retailing.

For a good many of those who have purchased their shops even the investment in bricks and mortar does not pay off. Our preliminary analysis of information gained from some of the traders who retired or went out of business within a year or so of our initial interview programme suggests that considerable losses are incurred in real terms. Many found themselves selling the property at little more than what they paid for it, even after ten years, and none derived from the sale of their shops any sizeable capital sum with which to face retirement. In twenty-two cases where we have details, the median price obtained for the shop was £1900 and the median value of stock amounted to only £600 – and against these sums there were invariably many claims. In four cases the entire capital sum was required to pay off debts to wholesalers, or repay the outstanding portion of the original purchase price, or meet the demands of the Inland Revenue. In a number of cases the declared price at which the shop was sold turned out to be largely a notional sum, for with no loan available the new 'owner' offered a minimal down payment and the balance of the agreed price was to be met from future profits. The acceptance of such terms of sale indicates that many counted themselves 'lucky' to have disposed of their businesses. Except for those whose premises were in highly favoured central-city sites, the retailers made little or nothing out of owning their shops. The market in small shops confers none of the benefits of owning your own house.

THE WORK SITUATION

If we compare the shopkeeper with the better-paid manual workers it seems that the only real advantage or privilege that he enjoys is that of independence. Certainly he has little real authority for he typically employs very few staff and those mostly from his own family. Although our sampling frame permitted up to three full-time employees (or six part-timers), 84 per cent of the sample have less than two full-time (or equivalent) employees. For the entire sample the average is one full-time assistant for each owner and almost 20 per cent have no help at all. If we exclude from these calculations paid family assistance we find that 44 per cent have no paid help at all. Our study confirms the picture painted in the earlier literature on the small shop as essentially a family business, and as far as we were able to judge from responses to our questions this situation has changed very little in the last few years. Seventeen per cent claimed they had decreased the number of employees over the previous five years but 10 per cent said they had taken on more staff.

Nor have the disadvantages of the work situation been overdrawn in the previous studies. Shopkeeping is an arduous business. One quarter of the sample kept their shops open for more than eleven and a half hours each day and were therefore actually working for more than twelve hours. The median time for the shop being open was 9.7 hours and the median working day 10.6 hours. The pattern continues day in, day out, and for some even Sunday brings no respite – a third of our sample opened on that day for an average of seven hours. More than 50 per cent do not close for lunch, 28 per cent have no half-day, and a further 14 per cent shut up shop for an afternoon but spend their time on business matters.

We could continue building up the picture in this way but mere statistics are inadequate to describe the situation. Statistics do not convey the gloomy and uncomfortable physical conditions under which many retailers work nor the boredom of those empty periods when there are no customers. The central figure in Malamud's novel reflects upon a lifetime spent in a small shop, on the long hours and the oppressiveness of his cramped, fly-blown surroundings in which he feels himself 'entombed'. The impression we have gained of the life and conditions of at least a sizeable minority of our sample suggest that the metaphor is well chosen.

If the money is relatively poor, if there is little security, if the hours are long, why do so many continue with it?[8] To answer that question we need to examine their perceptions of the occupation and in particular the ways in which they evaluate it against their previous work experience or against other jobs that they know about. Towards the end of the interview we asked how being a shopkeeper compared with their previous work, and the most frequent responses referred to 'independence and responsibility'. Clearly, the autonomy and opportunity to order their own working lives was much valued. Money was mentioned by less than half the sample and most of these indicated that the rewards of shop-keeping were rather better than those in their previous jobs. The financial returns may be modest but for some they are no worse than those experienced elsewhere. On the other hand, there was no doubt that many found irksome the long hours and consequent restrictions that this placed on leisure activities and holidays, and a good number disliked the actual content, the day-to-day routines of the job. We had expected that the rate of 'mortality' of small businesses and the wide-spread notion that small shopkeepers are 'disappearing' would produce a good deal of comment on the insecurity of the job. In fact very few mentioned it and from the responses to a question specifically related to this issue it is obvious that the vast majority (75 per cent) regard their job as 'secure'. Not only that, most thought it compared favourably with named occupations, for instance that of schoolteacher. So, part of the answer to our question lies in the fact that for many shopkeepers the job compares reasonably well with others they have had or know about. The money is not often worse and though the conditions of work may not be too good, the fact that a man can be his own boss counts for a lot. However, there is no doubt that many remain as shopkeepers for less positive reasons. Finding a job which was significantly better paid would be hard (given their rather modest educational attainments) and, indeed, for many their age would make it difficult to obtain any employment at all.[9] We asked all our respondents whether, if they had a completely free choice, they would stay in the same job. If we leave out those who intended to retire, rather more than 50 per cent indicated that they would like to get out of retailing. Thus, like men in a great many other jobs a sizeable number continue in the occupation because they are 'trapped'.

Finally, we should consider what attracts men to retailing in the first place. Early in our interviews we asked why they had taken up this job and the replies were interesting. 81 per cent gave 'independence' as an important or very important reason, 72 per cent regarded 'money' as important, and 62 per cent stressed 'getting ahead'. There is little doubt that it is the image of the small businessman as one who has autonomy and who may through his own efforts make a success of his job that continues to draw new recruits to the occupation.

The salience of the 'independence' idea is also brought out by our examination of the patterns of trading. In our original paper we had followed some of the existing writing and predicted that though 'being your own boss' would be important, the present market conditions would ensure that a good many small retailers would give up some independence by joining or forming collective buying groups in order to become more competitive. After all, there are considerable advantages to be gained, not only in the economies that come from bulk purchasing, but also in the expertise in promotions and advertising that is available to chain members, plus the advice and occasionally even the finance for improving the mode of selling or the premises themselves. But in fact very few of our sample did belong to such organizations, 92 per cent remaining entirely independent. The reasons for this lie partly in the fact that though shopkeepers who join them reap some advantage, the chains have been initiated by, and are run largely in the interests of, the wholesalers, and it is they who establish the criteria of eligibility.[10] Interviews with managers of voluntary chains in Edinburgh indicated that they tried, not always successfully, to restrict membership to retailers with a turnover of around £500 per week, and threequarters of our sample would on this point be judged 'too small' or 'unpromising'. It is also true that such collective organizations do not exist in all areas of business and national data indicate very clearly that voluntary chains are really well established in only the grocery trade. However, it is plain that the small shopkeepers are not always well informed about the existence of voluntary buying groups; 24 per cent of the grocers for instance explained that they did not belong to a buying chain because 'there are none in our kind of business'! And even when they are well-informed there are still those who would not join because to do so means ceding some of their independence to a collective body. When we enquired about the Union of Small Shopkeepers we encountered the same tendency. Only nine persons belonged to the union, whose existence can hardly be unknown since its spokesmen are frequently asked to comment on economic and fiscal matters as they affect the retailer. The Scottish Secretary of the union admitted that a great many small shopkeepers were reluctant to join either the union or the voluntary chains because: 'Shopkeepers are the most individual minded people. They will not be told how to run their business. They will not brook any interference. You rarely find that they'll co-operate with each other . . . because they're the one type who are completely independent.'

VALUES AND IDEOLOGY

We suggested earlier that the general approach to business affairs might be described as 'economic traditionalism'. Summarizing the material already discussed and attempting to abstract the common elements of their economic vision we arrived at three key elements:

1 A deeply held belief in the advantages of 'independence'. The implied virtues of working for yourself, of succeeding through your own efforts reflects a moral rather than an economic assessment;

2 A distaste for what may be regarded as the 'rational–legal' elements of our society. Thus, large, bureaucratically structured organizations are mistrusted. There is a fear of 'control' and 'intervention' and scepticism of the notion of rational planning;

3 A dislike of change. Their outlook is not that of the determined entrepreneur. What matters is stability and continuity and the 'traditional' way of doing things. The reluctance with which they view changing the manner of trading and their general economic conservatism are only partially explained by financial constraints. They are essentially matters of general economic orientation.

Such views are obviously not the exclusive preserve of shopkeepers. Indeed, from the reasons given for starting up in business and from other data we must infer that these attitudes have been nurtured in other *milieux*, in other occupational settings. At the same time it is plain that the work situation of the independent trader provides a suitable climate for the sustenance and development of these ideas. This is one of the reasons why shopkeeping remains attractive. For those who hold such an economic orientation the opportunities of finding a job in which these values may be realized are few; if the level of education is relatively low and there are only modest amounts of capital available the appeal of shopkeeping becomes even clearer. The small shop is the most accessible form of self-employment for those who cherish independence but who lack formal skills or sizeable economic resources.

Accounting for the origins of these economic dispositions, however, is not easy. Shopkeepers come from diverse social backgrounds (as we shall discuss below) and this fact, together with the limitations of our data on family of origin, precluded simple hypotheses about values acquired from parents. However, it is possible that early associations with non-bureaucratic employment (being brought up in a family of independent artisans for example) may be important to those who do not come from middle-class backgrounds. The very extensive information collected on the occupational careers of the Edinburgh sample yields no one simple route into shopkeeping, but it is striking that large numbers had some prior experience of working in retail firms.[11] The general economic conservatism is almost certainly linked to their lack of geographical mobility: 64 per cent were brought up in Edinburgh or within ten miles of the city and 79 per cent are from the central belt of Scotland. They are then overwhelmingly 'locals' and they seem to see the problems of their trade in very parochial and 'traditional' terms.[12]

The constellation of economic beliefs and values has obvious implications for the shopkeepers' political commitments and we would expect to find evidence of what Goldthorpe and Lockwood (1963) called 'radical individualism'. From the information contained in the politics section of our interview schedule we can abstract some themes which go some way to fulfill that expectation. First, there is the concern with possessive individualism and the support for political parties or programmes which seek to maintain a 'property-owning democracy'. Related to this is the interest in preserving a free market economy, and a climate in which the individual has open to him the widest opportunities for economic advancement and the requisite incentives to encourage his efforts. The desirable social order is one in which a man is rewarded for hard work and initiative and it is on this basis that work is assigned and structures of inequality justified. Along with these features goes, very naturally, an unremitting opposition to those policies and political groupings which would seek to reduce a man's economic freedom and which aim at some deliberate shaping and planning of economic and social systems through increasing central control.

Tables 5-9 present some of the political data. *Table 5* indicates clearly enough that support for the Conservative Party is strong and that Labour can hope for few votes from this group. More important than these figures on voting intention are the data on voting histories which show the consistency with which shopkeepers have voted for the right-wing party. We have information on all elections back to 1945, so that given the average age in our sample we are dealing with a large number of observations. Furthermore, our definition of a 'solid' supporter is a very stringent one so there can be no doubt about this group's regular attachment to the Conservatives. Equally, their disinclination to vote for Labour is made clear. Recently, King (1972) showed that only 70 per cent of the electors voted for the same party in both 1964 and 1966. Comparable figures for our sample indicate that 81 per cent of the men and 83 per cent of the women gave their vote to the same party – a considerably higher level of 'stability'.

Responses to an open-ended question on 'what the parties stand for' produced interesting results. The Tory party was clearly identified with *laissez-faire* economics, with 'free competition and enterprise', with an economic climate where the individual could succeed through his own

TABLE 5
Voting intention of owners

	percentage	N
Conservative	65.9	247
Liberal	4.0	15
Labour	14.7	55
Scottish Nationalist	6.1	23
abstain	5.1	19
don't know	4.3	16
	100.1	375*

* 16 respondents refused to answer; no information for 3 respondents; 4 respondents not eligible.

TABLE 6
Voting history of owners

	percentage	N
'solid' Conservative	54.3	201
'solid' Labour	20.0	74
other	7.3	27
changers	13.3	49
uncommitted	5.1	19
	100.0	370*

* 11 respondents had voted only once or were ineligible. On 17 cases there is inadequate information.

'Solid'—those who a) voted whenever eligible – always for the same party

b) may have abstained as often as they voted – but always voted for same party.

'Other'—a combination of several groups originally coded 'deviationists'. Basically those whose record shows movement between the parties other than that between Conservative and Labour.

'Changers'—those who have voted for both Conservative and Labour

'Uncommitted'—those who abstained on every occasion, or who abstained four times or more and cast only one vote.

efforts; it held the promise of 'economic prosperity' for all who were prepared to work hard. By contrast, notions of what the Labour party stood for were by no means as clear cut, but the commonest single response linked the party with 'nationalization, planning, and control', and these things were all regarded with considerable hostility. Many saw Labour as a party determined to produce a new and more equitable division of the nation's resources but half those giving this response disapproved of this political goal. Overall, the answers to these questions are striking because they are so diverse and because so many of them carry powerful tones of opposition to socialist policies. Though the numbers involved were small it was necessary to retain separate codes for responses which identified Labour with 'bad, weak government', with 'dishonesty' and with 'communism'. We also asked 'what kind of people do you think tend to vote for the different parties?' and the Labour voters were, as one would expect, seen largely in terms of the 'working class' or 'manual workers', but again we found our respondents remarkably forthright in their antipathy to left-wing supporters. We were surprised to find so many answers carrying distinctly negative characterizations of those who vote Labour; in particular, the linking of the party with 'layabouts', with those who 'want something for nothing', seems important, for it underlines that moral evaluation of work that we encountered in their purely economic views.

TABLE 7

'Trades Unions have too much power in the country'

voting intention	agree	disagree	D.K.	N
Conservative	82.6	13.4	4.0	247
Liberal	86.7	13.3	0.0	15
Labour	56.4	38.2	5.5	55
Scottish Nationalist	69.6	21.7	8.7	23
abstain	68.4	26.3	5.3	19
don't Know	80.0	13.3	6.7	15
				374*

Agreement that trade unions have too much power is widespread, and even among the Labour supporters rather more than 50 per cent concur in this assessment. Such a view is, of course, congruent with those highly individualistic attitudes that many expressed in answer to

TABLE 8

'*The State interferes too much in the lives of individuals in this country*'

voting intention	agree	disagree	D.K.	N
Conservative	74.9	23.9	1.2	247
Liberal	73.3	26.7	0.0	15
Labour	50.9	47.3	1.8	55
Scottish Nationalist	69.6	30.4	0.0	23
abstain	47.4	42.1	10.5	19
don't know	66.7	26.7	6.7	15
				374*

TABLE 9

'*Big Businessmen have too much power in the country*'

voting intention	agree	disagree	D.K.	N
Conservative	45.9	46.7	7.3	246
Liberal	46.7	40.0	13.3	15
Labour	70.9	23.6	5.5	55
Scottish Nationalist	47.8	47.8	4.3	23
abstain	52.6	47.4	0.0	19
don't know	46.7	33.3	20.0	15
				373*

See note to *Table 5*. No information on one further respondent in *Tables 7* and *8*, and 2 respondents in *Table 9*.

questions on economic matters. Similarly, the idea that the State interferes too much in the lives of individuals received a good deal of acceptance, and though the responses from the intending Labour voters are distinctive, they do not indicate thorough-going rejection of the statement posed. Attitudes to the power of big business show a rather different pattern. Here only the left-wing voters provide clear support for the view that big business in Britain is too powerful and the other replies suggest a measure of uncertainty about the matter. This reflects the ambivalent attitudes towards big business that we encountered in other parts of the interview. It is clear that the relationship between large commercial concerns and small retailers is highly variable and complex. There are considerable differences from one trade to another and in many instances the relationship is perceived by the shopkeepers as symbiotic rather than conflictual.

So far we have treated the sample as though it were undifferentiated, and in particular as though basic variables like age, sex, and social origins made little difference to our findings. Whether we judge their political sentiments by 'voting intention' or by 'voting history' it is the case that women are more likely than men to support the Conservative party and there is a fairly clear relationship between age and vote such that older electors are more likely to be Tory than the relatively young. However, when we come to social origins we find that there is no simple relationship between the social background from which the retailer comes and his voting intention. Certainly, support for Labour is more likely to be found among those whose fathers were in manual occupations than among the sons of middle-class parents, as we see in *Table 10*, and the same relationship holds when we look at voting histories. But in both cases it has to be remarked that a very sizeable majority of those from working-class backgrounds support the Tories and that the highest levels of Conservative attachment are found in the 'intermediate' strata and among those whose fathers were shopkeepers.

TABLE 10

Social origins of owners by voting intention

occupational status levels of owner's father	Con.	Lib.	Lab.	Party Scot. Nat.	Abst.	D.K.	N.
upper middle	66.7	4.4	15.6	8.9	2.2	2.2	45
lower middle	56.9	6.9	8.6	12.1	10.3	5.2	58
shopkeeper	74.6	1.5	10.4	3.0	7.5	3.0	67
intermediate	72.7	0.0	13.6	4.5	4.5	4.5	22
manual	64.2	4.5	18.4	5.0	3.4	4.5	179
							371*

* Inadequate information in 27 cases.

There is not space here to discuss more than a part of the political data, but what has emerged so far in our analysis is not only the substantial support for the Tories but, more importantly, the opposition to policies with a socialist flavour and the marked reluctance to give much backing to the Labour party. The adherence of the small shopkeepers to the right-wing party should not be interpreted as evidence of a powerful commitment to Conservative ideology but rather as a somewhat sceptical acceptance of this party as the lesser of two evils. Certainly in our interviews we found echoes of the Poujadist's distaste for any centralized administration (Labour or Tory) and almost 40 per cent thought that it made no difference which party was in power.[13] The co-existence of high and consistent support for the Conservatives with this disbelief on the part of so many that the outcome of elections will make any difference is, in our view, to be explained by the detachment of this stratum from the political and economic interests of either party. The shopkeepers will back the Conservative party because they identify it as the party of the 'middle class' and because its policies appear less likely than those of Labour to be detrimental to their chances of advancement or survival.

SHOPKEEPING AND SOCIAL MOBILITY

We commented earlier that this occupation was characterized by high 'mortality' rates among the businesses and by a steady flow of new recruits to replace most of those who left the trade. Many earlier studies had commented on this and also on the fact that the stratum drew its members from a wide spread of social backgrounds. Our own sample provides some demonstration of this diversity, 49 per cent coming from manual households, 39 per cent from the lower-middle class and 11 per cent from the upper-middle class. For the most part their education has been modest. Many of the men (74 per cent) left school at the earliest opportunity and 70 per cent have no secondary-school qualifications. Among the female owners fewer had left school so promptly (58 per cent) and only 61 per cent were without any school certificates. At the other end of the scale, over 9 per cent of the men and 10 per cent of the women owners have higher educational qualifications in the form of professional certificates or degrees. Between these two extremes we find a wide variety of educational experiences – with rather more than 40 per cent of the men and a little less than 40 per cent of the women having taken some part-time further education.

Shopkeeping, then, is open to a diverse population. It is accessible to people with little education and no skill or specific expertise. The nature of the occupation and especially its work situation is such that it offers *occupational* mobility without *social* mobility and herein lies one of its most intriguing aspects for the student of social stratification. It is possible to bring to this job widely divergent orientations and aspirations and it is possible to carry out the day-to-day routines without these necessarily affecting patterns of social relationships developed in very different occupational settings or social *milieux*. For example, a manual worker may acquire a shop and yet voluntarily maintain close links with existing kin, friends, and former workmates. There are no occupational pressures upon him to establish close contacts with a particular status group, no necessity to join voluntary organizations or associations of a predominantly middle-class kind. Where in most occupations the social patterns and values of workmates impinge upon the new recruit in many subtle ways, the isolation of the shopkeeper leaves him free to cling to old ways or to develop new ones almost at will.

Thus, though we may regard the occupation 'shopkeeper' as placing the owner in the 'petite bourgeoisie' or less satisfactorily 'the middle class', it is obvious that this is compatible with the maintenance of 'working-class' normative and relational patterns.[14] There is certainly a small group (approximately 10 per cent of the sample) who come from manual backgrounds, who run shops in working-class districts, and who live in those same areas. It is entirely possible that some of them will share working-class culture in a great many respects.[15]

Given this heterogeneity, the orientation we referred to earlier as 'economic traditionalism' must encompass more than one cluster of beliefs and attitudes. 'Independence' for example may have a dual meaning. It can be viewed as a condition of positive freedom, of freedom to act or think in a particular way, or it may be seen negatively, – as freedom *from* some set of constraints. Not only has this duality of freedom been long recognized,[16] but the idea that owning a small business is seen as an escape from the alienation of the manual workers' world is far from new.[17] Shopkeeping then may be desirable as a relief from hierarchical authority, and as a chance to have some of the 'good things' in life. Thus, one can imagine a working-class pattern of attitudes and beliefs quite compatible with shopkeeping. Some will enter the occupation from manual backgrounds without aspirations for upward *social* mobility. They can gain the benefits of autonomy (and possibly some economic advantages as well) without having to move into new social worlds with new and inescapable relationships and unfamiliar, alien values.

Others, however, *will* see the occupation as offering them social mobility. They will wish to adopt new sets of social relations and new normative standards. They will identify with other established middle-class groups and will seek the opportunities both for themselves and for their children which this occupation may be able to provide. They will want to give their children a 'better start', to set them on the road to solidly middle-class positions, and in this they will be conscious of the need for planning, for 'sacrifice', and for the establishment of clear 'projects'.

Within our sample it is possible to see some evidence of this. Family size is small, with the mean at 1.82 in what is a fairly elderly group, most of whom have completed their families. There are 9 per cent who never married, a further 14 per cent have no children, and 25 per cent have only one. Only 8 per cent have four children or more. Educational aspirations for the children are high, with more than half of those with children wanting some kind of selective, fee-paying secondary schooling.[18] If we look at the first-born children we find that 25 per cent did attend such schools. The desire for such educational opportunities and the extent of its attainment certainly suggests that, for some, shopkeeping is associated with the formation or maintenance of values that distinguish them from manual workers. Analysis of the occupational achievements of the children is based on very small numbers (most are still in full-time education) but it suggests that the majority find their way into at least lower middle-class jobs.

Control over the life-chances of one's children is an important element of class situation and, in this respect, the contrast with the affluent workers previously studied (Goldthorpe *et al* 1969) is striking. It is not that the shopkeepers' aspirations are so much higher but that they are far more likely to see these ambitions for their children fulfilled. Direct economic power is of some importance (in the payment of fees for example) and knowledge of the workings of the local education system is certainly well developed among many. Most important, however, is the transmission to children of a system of values and beliefs which many small shopkeepers hold and which emphasizes the importance of success through one's own efforts and, critically, the *possibility* of such success.

The diversity of social background from which the retailers came indicates that this stratum is of interest for another reason. As S. M. Miller (1960) pointed out a good many years ago, students of social mobility should pay more attention to the nature and extent of *downward* mobility. The ease with which shopkeeping may be entered is of advantage not only to those from manual backgrounds. It becomes a 'refuge' for some from solidly middle-class homes who have failed to acquire the kinds of skills and competences demanded by most of the better paid white-collar jobs. Some hints of this are found in our educational data. For example, 42 per cent of those from 'upper middle-class' backgrounds left secondary school with no qualifications at all and 40 per cent left at the earliest opportunity.

Another important attraction of this occupation to those from middle-class origins is plain enough. Independence is, at least traditionally, a hall-mark of the most respected occupations in our society and shopkeeping provides a chance to realize this symbolic value. Then again the social isolation that is possible, and to some extent enforced, may insulate those who are downwardly mobile from the relational pressures which commonly accompany such changes in social position.

Thus, the true marginality of shopkeeping becomes clear, revealing the stratification processes are not crudely deterministic; rather there is for the individual an element of purposive action involved. The occupation affords just enough power and privilege to enable those with the necessary ideology and value-orientation to ally themselves with the fortunes of the middle class. At the same time, for those who so choose, it is compatible with the values and life-styles of the working class.

CONCLUSION

In this section we can return to some of the general themes with which we begun. If we ask where the shopkeepers stand in the class structure of contemporary industrial society, the answer is 'outside it'. In a very real sense the petite bourgeoisie is detached from the concerns of the working and middle-classes. To a large extent the small businessman finds himself a mere spectator at the arena in which the forces of labour and big business confront each other. His economic and political interests are not represented by any major parties in western democracies and if he throws in his lot with the right-wing parties it is largely because they seem more likely to sustain traditional values with which he agrees. It is not that they invariably defend his economic interests. In our sample, for example, support for the Tories was tinged with scepticism. The Conservative party seems well aware that the small business stratum is an important constituency and its election manifestos make some obvious appeals to this group; but in office the pledges of the hustings are rarely redeemed. To a party in power, it is big business that matters, not the small traders.

There is little that is new in the situation of the small shopkeepers. They have always been regarded as marginal. Even in the eighteenth century, when we may more properly speak of a 'bourgeoisie', they were treated as very doubtful members of that class. Always there was suspicion that they lacked certain qualities, that they could not be assumed to be *vivant bourgeoisement*.[19] In nineteenth-century Britain similar doubts were expressed. The historical picture is rather confused, with Marxists like Foster (1968) insisting that shopkeepers were black-listed and coerced into voting for the interests of the workers, while others like Vincent (1967), Nossiter (1972), or Davis (1966) discuss their similarity to the artisans and the sizeable radical vote which they produced.

It is worth reflecting briefly on the traditional concerns of the 'bourgeoisie'. In Europe's pre-industrial cities the merchants and traders sought the overthrow of a feudal system of domination. They struggled to establish rights that guaranteed freedom for the individual, among these the rights to own property and to trade. Thus, 'property' and 'autonomy' are important motifs in the history of this stratum. They appear just as clearly among the radical shopkeepers of an industrializing Britain as among the traders of medieval city states. It seems as though the focal concerns have changed little down the years; that yesterday's 'Radicals' and to-day's 'Conservatives' would find much to agree about.

If this is so, then perhaps we can argue that the petit bourgeois stratum is the repository of many of the traditional values upon which a capitalist social order was built. The shopkeepers' passionate individualism and the moral evaluation of work emerge clearly enough. So too does the vision of a *laissez-faire* economy in which men like themselves will prosper. Moreover, their belief that by hard work and wit you can succeed is crucial to the conception of ours as an open society. Thus, the symbolic significance of the stratum resides in the fact that, to many, their lives appear to demonstrate the possibility of individual mobility. Despite the modesty of their origins many have succeeded – succeeded that is, in terms quite fundamental to a capitalist society. They have won, albeit in small measure, property and autonomy.

Finally, we would argue that the significance of these central concerns in the political and social philosophy of the petty bourgeois is this: espousing an ideology of independence and hard work he is inclined to the belief that inequality is the result of the differential distribution of talent and effort. In doing so he buttresses the present system of inequality and offers it legitimation.

Notes

1 Among the most influential are Birch (1959); Fromm (1960); Hoffman (1956); Mills (1951); Trow (1967).

2 The *British Labour Statistics Year Book 1969* gave the average weekly wage for manual workers as £23. 15. 7 (£1236 per annum).

3 The figures presented in the *Family Expenditure Survey* (1969) show that among 'Professionals' 72 per cent were involved in house purchase. However, only 20 per cent were outright owners, the remaining 52 per cent had their property mortgaged.

4 In his novel *The Assistant*, Bernard Malamud (1967) provides a vivid picture of the precarious existence of the small retailer and of the effects of trade fluctuations.

5 In his discussion of traditionalism Weber (1961: 261) remarks on the 'general incapacity and indisposition to depart from the beaten paths' which would aptly describe the economic orientation of the shopkeepers.

6 In his description of the small farming community in which he grew up J. K. Galbraith remarks, 'Spending money even when it might mean more money was painful. And perhaps unwise. For with the increased prospect of gain came the increased prospect of loss'. Our shopkeepers seem to adopt a similarly canny approach.

7 No less than 77 per cent own their shops; 66.5 per cent own them outright.

8 There is not space here to discuss the 'survival of the stratum' but our study suggests that rather more than 10 per cent leave the trade every year. As our earlier work argued this must mean that something like 40,000 new recruits are found every year in Britain. Interestingly, the preliminary results of the 1971 Census of Distribution in *Economic Trends* (1973) confirm our claim that the total stratum size was relatively stable. Between 1966 and 1971 the number of independent shops remained almost unchanged.

9 Even top clerical grades earned, on average, little more than £1400 at this time. See The Institute of Office Management (1970).

10 On the origins of voluntary chains in Britain see Fulop (1962) and for a broader discussion of the 'politics of distribution' see Palamountain (1955).

11 The analysis of occupational careers shows that among the male owners 50 per cent of those with prior careers (N = 291) had experience of working in shops and 35 per cent were so employed immediately before opening their own businesses.

12 This may be more marked in Edinburgh than in other large towns and cities. Edinburgh has experienced very little immigration largely

because it provides few opportunities for unskilled or semi-skilled workers.

13 Much of the traditional literature describes the petite bourgeoisie as a very 'conservative' stratum. Richard Hamilton in an as yet unpublished paper tries to show that there is 'a myth of small business conservatism', and using data for the U.S. he makes a fairly convincing case that on a great many issues, as well as party support, this group is no more conservative than many others in the middle class. Our findings relating to a more narrowly defined group in the UK suggest that the conservatism is no 'myth' but this does not mean that there is commitment to any extreme right-wing ideology.

14 See for example R. Roberts (1971: 5). Roberts, himself the son of a small shopkeeper describes life in Salford in the Edwardian era. 'Shopkeepers, publicans and skilled tradesmen occupied the premier positions, each family having its own sphere of influence. A few of these aristocrats, whilst sharing working class culture, had aspirations. From their ranks the lower middle class, then clearly defined, drew most of its recruits.'

15 At the present time our analysis of the relationships between social origins, place of business, and place of residence is incomplete.

16 See e.g. E. Fromm (1960).

17 See, notably G. Chinoy (1955).

18 The Edinburgh situation is peculiar. Until last year there was a small number of corporation schools that were highly selective and for which small fees were payable. The existence of these schools obviously inflates the proportion wanting fee-paying education, but it does not alter the fact that demand for education in grant-aided or public schools is high.

19 See for instance E. Barber (1955: 16).

Additional Note

It may be objected that in our interpretation of the political data we over-emphasize the degree of conservatism and that the low response rate has led to unknown biases. In fact we have a good deal of information on those who declined to be interviewed. They are for the most part, old and female and for those reasons likely to be *at least* as right-wing as the rest of the sample. Moreover, we made an analysis of reasons for refusal which indicated clearly that many are committed to highly individualistic, right-wing views.

References

BARBER, E. 1955. *The Bourgeoisie in Eighteenth Century France* Princeton University Press.

BECHHOFER, F. and ELLIOTT, B. 1968. An Approach to a Study of Small Shopkeepers and the Class Structure. *European Journal of Sociology* 9.

BECHHOFER, F., ELLIOTT, B., and RUSHFORTH, M. 1971. The Market Situation of Small Shopkeepers. *Scottish Journal of Political Economy* 18 (2).

BIRCH, A. H. 1959. *Small Town Politics*. London: Oxford University Press.

CENTRAL STATISTICAL OFFICE, 1973. *Economic Trends* No. 232 London: H.M.S.O.

CHINOY, E. 1955. *Automobile Workers and the American Dream*. New York: Doubleday and Co.

DAVIS, D. 1966. *A History of Shopping*. London: Routledge & Kegan Paul.

DEPARTMENT OF EMPLOYMENT, 1971. *British Labour Statistics Year Book, 1969*. London: H.M.S.O.

FAMILY EXPENDITURE SURVEY. 1971. *Report for 1970*. London: H.M.S.O.

FOSTER, J. 1968. Nineteenth Century Towns: A Class Dimension. In H. Dyos (ed.) *The Study of Urban History*. London: Edward Arnold.

FROMM, E. 1960. *The Fear of Freedom*. London: Routledge & Kegan Paul.

FULOP, C. 1962. *Buying by Voluntary Chains*. London: Allen & Unwin.

GALBRAITH, J. K. 1964. *The Scotch*. Cambridge, Mass: Houghton Mifflin and Co.

GOLDTHORPE, J. H. and LOCKWOOD, D. 1963. Affluence and British Class Structure. *Sociological Review* 11.

GOLDTHORPE, J. H., LOCKWOOD, D., BECHHOFER, F., and PLATT, J. 1969. *The Affluent Worker in the Class Structure*. Cambridge: Cambridge University Press.

HAMILTON, R. 1972. The Politics of Independent Businessmen. Unpublished mimeo.

HOFFMANN, S. 1956. *Le Mouvement Poujade*. Paris: Armand Colin.

INSTITUTE OF OFFICE MANAGEMENT. 1970. *Clerical Salaries Analysis, 1970*. London.

KING, A. 1972. Politics. In P. Barker (ed.) *A Sociological Portrait*. Harmondsworth: Penguin.

MALAMUD, B. 1967. *The Assistant*. Harmondsworth: Penguin.

MILLER, S. M. 1960. Comparative Social Mobility. *Current Sociology*, 9 (1).

MILLS, C. W. 1951. *White Collar*. London: Oxford University Press.

NOSSITER, T. J. 1972. Shopkeeper Radicalism in the Nineteenth Century. In T. J. Nossiter, A. H. Hanson, and S. Rokkan (eds.)

Imagination and Precision in the Social Sciences. London: Faber and Faber.

PALAMOUNTAIN, J. C. 1955. *The Politics of Distribution*. Cambridge, Mass.: Harvard University Press.

ROBERTS, R. 1971. *The Classic Slum*. Manchester: Manchester University Press.

TAWNEY, R. H. 1921. *The Acquisitive Society*. London: Bell.

TROW, M. 1967. Small Businessmen, Political Tolerance and Support for McCarthy. In L. Coser (ed.) *Political Sociology*. New York: Harper Row.

VINCENT, J. R. 1967. *How Victorians Voted*. Cambridge: Cambridge University Press.

WEBER, M. 1961. *General Economic History*. New York: Collier Macmillan.

ZYGMUNT BAUMAN

Officialdom and Class: Bases of Inequality in Socialist Society

The following is an attempt at constructing a theoretical model of the *power structure* of socialist society as distinct from the *stratification* model. The essential differences between these two ways of accounting for the phenomenon of social inequality can be summarized as follows:

1 the power-structure model aims at depicting the *differentiation of opportunities of action*, of influencing events, and of access to appropriate resources – as seen, in principle, by an outside observer; the stratification model attempts to systematize and make coherent the disparate assessments of these qualities, possessions, and accomplishments of members of the society, which are selected as important and significant by the members themselves. All in all, while the power-structure model starts from situations as its raw data, the stratification model is focused on evaluative patterns;

2 while the stratification model *compares* the values assumed by selected variables in differentiating groups within the population (without pre-empting the question of relations between the groups) – the power-structure model attempts to represent the *web of dependencies*, which both unites and opposes groups within a society. 'Dependency', which is the meaning ascribed by Marx to the notion of 'social relation', stands here for any constraints that one group exercises on the other group's claims to either consummatory or instrumental resources;

3 the intention behind the power-structure model is to reveal the conditions which are *likely to generate* important disparities in behaviour given a certain conjunction of circumstances. The stratification model, on the other hand, is set on describing existing variations in behaviour; the question whether observed variations have a systemic, or a contingent (even if monotonous) nature may be asked in this connexion, but it does not belong to the logic of the stratification model;

4 the power-structure model employs the logic of *typology*: it normally sets apart distinct types of systematically determined situations, which are defined in opposition to each other and which tend to be mutually exclusive. The stratification model, by contrast, uses the logic of a continuum defined by a specific relation between any pair of points selected at random (e.g., 'more and less prestige') – rather than by its sharply determined poles. By detecting discontinuities in what is essentially an uninterrupted line, the stratification model arrives eventually at the logic of *classification*:

5 last, but not least, the stratification model is a linear one; the power-structure model is not. A single set of values may, of course, be applied in retrospect with the effect of arranging the units of the power structure in a linear order; but this operation would not belong to the logic of the model. The same operation is, however, the principle underlying the construction of the stratification model, and thereby constitutes its inherent element. The linearity (portrayed ordinarily as verticality) of the stratification model is therefore determined by its own logic and as such is necessarily given. An important consequence of this distinction is that the power-structure model is *not* distinguished from the stratification model merely by the selection of power as its central variable; indeed, one may easily construct a stratification model of power.

The class model of capitalist society elaborated upon in Marx's writings is a foremost example of the category of power-structure models; so is Weber's market-based dimension of social differentiation; recently a clear scheme of the same kind has been suggested by John Rex (Rex 1972) for contemporary British society. Rex's model possesses all the elegance sought for by Marx in his pursuit of the *necessary* relations that underlie the flow of contingent events on the surface of political history. The distinctive marks of the two models, each set in its own and independent system of logic, are in a sense so apparent that they would hardly have to be spelled out if it were not for their persistent, though erroneous, treatment as two alternative and comparable accounts of the same facet of social reality in tension with each other.

PRAXIS AND THE MULTIPLICITY OF POWER STRUCTURES

There is much to be said on the possibility of applying a single model of stratification to a given society at a given moment. The models proposed by sociologists usually pretend to enjoy exactly this kind of monopolistic status. This is due less to methodological blunders committed by their authors than to the multitude of conflicting standards typical of any modern society. Such cohesion, and the air of finality which the proposed models seem to possess, should be ascribed as much to the authors' attempts at conceptual ordering as to the intrinsic coherence of the reality they describe. But this is not the subject I wish to analyze in this paper.

We have to ask, however, whether the one-to-one relation with a selected facet of social reality – the status we are inclined to deny to stratification models – can be a privilege enjoyed by the power-structure models. In other words, whether, for a given society at a given time, there is one and only one power-structure model which accounts for it adequately. Since the term 'power', contrary to the terms used in stratification models, stands for the 'potentiality of action' rather than for action which has already occurred, we ask in fact whether at any moment the future state of society, its 'future history', is pre-ordained by existing conditions in an unequivocal way, so that only one 'potentiality of action' may be assigned to it, at least in the (sufficiently) long-run.

There may be, theoretically, two types of answer to our question. The first is frequently found in popular interpretations of the Marxist theory of society (for a sophisticated version of this type see Marcuse 1969: 23 ff). There is, so we are told, one 'real' power structure in any society, and it is related to the 'real' network of interests. These interests and groups (units of the structure) define each other, i.e., the interest is what maximizes the satisfaction of vital needs of a particular group; and any X is considered a member of the group if this group's interests are simultaneously his own. Along with these real interests there are, however, 'immediate' interests as well. (The two terms are viewed as mutually opposed.) The 'immediate' interest is marked off by its opposition to the real one, or it is a truncated, garbled, or inadequate reflection of the real interest. A derogatory, morally reproachful sense, is attached to the term 'immediate interests' by the Soviet version of official Marxism; the pursuit of immediate interests is a form of inferior and unworthy conduct by an immature or hoodwinked class; while pursuing its immediate interests, the class is led astray, away from its real historical calling, away from the condition in which its real interests can be met – etc. To support this usage one needs a vision of a tough, inflexible, solid 'structure', somehow independent of mass human actions and so remaining unchanged and unaffected whatever the vicissitudes of the empirical historical action of classes. One can easily point to a number of Marx's statements that warrant such an interpretation. These stand, however, in jarring opposition to the basic 'open-endedness' and inconclusiveness of human praxis, on which Marx repeatedly insisted throughout his work. One can relate this contradiction (as Gianfranco Poggi has recently done) to the 'deterministic streak', which Marx never completely got rid of himself, and to the obvious mobilizing superiority of the politician's 'it *will* happen' over the scientist's circumspect 'it *can* happen that . . .'

The second answer is founded on the image of the power structure as co-extensive with historical praxis, and existing in virtue of the praxis and through it – rather than as a mysterious separate entity in its own right. According to this theoretical assumption, the questions concerning power are meaningless or at least unanswerable, unless predicated on a specific set of classes-in-action which pursue specific objectives, thereby drawing the frontiers of the competing camps and potential alliances. The power structure therefore emerges as a product of both objective factors (chances) and subjective factors (objectives which select the relevant set of chances) rather than as a solid 'objective' entity, which can be rightly or wrongly, but always *a-posteriori*, reflected by human ideas and action.

And so, in a given society at a given time, there will be one structure in which the classes are at each other's throats, set on nothing less than a thorough re-moulding of society and the maximization of their own demands. But it will succumb to a very different one the moment the multitude of people return to their routine, monotonous, and predictable conduct, and the group will and vision cease to transcend the limitations set by and for everyday, commonsense activity. This is the difference between the fourth and the rest of Rex's power structures ascribed to current British socio-political reality. This is, as well, the difference between the dichotomous, polar image of the class structure as drawn by Marx in the Communist Manifesto, or in the chapter on 'tendencies' in the first volume of the Capital, and the intricate web of divisions and sub-divisions finely spun by the same author in the *18 Brumaire of Louis Bonaparte*. The outstanding Polish Marxist Julian Hochfeld described the two distinct power structures as, respectively, the 'polar' and the 'developed' models (Hochfeld 1963: 149 ff).

On the whole, we can say that more than one power structure may be detected in each society at any given time. Either one or another can become conspicuous – can 'dominate' the societal stage – when illuminated by a specific historical praxis. There is, in other words, a stock of potential power structures in each society, among which praxis plays the role of main selector.

Vilfredo Pareto's distinction between 'real' and 'virtual' systems here comes immediately to mind as a singularly apposite analytical framework (Pareto 1902, vol. 1: 78 ff). The 'real', in this context is in a sense opposite to the 'real' as defined by the previously discussed dichotomy: the 'real systems' are by no means the necessary, or the only true, or the most compelling ones; their only distinctive mark is that they happened already to be actualized and therefore are accessible to empirical observation. But 'virtual' systems are not a bit less *realistic*; given appropriate circumstances, they also may actualize and become real. They can be discovered by the social scientist even before this metamorphosis takes place – by means of theoretical experiment however, rather than by straightforward empirical observation. One has only to spell out the set of circumstances necessary for the metamorphosis to take place.

The set of virtual power structures ascribable to a given network of social relations called society can be, though only metaphorically, compared to Alfred Schutz's set of 'finite provinces of meaning' (Schutz 1967: 230 ff). There is no clear passage from one to another; neither are there trivial rules of translation allowing for an exhaustive expression of the experience intrinsic to one in the language of another. Each 'province' has its own, distinct criteria for distinguishing the real from the unreal and the relevant from the irrelevant. In Schutz's words, the switch from one 'province' to another requires a sudden and abrupt 'shock'. The many descriptions of 'revolutionary situations' may be seen as attempts to record the conditions likely to generate such a shock, i.e. to 'switch off' the everyday and monotonous power structure, and to 'switch on' the simplified, cruder, blatantly conflict-charged one. The latter structure is hardly able to support the 'normal' functioning of the society in its 'normal' state, but is necessary to generate a situation of upheaval. Their differences notwithstanding most descriptions accept that for the 'revolutionary situation' to emerge, the routine power structure must for some reason cease adequately to constrain the behaviour of actors – either because of the dwindling strength of the constraints themselves, or because some classes have taken on objectives which render the constraints unimpressive or irrelevant. The question whether the polarized and one-dimensional, or the multifaceted 'developed' power structure is more adequate as a description of a given society is unanswerable, unless put in the context of changing historical praxis.

In this paper I limit myself to one task only: I wish to sketch the theoretical framework that I think is both necessary and adequate for the description of the routine, everyday power structure of socialist society, as it matured historically in eastern and central Europe. As the socio-political systems there entered their 'system-management' phase, 'the regime and the masses have come to accept each other for granted'. And the sheer longevity of authority, which 'converted compliance into habit', and turned organizational and operational patterns into routines, also transformed 'the radical criticism of the past and millenial expectations' into 'a much more conservative theory of state, in which criticism turns into apologetics' (Meyer 1967: 98–101). Time has its effect even if a 'contrived revolution' marked its beginning. It is this power structure which sustains the 'normal', regular functioning of the system and which generates most of its current political and social history – short of the moments when the fate of the system as a whole, complete with its 'everyday' patterns of superiority and subordination, is put on the agenda, and its perfunctory routine is swept aside or suspended by the 'great simplifier' of a revolutionary situation.

'FUTURISTIC' LEGITIMATION AND THE PARTYNOMIAL AUTHORITY

Having spelt out the traditional, the charismatic, and the legal as the three basic types of authority, Weber hastened to qualify the completeness of his typology (Gerth and Mills 1948: 299–300): 'We do not claim to use the only possible approach nor do we claim that all empirical structures of domination must correspond to one of these "pure" types. On the contrary, the great majority of empirical cases represent a combination or a state of transition among several pure types ... They can be understood only as combinations involving several concepts.' Weber's scattered comments about his own typology were not particularly consistent. In *Wirtschaft und Gesellschaft* he seemed to feel a need for four distinct bases of legitimacy rather than three – in keeping with the four-fold typology of social action to which he attached fundamental importance. In Weber's analysis of social action the concept of *Wertrational* (action oriented to absolute values) had been given a prominence which is less evident in his study of religions. In concert with the four types of social action, Weber saw four ways in which the acting subjects may ascribe legitimacy to a social order. Along with the traditional, emotional, and legal legitimations, of which much had been made in his other studies, particularly in historical–comparative essays, there was a fourth which has all but disappeared in other contexts as well as in most popular digests of Weber's ideas: ascribing legitimacy to an order 'by virtue of a rational belief in its absolute value, thus lending it the validity of an absolute and final committment' (Weber 1964: 130). To the best of my knowledge Weber was never very specific on this subject; in particular, he supplied little information – in comparison with ample historical applications of the other three types – on the concrete empirical forms the order based upon 'substantive rationality' may take on. In the quoted passage Weber points to the belief in Natural Law as the only example. He is somewhat more informative in the chapter on economic action:

'There is an indefinite number of possible standards of value which are "rational" in this sense [i.e. of 'substantive' instead of 'formal', *Wert* instead of *Zweck*, rationality – Z.B.]. Socialistic and communistic standards which, though by no means unambiguous in themselves, always involve elements of social justice and equality, form only one group among the indefinite plurality of possible points of view. Others are action in the interest of a hierarchy of class distinctions or in furtherance of the power of a political unit, particularly by war.' (Weber 1964: 185–6)

Two comments are in order. First, the unusual vagueness of Weber's discussion of substantive rationality, which is in such sharp contrast to the eloquent, detailed analysis of the other three types of action and legitimation, was probably due to the fact that little, if any, historical societies were available at the time as suitable examples of this type. Of socialism, Weber together with his contemporaries was given no choice but to share Pareto's view that although socialism 'a été, au moins indirectement un élément essentiel de progrès dans nos sociétés', t 'n'a pas pu faire du bien, par des mesures qu'il aurais inspirées directement' (Pareto 1902: 63). Emile Durkheim, Werner Sombart, Gustav LeBon, and other prominent sociologists who dedicated voluminous studies to the analysis of the new and perturbing phenomenon, saw socialism as a set of postulates and values, as a political programme, a psychic or moral attitude – but emphatically not as a name for a distinct, empirically analyzable society. Weber could have hardly been an exception to this rule.

Second, for the purpose of typology Weber puts 'socialistic and communistic standards' into the same category as the 'interest of a hierarchy', which he saw in other places as a rather prominent component of traditional authority, and particularly of its patrimonial sub-type. This association is certainly too cursory to be taken as an expression of Weber's considered and theoretically grounded view, but definite enough to warrant a suggestion that Weber would perhaps have explored

further the affinity between socialist legitimation of the social order and
the patrimonial-like features of authority – had he been given the
chance of investigating an empirical sample of the type.

My contention is, first, that the socialist societies which emerged in
the last half-century in eastern Europe do not fall into any of Weber's
three widely discussed types, thus requiring us to design a separate,
fourth category; and, second, just such a category may be found in close
analytical proximity to Weber's 'patrimonial' type.

It goes without saying that Weber's description of patrimonialism
cannot be applied unaltered to socialist societies. The concept had
been coined by Weber in the course of exploring the attributes of
traditional societies, and it bears clear marks of its origin. To be of any
use at all to our purposes, if only as a source of inspiration, it must be
first dissociated from the confinements of its original context, in the
same way as Hermann Schmalenbach dissociated Toennies' *Gemein-
schaft* from its bonds with *Blut und Boden*, thus arriving at a highly
useful notion of *Bund*. In our case, the concept of patrimonialism needs
to be detached from two historically specific phenomena which loomed
large in Weber's description: the personal basis of supreme power
(the notion of 'the ruler'), and the traditionalistic legitimation of
authority. The moment this drastic operation is carried out the striking
appropriateness of the remainder of Weber's analysis to a systematic
description of prominent features of socialist society will become apparent. (Cf. particularly the points of divergence between the formal
rationality of bureaucratic orders and the substantial rationality of
patrimonial rule – Weber 1964: 342 ff, 185 ff.)

For want of a better name, I propose the term 'partynomial' to
describe the type of authority characteristic of socialist societies.
(This is not the place to discuss the plausible suggestion that socialist
societies are not the only contemporary societies that fall within this
category.) In the same way as traditional authority is associated with
traditional types of social action – the charismatic with the emotional,
and the legal with the *Zweckrational* – partynomial authority, as an
ideal type, is intimately attached to *Wertrationalität* as the prevalent
mode of action. I shall try to enumerate, in logical order, the major
characteristics of partynomial rule.

1 Whatever may be said about the practice of socialist government,
   its sole and indispensable *legitimation* is in the future; the rulers of
   any socialist state justify their rule and demand obedience in the
   name of an ideal society they are set on building; the future shape

of a better society is 'given' in an ideal form and is called to play the role of the sole and ultimate judge of whatever decisions may be made at present. The 'futuristic' nature of their legitimation excuses the rulers from submitting their policy to the judgment of 'the masses'. If 'the masses' happen to disagree with the course chosen by their rulers, this bears evidence only to the 'immaturity' of the masses themselves, to their inability to grasp the far-sighted wisdom of the leadership. This is accounted for by reference to regrettable drawbacks in mass education or propaganda, or explained away as the baleful legacy of pre-socialist ideology. The advantages of the future society as well as the roads leading to it are clearly visible only to the eyes of the vanguard, which in *principle* (though an alternative formula may be temporarily launched) is organized in the party. Therefore the party, as the repository and the guardian of the ideal society to come, needs no endorsement from its contemporaries; much less can it allow itself to be diverted from its path by the sluggish pace of the unenlightened, and thereby retarded, majority. (Though every effort is made to aid popular opinion to 'catch up' with the advanced ideal.) It is true that with the passage from the system-building to the system-management stage less emphasis is placed on the 'futuristic' ideology, and it is superseded by an increasingly utilitarian, pragmatic idiom. But the ideological shift takes place within the established organizational framework without challenging the position of the party and its 'futuristic' mission. If previously the party sought to impose its control over *functional divisions* of society, today it seeks to co-opt the scientific, economic, military, engineering, educational, cultural, and professional elite into the top levels of the party leadership, and thus 'assimilate' whatever potential leadership accumulates outside its ranks (cf. Meyer 1967: 105). The 'vanguard' image of the party is anchored now in a different practice – but it still remains unchallenged, although increasingly spelled out in meritocratic terms.

2 In the same way in which the defence of tradition buttressed patrimonial authority as described by Weber, the commitment to the implementation of the ideal society by an enlightened elite lends support to partynomial rule. Loyalty to the party takes the place of obedience to the person of the ruler, and faith in the desirability of the socialist order replaces the respect for tradition. Weber's pertinent description of the components of patrimonialism can accordingly be re-phrased. Thus the administrative staff is

typically recruited on the basis of ideological loyalty to the party from among those who, according to the party's own assessment, 'have of their own will entered into a relation' of ideological loyalty. The five marks of a 'perfect bureaucracy', whose absence Weber noted in a patrimonial order, are not present in a partynomial system either – even as an ideal type; 'In place of a well-defined impersonal sphere of competence, there is a shifting series of tasks and powers commissioned and granted' by the party through more or less arbitrary decisions. 'In contrast to the rational hierarchy of authority in the bureaucratic system, the question who shall decide a matter' can be subject to the arbitrary decision of the party. 'Whenever (the party) intervenes, all others give way' to its will. Any checks 'from below' aimed at effectively reducing the arbitrariness of these decisions would be emphatically dismissed as an attempt by the ideologically retarded to shape the imperatives of the future, of which the party is the sole interpreter.

3 The vanguard legitimation of partynomial authority requires the teleological, not the genetic, determination of macro-social processes. The Plan is the major instrument of such a teleological determination. One speaks of the *emergence* of capitalism, but of *construction* of socialism; the advent of a socialist or a communist society can only come about through a conscious and persistent effort of planning and the implementation of plans. Hence the uniqueness of socialist plans, which are often wrongly understood as an exercise in market forecasting. The plan we discuss here 'can be defined as guidance of economic activities by a communal organ through a scheme which describes, in quantitative as well as in qualitative terms, the productive processes to be undertaken during a given future period' (Landauer 1931: 220). The plan, of course, commands and guides much more than just productive processes. If the plan covers a major part of the national economy, it holds under its sway virtually all spheres of politics, social life, and culture. Now to plan, as a teleological activity, is the more successful (effective), the larger the resources which remain under the direct control of the planning agency. This control can be never complete; the informational blockages in the economy constitute one obvious limit to control. Even more important, however, is another equally unavoidable constraint; short of opting for a pernickety regimentation of labour and distribution of goods (job-placement and food rationing), even the most detailed

planning can only indirectly influence the decisions of consumption and production on the level of individual action.

4 Since all recommendations of the plan are implemented if at all, on the level of individual action – production and consumption decisions must enter the planning process as its major variable. Except for the unacceptable solution mentioned above, there is no way of controlling this variable directly. Still, to be of any use in planning, it must be at least predictable, within as widely drawn limits as possible. Producer-consumer behaviour is predictable to the extent to which individuals submit to the routine, monotonously recurring patterns of conduct. They are likely to behave regularly and respond to stimuli in a repeatable, easy to forecast way, in conditions of relative certainty, guaranteed by the formal rationality of the market (where it will be reasonable to assume the reciprocity of *zweckrational* motives and corresponding conduct). The plan, therefore, not only tolerates, but needs and generates market behaviour on the individual level. A severely restricted market can, however, hardly generate enough rationality to render individual behaviour sufficiently predictable to be taken as a stable factor in the process of planning. On the other hand, a market with enough freedom to turn out the required volume of formal rationality (and hence predictability) may well bite away a solid chunk of the resources which the plan, to be effective, must keep under direct control. To this contradiction there is no easy solution. The relation between plan and market is a typical love-hate relationship; attacks and retreats alternate throughout the history of this tense and uneasy marriage, but hardly ever are they likely to terminate in divorce, since the two partners need each other as intensely as they suffer each other's presence.

5 All in all, the members of a socialist society are exposed, as individuals, to a typically impersonal, *zweckrational* situation of the market; and their exposure is built into a most vital field of their life activity – that of productivity and need-satisfaction. Within socialist society, partynomy on the authority level and market-type rationality on the level of social action coexist on a permanent basis; and there are many ways in which they are incompatible. Each defines in its own way the criteria of rational behaviour. One requires qualitative, the other quantitative thinking, the two modes of reasoning being not easily translatable. Each fosters and facilitates conspicuously different modes of action. Each propagates

different, hardly reconcilable values. Most important of all – each generates a different network of power and influence.

This point is of crucial importance – all the more so since it has been continually neglected by most accounts of inequality in socialist societies. It has been taken for granted by virtually all authors – if only implicitly – that there must be a single and all-pervasive standard of differentiation which underlies social inequlity in socialist society similar to that which characterizes capitalist societies. More often than not market-generated income has been the universal standard in question, with the 'functionalist' division of labour as the runner-up. Accounts of social inequality have, in fact, been limited to the problem of stratification rather than class structure. In some cases the dominant value-standards of capitalist society were thrust upon a reality to which such standards were inappropriate; in other cases the ideological self-image generated by partynomial rule was adopted in good faith as a total and sufficient account of reality. Both kinds of image certainly convey part of the truth; they sometimes possess a considerable informative value, particularly when inspiring the student to an assiduous though wearisome scrutiny of disparate and scattered data. Such attempts are doomed, however, to remain partial (and, worse still, divested of explanatory potential) insofar as they pay no heed to the power structure of the system type as a whole, which ultimately undergirds and generates whatever social inequality is to be found in socialist society. Only these standards of status assessment are relevant to the description of inequality in a given society – standards which have been *made* relevant by the structure of the society in question; only these may provide the analytical basis for understanding this society's dynamics and the conflicts which actuate its history. This is why all analysis of social differentiation should start from an inquiry into the type of authority and the bases of social action in the society under investigation, rather than from the assumption that the main indices of inequality are known beforehand.

TWO POWER STRUCTURES: THE DIALECTICS OF COEXISTENCE

What follows from our inquiry so far is that in the socialist societies of eastern Europe each individual's situation is shaped by two *relatively autonomous and to an extent antagonistic power structures, neither of which is entirely reducible to the other*. I am inclined to consider this as a permanent and structurally determined feature of the societies in question. The two power structures are: officialdom and class.

The first power structure is generated by the authority level of the social system. It stems from the party, as the main repository of control, and permeates the whole of society by virtue of the fact that in socialist society the traditional distinctions between economic, political, social and cultural actions are blurred to an extent unthinkable in late capitalist society with its increased power of the political state. Officialdom is ultimately rooted in the partynomial rule, but – contrary to popular oversimplifications – it does not resolve itself into the supreme power of the party as an aggregate of party numbers. Persons endowed with immense power within officialdom are not necessarily party members, nor are they necessarily highly placed in the hierarchy of the party organization; moreover, members of the party are not necessarily bestowed with much power as individuals. In short, the supreme power of the party is not tantamount to the supreme power of the party membership. There is a clear tendency for the top positions of 'lay' organizations to turn out a higher ratio of party members than the less influential layers of officialdom – as my own research in Poland, or Soviet studies by Semenow, Shubkin, or Shkaratan have testified (cf. Parkin 1969; Matthews 1972; Shkaratan 1971). But party rule is not the sum of individual members' influence and power. The major institution that sustains the power of the party is its supreme and unquestioned authority over all appointments to office in the many administrative bodies included in the official chart of the system; the unchallenged and monopolistic right of the party to appoint incumbents of offices, to determine and alter the range of their competence, and to dismiss them from office for any failure to meet these requirements which are determined or freely altered by the party.

The futuristic legitimation of partynomial rule serves simultaneously as the reason and the rationale for the party's monopoly of self-electing and self-coopting functions. The postulate of the party's supreme control over the distribution of power means in these circumstances a hardly concealed principle of a small, vanguard-type minority defending the purity of prospective ideals from being diluted or, worse still, contaminated by exposure to the hazards of 'majority judgment'. Hence the hardly disguised hierarchical nature of officialdom, generated 'from the top down', and the continual tendency of centralism to assert itself over and against 'democracy' in the contradictory formula of the party organization.

The power which constitutes the structure of officialdom is the ability to manipulate the distribution of resources and the conditions of access to them – i.e. to manipulate the structure of the situation which delimits the actors' freedom of action. As W. Ross Ashby put it, 'when a whole system is composed of a number of subsystems, the one that tends to dominate is the one that is *least* stable, the one that is nearest to instability ... The one nearest to instability rules' (Ashby 1966: 376). Which means that the volume of power associated with an individual-in-an-organization, or with his office, may be measured by the extent to which other members should, were they acting rationally, take into account his intended actions while planning their own behaviour; the greater the ability of X's response to influence the effects of Y's action, the stronger is the power position of X in comparison with Y. This ability, in turn, increases together with the degree of 'subjective irregularity', e.g. the unpredictability of X's action on the part of Y (for a more detailed analysis of power relations, see Bauman 1971). Contrary to Weber's equation between the 'free arbitrariness' of authority and its 'irrationality' (somewhat out of tune with his otherwise broad-minded view of historical variations in rationality), the notorious lack of clear, hard and fast rules determining and 'stabilizing' behaviour, or the criteria of such judgment the party supervisors may adopt, or such justice they may dispense, seems to provide a major constituent of the kind of 'rationality' peculiar to partynomial rule. Rather than being analyzed in terms of Weber's ideal type of bureaucracy, the party (as a basis of authority rather than its administrative capacity) should be seen as the 'collective ruler', whose obtrusive though invited presence is constantly felt, though never exactly seen. These 'rulers' in the Weberian bureaucracy enjoy the unique luxury of being concerned with means alone, while others take care of the ends; who, therefore, may fetter the hands of the bureaucrats with a plethora of minute, pernickety regulations which channel their behaviour in an (ideally) entirely predictable way, while the hands of the rulers retain (ideally) a complete freedom of movement. Weber never in fact rid himself completely of the tormenting awareness that while creativity (seriously discussed by Weber only in the context of charisma) draws its living impulse from communion with the divine and intractable absolute, rationality may flourish only in conditions of unfreedom. Ends and means, charisma and bureaucracy, value and fact – all the crucial and self destructive Weberian antinomies are nothing but obsessive harpings on the same tragic motif. The party as the base of partynomial rule would have been surely put by Weber into one box with ends and values; that is why it obstinately escapes his means oriented framework of bureaucracy.

Officialdom as a social body tends to encompass, exactly in the manner of market generated class structure, the whole of society and to grant each individual his proper official category. Due to the scarcity of rules making for stability of assignment, it is a relatively flexible and fluid body with an unusually high degree of social mobility, particularly in its middle levels. Neither a major shuffle nor a single exchange of position normally happens however other than under the auspices of the party. Hence the roots of all endemic personal insecurity are traceable to the party, thus perpetuating and reinforcing constantly its sway over individuals' actions and minds. Given enough time to assert itself, effective power will always generate enough self-fulfilling, 'realistic', and 'rational' legitimations to self-perpetuate itself within the framework of routine, everyday interaction.

This quality is by no means a distinctive feature of socialist society. What however seems to be its peculiar trait is its incapacity to subdue all relevant dimensions of human action to the scale in which the alleged superiority of the system sustaining values are measured and assessed.

The notorious Marx-Weber controversy on the nature of social inequality boils down to one major point of disagreement: to Marx, all facets of human differentiation in an established society tend, at least in the long run, to succumb to the divisions which determine the focal power structure of society – i.e. that related to the creation and distribution of goods.

In capitalist society, for example, the cultural, social, and political differentiation between large groups of people tends in the long run to approximate the essential inequality in the situation of action related to the ownership of the means of production. To Weber, on the other hand, the three major dimensions of social inequality (economic, social, political), are *per se* autonomous, and their overlapping or divergence cannot be conceived on theoretical grounds alone; it is not impossible that they do tend to merge, but whether this is indeed the case can only be discovered empirically – there is nothing 'necessary' in their congruence. We cannot give this controversy the attention it deserves in its application to capitalist society. But we cannot pass by its relevance to the issue here under discussion – the power structure in socialist society. My contention is that the two essential planes of inequality endemic to socialist society – officialdom and class – do not overlap; and that their incongruence has, given the fundamental structural principles of a socialist society, a necessary, i.e. theoretically deducible, character. In other words, the lack of a one-to-one correspondence between officialdom generated and class generated inequalities, as well as the constant tension between the corresponding power structures, stand and fall together with the type of socialist society which has been historically established in eastern Europe.

It is Marx's view of nineteenth-century capitalism that economics, understood as a network of ownership relations, subdued all other dimensions of social life, thereby reducing the bases of social inequality to a single principle. The differentiation of access to the control and use of the means of production unilaterally determined the structure of political and cultural relations. One doubts, however, whether such a neat and clear-cut uni-dimensionality may be presumed as a model feature of socialist society. The two power structures seem to resist all attempts to reduce them to any one over-riding principle; insofar as the market retains its relative autonomy towards the political structure and the state remains, at least theoretically, largely immune to the effects of the re-allocation of goods in the market, the two structures generate divisions which *can*, but *need not*, overlap. In spite of the authority which the state exercises over the economy, it must foster, however grudgingly and gingerly, the inequality generating capacity of the market.

I have tried already to show how, except for brief and atypical periods, partynomialism has always required, as its unavoidable supplement, an impersonal base of social action, at least on the level of individual decisions. Modern socialist societies retain the distinction between the 'public' and the 'private'; this distinction is even more pronounced under socialism than under capitalism, since between partynomialism and impersonalism there is a sharp opposition of standards, criteria of rationality, and logic which is all but absent in the combination of plebiscitarianism with impersonalism (Bendix 1969: 66 ff). While *Wertrationalität* rules in the public sphere, subject directly to party-nomial authority, *Zweckrationalität* is the only way of eliciting from the vast domain of the private the degree of regularity and certainty which may render it more or less manageable for planning and partynomial control. The individual is therefore exposed, within his 'private' life of a seller of labour force and a buyer of consumer goods, to an entirely market-type situation of impersonal, quantitative, means-oriented rationality. Maximizing of effects and minimizing of costs is the sole activity which his situation defines as rational. Zero-sum games, competition, and the differentiation of assets inevitably follow, as they always do whenever material strivings of men are organized in the market; control over the situation may be enhanced only through the appropriation of assets and money. In the long run individual differentiation coagulates into class-type groups, distinguished by their access to coveted goods. Since the goods are private possessions of individuals, they may be bequeathed and inherited, and full-fledged, hereditary classes therefore emerge.

Each individual in the society under discussion is therefore a member of two largely independent power structures: officialdom and class. They constantly tend to foreclose and subordinate each other's domain; money is repeatedly used to pave the way to the goods under the control of officialdom, and the holders of positions in officialdom struggle to translate their advantages into corresponding market prequisites. This tendency may frequently blur the distinction between the empirical manifestations of the two networks of inequality. Nothing short of structural change of the system will however remove the structural autonomy of officialdom and class, the endemic contradiction between the bases of their differentiating power, and between the standards of rationality they emanate. The relationship between them – as the relations between partynomialism and impersonalism, *Wertrationalität* and *Zweckrationalität*, plan and market – is one of tension and antagonism, of open battle or uneasy armistice.

The relative autonomy and opposition between the two power structures present in the socialist system may help us to explain the dynamics of socialist society, usually seen at the level of political history as a series of swings apparently inexplicable in any but thoroughly personal, palace revolt terms. The characteristic fitfullness and pendulum-like tendency of this history reveals its logic when viewed against the ambiguity of the dialectic between officialdom and class. The class structure continuously emanates and solidifies the kind of privileges the officialdom is set on destroying, though constantly forced to re-invigorate. Class privileges have their own base, largely independent of the direct control of officialdom, and therefore weaken the grip of partynomial rule over the whole of society. Individuals who enjoy a better position within the class structure do not owe their privileges to officialdom; such privileges they have are their own possessions, not just the perquisites of the office they hold; they may well become an inalienable property, if only their base – the market – is effectively protected from officialdom's interference. Officialdom's tendency to express the privileges of the incumbents of high office in market terms leads inevitably to a point at which large numbers of incumbents establish foundations of privilege which are bound to suffer from officialdom's supremacy. They will be then interested in institutionalizing their independence from direct partynomial rule; they will

F

wish to re-establish their position as that of a 'class of privileged' instead of remaining just a 'privileged category'; (the managerial call for decentralization, usually associated with an argument against artificial curbing of income inequality, is a typical example.) Whether we like it or not, the demand for freedom often means, in the context of a socialist society, the demand to liberate market forces from the control of partynomial rule, i.e. liberation of the class structure from the constraints imposed by officialdom.

At the same time, the underdogs of the class structure look naturally to officialdom for redress of their grievances. In spite of its ultimate responsibility for whatever inequality there is in socialist society, the party may therefore rely on the support of the workers, who see in officialdom the only body called to defend them against mounting deprivations in the market sphere. A sort of alliance between the party and the workers against the managers and professions (the groups who, apart from black-marketeers and the few extant artisans and private shopkeepers, constitute the most privileged classes in market terms) asserts itself more often than not as a persistent mark of the routine, everyday power structure. It will probably never become the only and constant structural principle of socialist society – for reasons I have tried already to spell out. No known socialist society has so far managed to do without the market, and therefore without classes; but it if did, the conflicts generated by officialdom would be laid bare for everybody to see and draw conclusions, and the alliance between workers and rulers would have been even less probable than it is in the present circumstances. As it is, the problem of equality is seen as located in the class structure, while the problem of freedom seems to be confined entirely to officialdom; there is little chance therefore that the large groups whose interests are definable in the terms of freedom and equality, respectively, would act in concert, focusing their attention on the same objectives and the same enemies. In this 'everyday' divergence of interests and correlated dissent, which is a consequence of the irremovable duality of power structures, one can see the roots of the survival ability of the eastern-European type socialist society. Thus far, eastern European socialist socieites have amply demonstrated their inability to enhance freedom and equality at the same time. There were times in which the regime produced neither; at other stages a significant increase in freedom combined with a parallel increase in social inequality; contrariwise, a dash for great equality coincided as a rule with an additional curb on freedom. This inherently contradictory paradigm can generate a wide range of dividing lines and alliances – among which an alliance of the better-off workers with their managers against the heavy-handed control of the party is a union which cannot be dismissed off-hand. A social structure able to generate simultaneously freedom *and* equality is still to be found. The Yugoslav experience has done little to warrant the hope that the institution of self-management would offer the sought for solution. One can, however, see in the same structural feature of the socialist system a permanent source of violent conflict, vehement enough to disrupt the routine structure of society and to expose its other structure of interests normally kept in the shadow by everyday necessities and usages. That may happen if various kinds of dissent join together not so much from a common root (which they do not possess), so much as from the fact that they all represent dissatisfaction with a social reality perceived as unbearable. This event, called a revolutionary situation, is not however sufficiently determined by the everyday power structure. As is always the case, the role of catalyst may be played only by a creative and refractory historical praxis, which alone is able to weld together diffuse and manifold deprivations and to forge them into revolutionary praxis.

References

ROSS ASHBY, W. 1966. The Application of Cybernetics to Psychiatry. In Alfred G. Smith (ed.) *Communication and Culture*. New York: Harcourt, Brace and World.

BAUMAN, Z. 1971. Uses of Information. *The Annals of the American Academy of Political and Social Science* **393** January: 20-31.

BENDIX, R. 1969. *Nationbuilding and Citizenship*. New York: Doubleday.

GERTH, H. H. and MILLS, C. WRIGHT. (trans. and eds.) 1948. *From Max Weber*. London: Routledge & Kegan Paul.

HOCHFIELD, J. 1963, *Studia o Marksistowskiej teorii Spoleczenstwa*. Warszawa: PWN.

LANDAUER, C. 1931. *Planwirtschaft und Verkehrswirtschaft*. Munich: Duncker und Humblot.

MARCUSE, H. 1969. *Soviet Marxism, A Critical Analysis*. London: Routledge & Kegan Paul.

MATTHEWS, M. 1972. *Class and Society in Soviet Russia*. London: Allen Lane.

MEYER, A. G. 1967. Authority in Communist Political Systems. In Lewis J. Edinger (ed.) *Political Leadership in Industrial Societies*. New York: John Wiley & Sons.

PARKIN, F. 1969. Class stratification in Socialist Societies. *The British Journal of Sociology* **20** December: 355-374.

PARETO, V. 1902. *Les Systèmes Socialistes*. Paris: V. Giard et E. Brière.

REX, J. 1972. Power. *New Society* **22** (525) October 5: 23-26.

SCHUTZ, A. 1967. On Multiple Realities. In *Collected Papers*, vol. I. The Hague: Martinus Nijhoff.

SHKARATAN, O. A. 1971. *Rabotchi Class v S.S.R.R.* Moscow: Mysl.

WEBER, M. 1964. *The Theory of Social and Economic Organization* (trans. by A. M. Henderson and Talcott Parsons). New York: Free Press.

RICHARD SCASE

Conceptions of the Class Structure and Political Ideology: Some Observations on Attitudes in England and Sweden[1]

Many discussions about workers' images of society have emphasized the need to investigate actors' immediate social relationships. Lockwood, for example, has stated that, 'for the most part men visualize the class structure of their society from the vantage points of their own particular *milieux*, and their perceptions of the larger society will vary according to their experiences of social inequality in the smaller societies in which they live out their daily lives' (Lockwood 1966: 249). He goes on to suggest that 'the industrial and community *milieux* of manual workers exhibit a very considerable diversity and it would be strange if there were no correspondingly marked variations in the images of society held by different sections of the working class' (Lockwood 1966: 250). Similarly Inkeles, in a comparative study of attitudes in different industrial societies, has argued that '... people have experiences, develop attitudes, and form values in response to the forces or pressures which their environment creates. By "environment" we mean, particularly, networks of inter-personal relations and the patterns of reward and punishment one normally experiences in them' (Inkeles 1960–61: 2). He suggests that '... within broad limits, the same situational pressures, the same framework for living, will be experienced as similar and will generate the same or similar response by people from different countries' (Inkeles 1960–61: 2). A task for empirical enquiry, then, is to see how far systematic variations in patterns of social relationships are related to differences in actors' conceptions of social reality.

However, the processes whereby these social relationships are conducive to particular types of subjective response are unclear. For example, it has often been suggested that roles that bring employees into close personal contact with their employers will lead workers to adopt deferential attitudes. But it could also be argued that these relationships are conducive not necessarily to deference but to workers making comparisons with their employers such that they feel relatively deprived and resentful, and thus adopt radical attitudes. If this is a possibility, why has deference been seen to be a more likely outcome than radicalism? Of course there is empirical evidence, although of a limited kind, to indicate that these patterns of relationships do indeed lead to deferential attitudes,[2] while there is little to indicate that they are conducive to radicalism.[3] But is this a function of specific social relationships as such, or is it more a consequence of the procedures whereby these relationships have become *defined* and invested with social meanings?

The point can be further clarified by reference to Lockwood's typification of the 'proletarian traditionalist'. He states that '... the dominant model of society held by the proletarian traditionalist is most likely to be a dichotomous or two-valued power model. Thinking in terms of two classes standing in a relationship of opposition is a *natural consequence* (my italics) of being a member of a closely integrated industrial community with well-defined boundaries and a distinctive style of life' (Lockwood 1966: 251). But why should such an image of society be regarded as an inevitable outcome of social environments of this kind? In fact Moore (1972), in a study of mining communities in Durham, found that in some circumstances there was little evidence of a heightened awareness of class consciousness among miners. He states, 'It is clear that the miners have developed a strong sense of occupational community (unlike the traditional deferential worker), but this does not mean that class consciousness emerged from this' (Moore 1972: 30). He goes on to add, '... Lockwood does not consider the possibility that men have to be *converted* to a traditional proletarian outlook in certain situations' (Moore 1972: 32). Consequently he argues that in order to see whether miners will adhere to 'traditional-proletarian' images of society it is necessary to consider the role of ideas and ideologies in shaping actors' definitions of social reality; in the case of the Durham miners, the relative influences of Methodism, Trade Unionism, and the Labour Party. Indeed, Moore's argument lends weight to Parkin's claim that, 'although there is a factual and material basis to class inequality, there is more than one way in which it can be interpreted. Facts alone do not provide meanings, and the way a person makes sense of his social world will be influenced by the nature of the *meaning-systems* he draws upon' (Parkin 1971: 81). These meaning-systems, according to Parkin, are a function of the influence exercised by different groups in society.

These arguments do not, of course, refute the significance of social relationships in shaping individuals' images of society. But they do imply that a consideration of *only* these factors is insufficient, and that it is necessary to investigate the processes whereby these relationships become defined by the actors involved. These arguments would also suggest that this is particularly necessary in the comparative study of attitudes in different industrial societies where writers have frequently implied that the institutions of advanced capitalism generate similar patterns of attitudes among workers in different countries that tend to over-ride differences generated by national, political, and cultural factors.[4]

This issue is investigated in the present paper in relation to the attitudes of workers in two industrial societies – England and Sweden.[5] The objective is to ascertain whether or not workers in similar structural positions within the two countries have similar conceptions of their respective class structures and of social mobility within it. If they do, it would indicate that institutional social environments have major consequences for shaping individuals' conceptions of social reality. But if they do not, it would suggest the significance of other factors which may have been neglected in discussions of the sources of class imagery.

METHOD

In order to test these ideas a comparison was made of two groups of English and Swedish workers, who were both subject to relatively similar institutional constraints. They were chosen from two factories which shared a number of common characteristics. First, both factories manufactured similar products; in each case the work process consisted of producing a wide range of engineering goods and components. Second, the technologies were more or less similar, except for the fact that the Swedish factory was more highly capitalized; tasks undertaken by machinery in the Swedish factory were often performed by manual labour in the English workshops. In both places, productive techniques enabled employees to communicate with each other while they were working, and a number of the tasks were undertaken by work teams: the division-of-labour was much less complex than that normally associated with assembly-line technology as found, for example, in the automobile industry. Third, both factories produced goods for relatively static or even contracting markets: there had been no expansion over recent years and there was little expectation by either management or workers that this was likely to occur in the foreseeable future. At the time of the investigation, neither factory had been confronted with the threat of redundancies, and there was an assumption by both groups of workers that employment was relatively secure.

Although the two factories were similar in terms of these characteristics, they differed in at least two important respects. First, work and employment conditions, by any absolute standard of comparison, were much better in the Swedish factory. This was evident in the quality of heating, lighting, and ventilation, in the provision of social and recreational amenities, and in regulations relating to industrial safety and the use of machinery. Second, there were differences in the sizes of the two factories: the English unit employed 972 manual workers, compared with the 298 in the Swedish. Unfortunately it was impossible to choose two factories of a similar size that could also be matched according to other criteria: whether this affected attitudes between the two samples was not investigated and must therefore remain an open question.[6]

In terms of wage differentials, it was difficult to make accurate calculations because earnings in both factories, particularly those of non-manual workers, varied according to age and length of service. Furthermore, the management of the English workplace were reluctant to give detailed information; they were only prepared to disclose 'approximate' earnings. However, the information they made available suggested that differences between the remuneration of the highest paid manual workers and senior management tended to be less in the Swedish workplace than in the English; whereas the earnings of Swedish senior managers were approximately two and a quarter times greater, those of their English counterparts were as much as three times as great. But on the other hand, differences between the earnings of the highest paid manual workers and white-collar employees were similar; by the age of 40, senior clerical officers and other higher grade employees could be earning about one-third more than blue-collar men.[7]

The two samples were taken from manual workers between the ages of twenty-five and fifty-four in order to eliminate both those whose careers had yet to become firmly established, and those approaching retirement.[8] The investigation also concentrated almost exclusively upon married men; these comprised 85 per cent or more of both samples.

Of course the samples cannot be regarded as representative of workers in each of the two countries; they were matched according to a number of variables and so their general representativeness is limited. They were chosen from specific industries which, like all industries, have characteristics peculiar to themselves; traditions of historical development, industrial relations, and technological change.[9] Consequently, these factors limit the degree to which it is possible to generalize findings derived from this study. But the results can be regarded as at least *indicative* of patterns in the two countries which only more comprehensive enquiries will be able to substantiate.

The data were collected by interviews in the spring and summer of 1970, using schedules printed in English and Swedish, but neither sample was aware of its participation in an international comparison.[10] Both samples were asked a large number of specific questions about their life-styles and employment conditions, and about various aspects of social and economic inequality. But at the same time, they were asked a number of more general and abstract questions about the social structures of their respective countries.[11] The response rates were high – 87 per cent for the Swedish sample and 73 per cent for the English: this provided 122 completed Swedish schedules and 128 English schedules, upon which the present discussion is based.

RESULTS OF THE INQUIRY

Both samples were asked, 'Some people say that there are no longer social classes in this country. Others say that there are. What do you think?'. An overwhelming majority of both groups stated that they do exist: 97 per cent (N-118) of the Swedish and 93 per cent (N-119) of the English workers.[12] These respondents were then asked the open-ended question, 'Why do you think this is the case?'. The coded responses are shown in *Table 1:*

Any similarity between the two samples in terms of their recognition of social classes evaporated when they described their reasons for the existence of these classes. As *Table 1* shows, half of the Swedish respondents referred to economic, and 20 per cent to educational factors. At the same time, only 2 per cent considered birth and family background to be important. By contrast, although one-third of the English workers mentioned economic factors, only 3 per cent referred to education but more than 10 per cent to 'birth' and family background. At the same time, as many as 25 per cent considered social classes to be an inevitable feature of life; they made such statements as 'you will always have leaders and followers'; 'some people are bound to be better than others'; 'breeding makes social classes inevitable'. Furthermore, the English respondents were more likely than the Swedish to describe the class structure in terms of notions of status and snobbery: more than 12

TABLE 1

'Why do you think this is the case?' ('That there are social classes')

Because of:	Swedish workers (N-118)		English workers (N-119)	
	%	Nos.	%	Nos.
'birth' and family background	1.7	2	10.9	13
'money', 'wealth', and various economic factors	55.1	65	37.1	44
status and 'snobbery'	5.9	7	12.6	15
educational qualifications and experiences	20.3	24	2.5	3
'an inevitable feature of life'	0.9	1	25.2	30
occupation	1.7	2	2.5	3
don't know	2.5	3	2.5	3
other and non-classifiable responses	11.9	14	6.7	8
Totals	100.0	118	100.0	119

per cent made comments like 'there are those who think they are better than others'; and 'some people will always look down their noses at you'.

A further question asked was, 'What is the major factor, do you think, which determines the class a person belongs to?'. Whereas the previous question tried to ascertain the characteristics used by respondents for describing their respective class structures, this question attempted to identify the criteria which they would use in allocating individuals to positions *within* these structures.

Table 2 shows that the Swedish workers considered an individual's class position was determined primarily by his economic circumstances and his level of education, while other factors, such as his birth and family background, were regarded as of limited importance.[13] Among the English workers, on the other hand, there was a similar recognition of the importance of economic factors but they were much more likely to emphasize the significance of birth and family background, and to give little weight to the role of education. Therefore the responses indicated that although both samples stressed the importance of economic factors for determining the class position of individuals, the Swedish workers were more likely to refer to 'meritocratic' factors than the English. Indeed, this pattern was confirmed by their descriptions of different social classes.

TABLE 2

'What is the major factor, do you think, which determines the class a person belongs to?' *

Factors mentioned	Swedish workers (N-118)		English workers (N-119)	
	%	Nos	%	Nos
'birth' and family background	10.2	12	37.8	45
educational qualifications and experiences	38.1	45	13.5	16
'money,' 'wealth', and economic factors	68.6	81	58.0	69
occupation	5.9	7	10.9	13
attitudes and appearances	3.4	4	5.0	6
patterns of social interaction	–	–	3.4	4
other and non-classifiable responses	9.3	11	10.9	13

* Most respondents mentioned more than one factor and so the figures add up to more than 100 per cent.

The workers that recognized the existence of social classes were asked, 'Which are the major classes in this country today?'. In reply to this question all respondents mentioned more than one class: 28 per cent of the Swedish and 29 per cent of the English workers conceived of a two-class model of society; 66 per cent and 60 per cent, respectively, a three-class model, and a further 5 per cent and 11 per cent a class model consisting of four or more categories. In other words, somewhat less than one-third of both groups of workers mentioned two, and a further two-thirds, three major social classes. In terms of their own class position, all the respondents in both samples who considered there were only two social classes placed themselves in the 'bottom' category. But among those who conceived of their society in terms of a three-class model, there was an important difference between the two groups. Whereas 47 per cent of the Swedish respondents adhering to this model allocated themselves to the 'intermediate' category, this was done by only 21 per cent of the English; indeed as many as 79 per cent placed themselves in the 'bottom' category.

Although there was a close relationship between the model of the class structure and reasons given for the existence of social classes among the English workers, this was not the case for the Swedish. For those Swedish respondents with either a two-class or a three-class model, approximately 55 per cent held that social classes were a result of economic factors. At the same time, about 20 per cent of both these groups emphasized the importance of education. Among the English workers, on the other hand, of those with a two-class model, 49 per cent mentioned economic factors, 20 per cent the inevitability of social class and 6 per cent the importance of birth and family background. But for those with a three-class model, 34 per cent referred to economic factors, 27 per cent to the 'inevitability' of social classes, and 10 per cent to birth and family background. In other words, whereas economic and educational factors were consistently considered to be important among the Swedish workers, despite any differences in their models of the class structure, ascriptive criteria were more likely to be mentioned by those English workers with a three-class model than by those with a two-class model of society.

TABLE 3

'Which are the major classes in this country today?'

'Labels' Mentioned	Swedish workers (N-118)		English workers (N-119)	
	%	Nos	%	Nos
'upper', 'top', 'higher classes'	20.3	24	74.8	89
'the wealthy', 'rich', 'those with plenty of money'	11.9	14	16.0	19
'social group I'	48.3	57	–	–
'middle class'	16.1	19	75.6	90
'white-collar people'	17.0	20	0.9	1
'educated people'	4.2	5	0.9	1
'social group II'	47.5	56	–	–
'social group III'	39.8	47	–	–
'working class'	39.0	46	74.8	89
'ordinary people', 'average people'	1.7	2	1.7	2
'lower class'	1.7	2	17.7	21
'the poor', 'the lower paid', etc.	5.9	7	6.7	8
negative evaluation ('those who don't want to work', etc.)	8.5	10	0.9	1
other and non-classifiable responses	12.7	15	10.9	13

The replies to the question, 'Which are the major classes in this country today?' were then coded, as far as possible, according to the actual phrases used by respondents. The results are shown in *Table 3*.

Both samples were then asked, 'Which of these classes would you say that you belong to?'; the replies to which are shown in *Table 4*.

TABLE 4

'Which of these classes would you say that you belong to?'

'Labels' mentioned	Swedish workers (N-118)		English workers (N-119)	
	%	Nos	%	Nos
'middle class'	9.3	11	19.3	23
'social group II'	25.4	30	–	–
'social group III'	21.2	25	–	–
'average people' 'ordinary people'	1.7	2	1.7	2
'working class'	39.0	46	69.8	83
'lower class'	1.7	2	5.0	6
'the poor'	–	–	3.4	4
other and non-classifiable responses	1.7	2	0.8	1
Totals	100.0	118	100.0	119

In view of the fact that replies to these questions were coded according to the actual terms used by respondents, it is interesting that they used relatively few categories in describing either the class structure or their own class position. This would suggest that in replying to these deliberately vague and ambiguous questions respondents did not consciously work out their own conceptions of their respective class structures but instead, 'gave back' a received cultural, ideological interpretation of them.

However, it is also clear that the two samples of workers had rather different reasons for explaining their own positions within their respective class structures. This is borne out by *Table 5* which correlates respondents' self-assigned class with the factors they regarded as important in determining an individual's class position.

This table shows that both groups of workers, irrespective of the specific terms that they used for describing their own class positions, considered economic factors to be the major determinants of an individual's placement within the class structure. But it is also clear that the Swedish workers persistently stressed the role of education to a degree unreflected in the English responses. In addition, although the number of Swedish workers that emphasized the importance of birth and family background was greater among those considering themselves to be 'working class', this did not equal the high frequency of this response found among the English 'working class' respondents. Indeed birth and family background were emphasized among these English workers to about the same degree as education among the Swedish respondents regarding themselves as 'working class'. In other words, *Table 5* suggests that while the Swedish respondents perceived their own positions within the class structure to be largely determined by economic and educational factors, the English sample, although recognizing the primary importance of economic criteria, were more

TABLE 5

Respondents' self-assigned social class related to the factors they considered important in determining an individual's position in the class structure (percentages)*

| | Respondents' self-assigned social class | | | | |
| | Swedish workers | | | English workers | |
Factors mentioned as important	'Social Group II' (N-30)	'Social Group III' (N-25)	'Work- ing Class' (N-46)	'Middle Class' (N-23)	'Work- ing Class' (N-83)
birth and family background	6.7	12.0	15.2	21.7	42.2
educational qualifications and experiences	40.0	40.0	41.3	17.4	12.1
money, wealth, and economic factors	86.7	72.0	58.7	56.5	57.8
occupation	3.3	4.0	8.7	4.4	14.5
attitudes and appearances	–	–	2.2	13.0	2.4
patterns of social interaction	–	–	–	4.4	3.6
other and non- classifiable responses	13.3	8.0	8.7	17.4	8.4

* Most respondents mentioned more than one factor and so the figures add up to more than 100 per cent. Only those class 'labels' used by a substantial number of respondents have been used in this cross-tabulation (see *Table 4*).

TABLE 6

Respondents' descriptions of 'Social Group I' and 'Upper Class'*

Respondents' desrciptions	Swedish workers 'Social Group I' (N-57)		English workers 'Upper Class' (N-89)	
	%	Nos	%	Nos
'lords and ladies', 'people with titles', 'the Aristocracy'	1.8	1	41.6	37
economic factors ('the rich', 'the wealthy', etc).	31.6	18	20.2	18
'big businessmen', 'directors'	52.6	30	53.9	48
'professionals' (or specific occupational title mentioned)	56.1	32	14.6	13
'higher white-collar workers'	28.1	16	1.1	1
'educated people'	26.3	15	4.5	4
'engineers'	12.3	7	–	–
'managers'	26.3	15	27.0	24
other and non-classifiable responses	19.3	11	30.3	27

* The figures add to more than 100 per cent since most respondents mentioned more than one factor in their descriptions.

likely to emphasize the role of birth and family background. In fact it is only among the English respondents describing themselves as 'middle class' that education is given as much importance as birth and family background.

Similar patterns emerged in respondents' descriptions of the 'top' social classes. In their models of the class structure there were no respondents who placed themselves in the top category. But it was considered useful to study their descriptions of this category to get some idea of what criteria they regarded as necessary in order to be part of a 'successful' and 'important' group in society. *Table 6* illustrates the samples' descriptions of the two groups that were most frequently mentioned in this category: for the Swedish workers, 'Social Group I', and for the English, the 'Upper Class'. These terms were mentioned by 49 per cent and 75 per cent of the Swedish and the English samples respectively.

This table indicates that both samples stressed the importance of economic factors. But, at the same time, the Swedish workers mentioned a number of occupations that require individuals to undergo relatively long periods of formal education and specialist training. Therefore various professional occupations, 'engineers', 'higher white-collar workers', and 'educated people' were frequently mentioned, while 'lords and ladies', 'the aristocracy', and other descriptions that would indicate that respondents perceived the class structure in traditionalist and ascriptive terms were absent. Among the English sample, by contrast, traditionalist attitudes of this kind were frequently expressed: no less than 42 per cent mentioned them in their descriptions of 'Upper Class'.

Clearly, the foregoing analysis suggests that the two samples had rather different conceptions of their respective class structures. From this it seems as though the Swedish workers would be more likely to conceive of the class structure as 'open' and as one in which there would be considerable opportunities for individual upward mobility. Among the English respondents, on the other hand, it would appear that their conceptions of the class structure would lead them to have limited beliefs in the possibilities of upward mobility, if only because of the importance given to ascriptive and traditional factors in determining individuals' class membership.

In order to test whether or not this was the case, those workers recognizing the existence of social classes were asked, 'Do you think that many people move from one class to another these days?'. Among the Swedish workers, 70 per cent (N-82) said 'yes' compared with 42 per cent (N-50) of the English respondents: more than two-thirds compared with less than one-half. These workers were then asked, 'What are the reasons for this?'. The coded responses are shown in *Table* 7.

Similar proportions of both samples felt that people could move from one class to another because of greater opportunities to improve their economic circumstances. But the factor mentioned most frequently by the Swedish respondents was that there were now better possibilities for obtaining educational qualifications; this was mentioned by only a few of the English workers. Instead, the latter were more likely to cite the need for 'personal contacts', and for individuals to exercise 'initiative', 'enterprise', and so on.

These results were further substantiated by the responses to a more specific question, 'How likely is the son of a factory worker to move from one class to another. Would you say that he was "very likely" "likely", "unlikely", or "very unlikely"?' No less than 98 per cent of the Swedish workers considered that he was either 'very likely' or 'likely', compared with 70 per cent of the English. Obviously both samples were optimistic about the mobility chances of the son of a

TABLE 7

'What are the reasons for this?'

('that many people move from one class to another these days')

Because of:	Swedish workers %	Nos	English workers %	Nos
opportunities to improve personal economic circumstances	33.0	27	38.0	19
possibilities for promotion at work	6.1	5	16.0	8
possibilities for obtaining educational qualifications	56.1	46	12.0	6
personal contacts	–	–	6.0	3
equal opportunity for everyone	2.4	2	4.0	2
individual effort and enterprise, etc.	–	–	12.0	6
other and non-classifiable responses	2.4	2	12.0	6
Totals	100.0	82	100.0	50

TABLE 8

'What would he (the son of a factory worker) have to do in order to move from one class to another?'

Responses:	Swedish workers %	Nos	English workers %	Nos
improve his personal economic circumstances	–	–	2.5	3
obtain promotion at work, or get a 'better' job	–	–	12.6	15
obtain some educational qualifications	95.6	113	51.3	61
make use of, or establish 'personal contacts'	0.9	1	1.7	2
exercise some 'individual effort', 'initiative', etc.	0.9	1	5.9	7
don't know	0.9	1	5.0	6
other and non-classifiable responses	1.7	2	21.0	25
Totals	100.0	118	100.0	119

TABLE 9

'What sort of people are more likely to have their sons at university?'*

'Sort of people'	Swedish workers (N-122)		English workers (N-128)	
	%	Nos	%	Nos
'educated people'	46.6	34	2.6	2
'the rich', 'the wealthy'	19.2	14	41.0	32
'professionals' (or specific occupation mentioned)	89.0	65	30.8	24
'big businessmen', 'directors'	19.2	14	53.9	42
other non-manual (or specific occupation mentioned)	11.0	8	19.2	15
'the aristocracy', 'lords and ladies'	–	–	2.6	2
'depends on parents'	4.1	3	2.6	2
'manual workers' (or specific occupation mentioned)	–	–	2.6	2
other and non-classifiable responses	1.4	1	14.1	11

* A number of respondents mentioned more than one 'Sort of People' and so the figures add to more than 100 per cent.

factory worker, but this attitude was held to a far greater degree among the Swedish respondents. Whereas there was almost complete acceptance of this opinion among the Swedish workers, a substantial minority of the English respondents – 20 per cent – felt that it was either 'unlikely' or 'very unlikely'. Both samples were then asked, 'What would he have to do in order to move from one class to another?'.

The results in *Table 8* show that the Swedish sample regarded the acquisition of educational qualifications as almost the sole means by which individuals could be upwardly mobile within the class structure. Although this opinion was shared by one-half of the English workers, it is evident that 'meritocratic' norms were held to be of far less importance.[14] But did the Swedish respondents consider that children from all social backgrounds enjoyed the same degree of participation within the educational system? To investigate this, both samples were asked, 'A lot of children stay on at school and go to university these days. Do you think that the sons of some people are more likely to stay on than others?'[15] Similar proportions of both samples – 60 per cent (N-73) of the Swedish and 61 per cent (N-78) of the English – agreed that the sons of some people were more likely to stay on than others.

These respondents were then asked, 'What sort of people are more likely to have their sons at university?'.

Table 9 shows that both samples were aware of inequalities within the respective educational systems. But it is also clear that the Swedish workers perceived of these in terms of advantages accruing to the sons of educated and other qualified, professional workers. By comparison, the English respondents rarely mentioned 'educated people' and they were less likely to refer to various categories of professional workers. Instead, they mentioned 'The Rich', 'The Wealthy', and 'Businessmen', but not 'The Aristocracy' and 'Those with Titles', which is perhaps somewhat surprising in view of the importance which they attached to these latter groups in their conceptions of the class structure. Clearly such people are seen not to require educational qualifications for their position in society!

The results of the interview survey suggest, then, that there were important differences between the two samples in terms of their conceptions of the class structure and of social mobility within it. Although both groups gave primary emphasis to economic factors in their descriptions, the Swedish workers attached greater importance to education, while the English workers were more likely to stress the significance of ascriptive and traditional characteristics. Furthermore, the Swedish workers were more likely to express a belief in the possibilities of individual upward mobility, and for this to occur they emphasized the need to obtain formal educational qualifications. When privileges within the educational system were recognized to exist, these were seen to be enjoyed by the sons of educated and other qualified people. For the English workers, on the other hand, possibilities of individual upward mobility were considered to be less likely, but when this was considered to be possible, fewer respondents mentioned the importance of education. In short, the Swedish workers were more likely than the English, to conceive of the class structure as 'open' and 'meritocratic'.

DISCUSSION

Any adequate explanation of the differences in the attitudes of the two samples would require a detailed discussion of a large number of factors. It would be surprising if the attitudes were not shaped, at least to some extent, by a whole range of historical processes as well as by a number of individual and group experiences.[16] Because this paper cannot consider all of these, emphasis will be given only to those factors which, *a priori*, seem most likely to explain the differences.

Obvious factors to consider are the samples' experiences of mobility at work, since it could be argued that their different conceptions of the possibilities for individual mobility in society are a consequence of these. However, the evidence does not support this. Asked about the possibilities for promotion, both samples were invited to name an occupation that they would be most likely to get if they were given promotion.[17] For both groups of workers 'foremen' and various supervisory manual occupations such as 'inspector' and 'chargehand' were most frequently mentioned – by well over 80 per cent of both the Swedish and the English samples. In other words, promotion was perceived in terms of movement within manual jobs, rather than into white-collar occupations. Indeed these were realistic assessments since in neither factory was there an effective scheme that would have enabled manual workers to become office employees. But the similarity in the samples' responses did not persist when they were asked, 'How likely is a factory worker to get promotion at work? Would you say that it was "very likely", "likely", "unlikely", or "very unlikely"?' Almost twice as many (73 per cent) of the English workers thought it either 'likely' or 'very likely' compared with the Swedish workers (39 per cent). Furthermore 80 per cent of the Swedish sample claimed their chances for promotion were either 'worse' or 'much worse' compared with those of white-collar employees, and only 3 per cent said that they were 'better' or 'much better'.[18]

Obviously the Swedish respondents' optimistic assumptions about mobility within the class structure cannot be regarded as a function of their conceptions of the possibilities for promotion at work.[19] Consequently it appears that their descriptions of the class structure were a function of factors other than those relating to immediate work experiences. Indeed, this claim can be supported by a consideration of the mobility patterns of respondents' sons. Those workers with sons at work (there were 45 and 52 among the Swedish and the English samples respectively) were asked to name and describe their sons' occupations. The results are shown in *Table 10*:

This table indicates that there were similar patterns of occupational mobility among the sons of both samples; only 16 per cent of the Swedish workers' sons were in non-manual occupations compared with 12 per cent of the English. Consequently the margin between these figures is too small to explain the differences in the two samples' conceptions of mobility in society. Again this suggests the need to

TABLE 10
Occupations of Respondents' Sons

Occupations of respondents' sons	Swedish workers %	Nos	English workers %	Nos
manual	80.0	36	73.1	38
non-manual	15.6	7	11.5	6
self-employed (not farmer)	2.2	1	–	–
farmer	–	–	–	–
farm worker	–	–	–	–
military (conscription and regular)	2.2	1	15.4	8
Totals	100.0	45	100.0	52

consider influences other than those directly relating to respondents' own immediate social experiences. But what are these?

An obvious factor to consider is the rate of social mobility in each of the countries. If this is higher in Sweden it could be one factor relevant to explaining the attitudes of Swedish workers. However, what evidence there is suggests that patterns of recruitment into various occupational roles, particularly those of a more prestigeful and highly paid kind, are very restricted in Sweden – certainly to a far greater extent than the beliefs of the Swedish sample would suggest. If there has been any increase in rates of inter-generational upward mobility, it has tended to be in terms of recruitment into the more routine, less qualified white-collar occupations. In the 1950s the rate of inter-generational mobility between manual and non-manual occupations appears to have been similar in Sweden, in Britain, and in a number of other European countries. Miller (1960), for example, in a re-analysis of various studies, has suggested that 26 per cent of the sons of manual workers in Sweden became white-collar employees compared with 25 per cent in Britain, 24 per cent in Denmark, 23 per cent in Norway, and 20 per cent in West Germany. But since the 1950s the rate of upward mobility, as measured in this way, appears to have increased in Sweden but not in Britain. This is borne out in *Table 11*, taken from a national study of mobility in Sweden, conducted in 1968.[20]

From this table it seems that 36 per cent of the sons of Swedish manual workers were in white-collar occupations in 1968, a noticeable increase compared with the 1950s. In Britain, on the other hand, there appears to have been virtually no change in the overall pattern.

TABLE 11

Social mobility among the Swedish adult population

| Father's social group* | Respondent's social group | | | | Total |
	I	II	III	Nos	%
I	50	37	13	254	100
II	11	45	44	1981	100
III	4	32	64	3274	100
Total	8	37	55	5509	100

Source: Erickson (1971:76)

* In this and the following tables, 'Social Group I' refers to senior civil servants, owners of large business firms, professional people, and senior managerial executives in private businesses; 'Social Group II' to lower-grade non-manual workers, owners of small businesses, independent artisans, and foremen; and 'Social Group III' to manual workers. This is the usual way in which Swedish social scientists describe the stratification system of their country.

MacDonald and Ridge (1972) suggest that in 1962, there were still only 25 per cent of the sons of manual workers employed in non-manual occupations. However, although there may now be greater mobility within the Swedish class structure than previously, this tends to be between lower-grade white-collar and manual occupations rather than taking the form of recruitment into professional, managerial, and administrative jobs. *As Table 11* shows, only 4 per cent of the sons of manual workers were employed in occupations of this kind. *Table 12* gives more detailed information on these patterns and shows the proportion of sons from different occupational backgrounds acquiring positions that have been classified in terms of Social Groups 'I' and 'III'.

Data of this kind confirm that the Swedish class structure in 1968 was still very rigid. For example, the son of a senior civil servant appears to have had about thirteen-times the chance of obtaining a 'Social Group I' occupation than a son of a manual worker employed in private industry. Even the son of a lower-grade white-collar worker employed in private industry had more than six-times the chance of getting such a position than a manual worker's son. In other words, these results are consistent with those of earlier Swedish studies, all of which have shown that recruitment into professional, managerial, and other highly rewarded

TABLE 12

Proportion of sons in Social Groups 'I' and 'III' according to fathers' occupation

Fathers' occupations	Sons' social group	
	I	III
senior civil servants	65.6	8.3
owners of large business firms, and professional people	52.6	8.2
senior managerial and executive in private business	50.7	18.5
lower-grade non-manual in private concerns	33.7	27.8
lower-grade non-manual in public concerns	24.4	32.0
owners of small business firms, and independent artisans	15.8	39.8
foremen	13.1	47.6
manual workers in public concerns	8.5	58.0
farmers	4.0	41.3
manual workers in private concerns	5.2	61.3
small farmers, fishermen	2.6	71.3
farm and forestry workers	3.3	75.7

Source: Erikson, (1971:95)

occupations, is highly restricted.[21] In fact these patterns appear to be much the same as they are for Britain.[22]

Clearly, the available evidence suggests that variations in the two samples' conceptions of their respective class structures cannot be seen to be solely a consequence of different mobility patterns, either in terms of immediate social experiences or the respective countries. Certainly the chances for the son of a manual worker becoming a lower-grade white-collar employee are greater in Sweden than they are in Britain, but the differences between the two countries in terms of overall patterns of social mobility are insufficient to account for the considerable variation in the attitudes of the two samples. How, then, are the differences to be explained? Since they do not seem to be a function of 'structural' differences it is pertinent to argue that they may be a consequence – if only partly – of certain normative influences: to follow Parkin (1971), those of a political kind.

Sweden, unlike Britain, is one of the few capitalist countries that has had a relatively continuous succession of Social Democratic governments. The Social Democratic party has been in office, either as the dominant partner in a coalition or as a majority government, since the 1930s and during this time it has claimed to represent the interests of the working class.[23] Most of its supporters are manual workers but there is also a substantial minority of lower-grade white-collar workers who also support the party.[24] Consequently, these governments have often enacted legislation with the intention of improving the economic and social conditions of its supporters, particularly those of industrial workers. Over the years priority has been given to economic growth, social welfare, housing, full employment, and factory legislation, all of which has improved the *absolute* living and working conditions of manual workers from among the worst in north-western Europe in the 1930s to the highest in 1972.[25] But on the whole, these programmes have had few consequences for the narrowing of differentials in the economic and social rewards of manual workers and those of other occupational groups.[26]

However if Social Democratic governments, despite their recent electoral appeals, have achieved little in reducing inequalities they have emphasized the desirability of establishing Sweden as a meritocratic society.[27] A society, that is, in which all individuals will be able to acquire occupational roles suited to their talents and skills and conversely, one in which recruitment into various occupations – particularly those which are prestigeful and highly rewarded – will be determined by 'competence' and 'ability' rather than by social background. Indeed, Parkin (1971) claims that Social Democratic governments in capitalist countries are more likely to emphasize equality of opportunity rather than equality of economic rewards. This emphasis in Sweden has been reflected in reforms of the educational system.[28]

Until the early 1950s, Sweden had a highly selective system of education. All children attended elementary schools, and in either their fourth or sixth grades, the more able were transferred to secondary schools where they pursued an academic curriculum before going to the *gymnasium* and subsequently to university. The rest – those not chosen for secondary education – continued their studies at elementary school before direct entry into the labour market, although some would also attend technical colleges. A consequence of this system, as in many other countries, was that the children from upper- and middle-class homes were more likely to attend the *gymnasium* than those from working-class backgrounds. For example, in a study of males born in 1934, Härnqvist (1958) found that only 35 per cent of pupils with the highest academic grades and from working-class homes transferred to the *gymnasium*, compared with 85 per cent of upper-class children attaining the same level of academic competence. Similarly, in terms of the social origins of university students, only 8 per cent of newly registered students came from working-class homes in 1947 (Israel 1968).

However, since the 1950s there has been a gradual introduction of non-streamed comprehensive schools, so that by the early 1970s Sweden will be the only country in western Europe with a completely non-selective educational system. Furthermore, there is little doubt that these reforms have improved the educational opportunities for working-class children: Reuterberg (1968) found that 87 per cent of working-class males born in 1948, and with the highest academic grades, transferred from secondary schools to the *gymnasium* – almost three times as many as among those born in 1934. But at the same time there has been a rapid increase in the proportion of university students from working-class homes. In the academic year 1962–3, working-class entrants accounted for 16 per cent of all places; by 1968, this figure had increased to 20 per cent (Statens Offentliga Utredningar 1971: 148–149).

But if reforms in the educational system have improved the opportunities for working-class children, these have not been as dramatic as the Swedish sample of workers tended to believe. Indeed, there remain important differences in the proportions of children from different social backgrounds that acquire higher educational qualifications. In 1968 it was found in a national sample that even among the youngest age cohort (20–29), the percentage of individuals with fathers in 'Social Group I' and with *at least* the *studentexamen* (taken at the termination of studies in the *gymnasium* and a necessary qualification for entry into institutions of higher education), was more than six times greater than for those individuals from 'Social Group III' homes (Johansson 1971). The complete figures are shown in *Table 13*:

The Social Democratic party has publicized these reforms of the educational system as providing the basis for the development of an open, achievement orientated, and meritocratic society. Consequently these changes have generated a set of beliefs that emphasizes the openness of the class structure and the possibilities of upward mobility for all; provided, that is, that individuals take the opportunities for obtaining the necessary qualifications in the much praised, 'democratized', and 'egalitarian' educational system.[29] But given government policies of this kind, it could be that as aspirations for upward mobility become heightened, so too could feelings of frustration, failure, and resentment when these expectations are not fulfilled. Indeed, these

TABLE 13

Percentage of individuals with the 'Studentexamen' or other higher educational qualification, according to age and socio-economic background.

Father's social group	Age of respondents		
	20–29	30–54	55–57
I	45	42	31
II	12	7	3
III	7	2	1
Total	12	6	3

Source: Johansson (1791:92)

attitudes are quite likely to develop in a country like Sweden where there are very restricted patterns of recruitment into the more prestigeful and highly rewarded occupations.[30]

Within the context of a Swedish economy which is overwhelmingly privately owned, it is difficult to envisage how recruitment into the more highly rewarded occupations can be democratized without an increase in government intervention. Otherwise, whether or not recruitment into these positions will change must depend upon the personal aptitude of managers and the controllers of private industry, who may be far from committed to the Social Democratic goal of greater social equality.[31] In fact this touches upon one of the major dilemmas confronting any Social Democratic government in a capitalist country: it may be committed to 'meritocratic' and even 'egalitarian' aims, and also to promoting the social and economic interests of its working-class supporters, but it often does so within the context of constraints imposed by the forces of a market economy.[32] Consequently it is questionable whether such objectives can ever be achieved without greater state control over these forces.[33] In Sweden, the Social Democratic pursuit of 'meritocratic' aims has led to various educational reforms and to the development of widespread beliefs in the openness of the class structure. Policies such as these have, so far, retained the allegiance of rank-and-file supporters, but in the long run feelings of resentment could emerge, particularly if the class structure remains as rigid as it is at present.[34]

In Britain, by comparison, 'meritocratic' norms have been less emphasized. Consequently, the class structure is still perceived to be shaped by a number of 'traditional' factors and there is less belief in the possibilities for upward mobility. Therefore it can be argued that manual workers will have limited aspirations for themselves and their children. As a result, feelings of failure are likely to be less pronounced among these workers and they are likely to perceive their own positions within the class structure as more or less inevitable.[35] But should Britain have a prolonged period of Labour governments, it could be that 'meritocratic' norms might become as widely emphasized as they are in Sweden. Certainly with Labour governments there have been attempts to equalize opportunities by making changes within the educational system.[36]

In conclusion, the foregoing discussion suggests that although workers' images of society may be shaped by their employment and other immediate social experiences, they are also conditioned by a number of wider normative influences. Accordingly, this paper has attempted to show that the English and Swedish respondents held rather different conceptions of their respective class structures because of exposure to different political norms. Of course this is not the only factor and a more comprehensive comparative study would doubtless disclose others. However, the evidence presented above does suggest that actors' conceptions of the class structure are shaped not only by 'objective' patterns of structural relationships but also by interpretations generated by wider social processes. In different industrial societies workers are subjected to relatively similar technological and social constraints. But this does not mean that they will necessarily have similar images of society, if only because they are also members of national, socio-political systems that vary considerably in ideological make-up. Consequently, in any investigation of workers' images of society, whether or not a cross-national comparative study, it is necessary to consider these macro-social factors as well as workers' immediate small-scale milieux.

Notes

1 The data in this paper were collected as part of a comparative study of social stratification in England and Sweden. The research is financed by a grant from the Centre for Environmental Studies, London, and the complete results will be published in a final report.

I am grateful to Derek Allcorn, Ray Pahl, Frank Parkin, Jack Winkler, and other colleagues at the University of Kent for their comments on an earlier draft of this paper.
2 This evidence is discussed by Lockwood (1966: 252-256).

3 However, Bell and Newby (1972) have suggested that in some work and community situations, agricultural workers, although generally in close personal contact with their employers, will adopt 'radical' attitudes.

4 See, for example, N. Birnbaum (1969).

5 England and Sweden are appropriate for a discussion of this issue because they are both highly industrialized societies with relatively similar occupational structures. Shortage of space prevents a documentation of their respective social structures but this is done in Scase (1972).

6 For a study of the relationship between organizational size and workers' attitudes, see G. Ingham (1970).

7 At the younger age levels there was often an overlap between the earnings of these two groups. It must also be stated that the differentials discussed here are for the *highest paid* manual workers. Of course, it would have been desirable to have had systematic evidence on the structure of earnings for all occupational and age groups, but the reluctance of management prevented this. Data of this kind, which would have included the earnings of low paid groups as teenage clerks and manual workers, would almost certainly have indicated that there were greater differentials *within* the two factories than those described in this paper. But in the absence of this information it was considered appropriate to describe differentials in terms of the *highest* earnings that members of each occupational category could hope to acquire.

8 It was considered that these factors would affect conceptions of social mobility. For a discussion of the relationship between age, stage in the family cycle, and attitudes, see H. Wilensky (1966).

The factories provided the names, addresses and ages of all manual employees so that the samples could be chosen.

9 In fact the two industries from which the factories were chosen were very similar in these respects. They both had low levels of conflict and relatively slow rates of technological innovation, by comparison with other industries.

10 Every attempt was made to ensure that the schedule was as similar as possible for both samples, but in a 'sociological' rather than a 'grammatical' sense. This was done by testing the schedule with Swedish sociologists and pilot respondents, in order to use questions that would convey similar meanings to both groups of workers.

A female Swedish research worker, normally resident in England, conducted the Swedish interviews and most of those in England; I am grateful to Anita Ehn-Scase for her assistance.

11 The practice of asking respondents 'poll-type' questions about things such as social class has been criticized on the grounds that 'class' means

very different things to different people. Consequently it is often argued that the resultant responses are of little sociological relevance. In the present enquiry there was an attempt to cope with this problem by asking respondents a number of questions about what they meant by the terms used in the questionaire, e.g. 'social class', 'promotion', 'inequality', etc. This probably did not completely solve the difficulties relating to respondents' interpretations of questions, but it would be a mistake to assume that their replies disclosed nothing about their conceptions of society. For a note about questions relating to the study of social class see J. Platt (1971); and for some favourable comments see G. Runciman (1966: 152-154).

12 Unless otherwise stated, the questions that follow were put to only these respondents.

13 These findings are consistent with those of other studies that have investigated this issue in Sweden. For a summary of these, see Scase (1972).

14 Indeed, of the twenty-five English respondents giving 'other and non-classifiable' answers, no fewer than 40 per cent (10) mentioned 'ascriptive' factors such as 'he would need to be born into the right family', 'make certain that he had a wealthy father', etc. Among the remaining, considerable importance was attached to 'luck' and 'chance'; they mentioned the need to 'win the pools', 'have a good bet', 'be left a fortune', and so on.

15 This question was put to all respondents and not merely to those who recognized the existence of social classes.

16 Industrialization and urbanization, for example, have been much more recent in Sweden. This, of course, has affected the structure of communities and possibly the development – or, rather, lack of – occupational sub-cultures.

17 This question was put after respondents had defined exactly what they meant by 'promotion'.

18 By contrast, the English workers held a more favourable opinion of their chances compared with those of white-collar workers; 34 per cent stated they were either 'worse' or 'much worse', but as many as 29 per cent suggested they were 'better' or 'much better'. There were a number of questions on the schedule which invited respondents to make comparisons between themselves and other occupational groups in society. For a discussion of these, see Scase (1974).

19 Indeed, the discrepancy between the Swedish respondents' conceptions of promotion in the factory and of mobility in society was such that it indicated the adoption of very different frames of reference in their consideration of these issues. They appeared to make a clear distinction between 'industry' and 'society' as institutional and normative systems. R. Darhendorf (1967) has argued this to be a feature of 'post-capitalist' societies.

20 R. Erikson (1971). The study was based on a random sample of individuals between the ages of fifteen and seventy-five years, drawn from the total Swedish population.

21 For a review of some of these studies, see Scase (1972).

22 For data on business directors, see G. Copeman (1955); for higher civil servants, R. Kelsall (1955); for university teachers, A. A. Halsey and M. Trow (1971); and for politicians, W. Guttsman (1963).

23 For a summary of economic and political developments in Sweden, see R. Tomasson (1970).

24 In the 1964 general election, for example, the Social Democratic party received approximately 75 per cent of the votes of industrial manual workers and about 45 per cent of those of 'routine' white-collar employees. See, Swedish Official Statistics (1965: 95).

25 According to almost all measures of material living standards – quality of housing, ownership of cars, telephones, television sets, deep freezers, and so on, as well as for such things as life expectancy and infant mortality – Sweden invariably appears in the international 'top three'. For a discussion of these achievements, see Tomasson (1970).

26 See Scase (1972).

27 In the 1970 General Election, the Social Democratic party adopted 'Increased Equality – For a More Just Society' as its election manifesto. This was supported by many other slogans with a similar theme which were financed by specific labour unions and the Trade Union Confederation.

28 For a summary of these reforms, see Härnqvist and Bengtsson (forthcoming). There is also a useful review in Tomasson (1970).

29 The Swedish mass media gives considerable emphasis to the opportunities available to individuals for obtaining educational qualifications that can be used for career advancement. In addition to their own courses, the radio and television services of the Swedish Broadcasting Corporation devote peak time to publicizing the various vocational and academic courses that are provided throughout the country. The Trade Union Confederation is also very active in this work: the Workers Educational Movement, for example, is an integral part of the trade-union movement and in 1970 it controlled 40 per cent of all adult education, providing courses for about one in ten of all adult Swedes. Some of these courses award *credits* which can then be taken into account for the purposes of obtaining university degrees. The Trade Union Confederation is currently negotiating with employers and the government about the possibilities of workers having time off from employment in order to study and obtain education qualifications. Furthermore, the government, over recent years, has conducted a massive advertising campaign in newspapers explaining the new opportunities that have been brought about by various reforms in the educational system.

It is interesting to speculate what proportion of English workers are aware of the opportunities provided by, say, the Open University. It is probably small; not surpringly, in view of the extremely limited publicity given to it by those sectors of the mass media with which most manual workers have direct contact.

30 Government policies explicitly geared to narrowing economic differentials between occupational groups appear to have been conducive to generating heightened feelings of relative deprivation among Swedish manual workers. See Scase (1974).

31 As Carlsson (1958: 126) has suggested, 'It might . . . be argued that the more general prevalence of higher education will make . . . employers more prone to take other things into consideration'.

32 This and many other problems that confront Social Democratic governments in capitalist countries are discussed by Parkin (1971).

33 There are signs that the Social Democratic government is increasingly prepared to pursue policies in this direction, possibly as a consequence of frustrated attempts to narrow economic differentials within the context of a privately owned economy. For example, it has recently been proposed that the State Pension Fund should be used to purchase stocks and shares and, ultimately, control in commerce and industry. A commission would be set up to oversee investments and it would consist of eleven members: five from trade unions, two from companies, two from local authorities, and a chariman and vice-chairman appointed by the government. By 1978 the State Pension Fund will have assets greater than those of all the Swedish banks and credit institutions combined.

34 In terms of economic differentials, this seems to have occurred already. See Scase (1974). If this resentment were also to develop in attitudes towards 'opportunities', then the allegiance of rank-and-file supporters to the Social Democratic party could become extremely problematic. The Social Democrats have always presented themselves as the party of social reform, social justice, and equality; it is in terms of these factors that they have asked to be judged at general elections.

35 A selective educational system is likely to enforce these attitudes. One of the main socializing effects of the secondary modern school is that it lowers the ambitions of pupils to accord with opportunities in the labour market. See, for example, M. Wilson (1953). Conversely, a non-streamed, non-selective educational system of the Swedish type is unlikely to lower the occupational expectations of working-class youth.

36 Changes, that is, towards comprehensive education. However, most of the schemes approved by the 1964-70 labour government included selective elements and they were generally far less egalitarian than the Swedish educational reforms.

References

BELL, C., and NEWBY, H. 1972. The Sources of Variation in Agricultural Workers' Images of Society. Mimeo. Paper presented to an SSRC Conference on *The Occupational Community of the Traditional Worker*. University of Durham.

BIRNBAUM, N. 1969. *The Crisis of Industrial Society*. New York: Oxford University Press.

CARLSSON, G. 1958. *Social Mobility and Class Structure*. Lund: Gleerup.

COPEMAN, G. 1955. *Leaders of British Industry*. London: Gee.

DAHRENDORF, R. 1967. *Class and Class Conflict in Industrial Society*. London: Routledge & Kegan Paul.

ERIKSON, R. 1971. *Uppväxtförhållanden och Social Rörlighet* (Childhood Living Conditions and Social Mobility). Stockholm: Allmänna Förlaget.

GUTTSMAN, W. 1963. *The British Political Elite*. London: MacGibbon & Kee.

HALSEY, A., and TROW, M. 1971. *The British Academics*. London: Faber & Faber.

HÄRNQVIST, K. 1958. *Reserverna for Högre Utbildning* (Reserves of Talent for Higher Education). Stockholm: Government Publishing House.

HÄRNQVIST, K., and BENGTSSON, J. (forthcoming) *Educational Reforms and Educational Equality*.

INGHAM, G. 1970. *Size of Industrial Organisation and Worker Behaviour*. London: Cambridge University Press.

INKELES, A. 1960-61. Industrial Man: The Relation of Status to Experience, Perception and Values. *American Journal of Sociology* **66**.

ISRAEL, J. 1968. Uppforstran och Utbildning (Socialization and Education). In Dahlström, E. (ed.) *Svensk Samhällsstruktur i Sociologisk Belysning* (Swedish Social Structure from a Sociological Perspective). Stochkolm: Almqvist and Wiksell.

JOHANSSON, L. 1971. *Utbildning – Empirisk Del* (Education – Some Empirical Data). Stockholm: Allmänna Förlaget.

KELSALL, R. 1955. *Higher Civil Servants in Britain*. London: Routledge & Kegan Paul.

LOCKWOOD, D. 1966. Sources of Variation in Working-Class Images of Society. *Sociological Review* **14**.

MACDONALD, K., and RIDGE, J. 1972. Social Mobility. In Halsey, A. H. (ed.) *Trends in British Society Since 1900*. London: Macmillan.

MILLER, M. S. 1960. Comparative Social Mobility. *Current Sociology* **9**.

MOORE, R. 1972. Religion as a Source of Variation in Working-Class Images of Society. Paper presented to an SSRC Conference on

The Occupational Community of the Traditional Worker. University of Durham.

PARKIN, F. 1971. *Class Inequality and Political Order.* London: Mac-Gibbon & Kee.

PLATT, J. 1971. Variations in Answers to Different Questions on Perceptions of Class. *Sociological Review* **19.**

REUTERBERG, SVEN-ERIK. 1968. Val av Teoretisk Utbildning i Relation till Sociala och Regionala Bakgrundsfaktorer (Choice of 'Academic' Education in Relation to Social and Regional Background). *Mimeo,* University of Gothenburg.

RUNCIMAN, G. 1966. *Relative Deprivation and Social Justice.* London: Routledge & Kegan Paul.

SCASE, R. 1972. Industrial Man: A Reassessment with English and Swedish Data. *British Journal of Sociology* **23.**

—— 1974. Relative Deprivation: A Comparison of English and Swedish Manual Workers. In Wedderburn, D. (ed.) *Inequality, Poverty and the Class Structure.* London: Cambridge University Press.

STATENS OFFENTLIGA UTREDNINGAR (SOU). 1971. *Val av Utbildning och Yrke* (Choice of Education and Work). Stockholm: Government Publishing House.

SWEDISH OFFICIAL STATISTICS. 1965. *Elections to the Parliament 1961-64.* Stockholm: Government Publishing House.

TOMASSON, R. 1970. *Sweden: Prototype of Modern Society.* New York: Random House.

WILENSKY, H. 1966. Work as a Social Problem. In Becker, H. (ed.) *Social Problems: A Modern Approach.* New York: Wiley.

WILSON, M. 1953. The Vocational Preferences of Secondary Modern School Children. *British Journal of Educational Psychology* **23.**

CHRIS MIDDLETON

Sexual Inequality and Stratification Theory

INTRODUCTION

With the recent revival of interest in feminist ideas, theories about the relationship between the sexes which had prevailed in adacemic sociology for many years have been subjected to much-needed criticism. Laudable as such criticism has been, it has nevertheless failed to emancipate itself from the paradigms that provided the framework for the very theories it sought to refute. In Althusserian language, the Women's Liberation Movement's critique of sexism has, with few exceptions, continued to operate on the ideological 'terrain' of sexism. Since the Marxist analysis of the oppression of women (by far the most significant alternative critique) suffers from a similar deficiency, our present understanding of the relationship between the sexes remains inadequate in the most fundamental respects.

The prospect is not entirely gloomy, however, for within the past two years the groundwork has at last been laid for a potentially much more sophisticated theory of the social condition of women under capitalism. Towards the end of the paper I shall give a brief outline of this promising theoretical development, which is founded on an application of the principles of historical materialism, but first I intend to present a selective review of some of the most significant literature in the sociology of sex-relationships, whether academic,[1] Marxist, or Feminist, to demonstrate how their theoretical weaknesses derive from a continuing subservience to the hegemony of sexist ideology.

All previous studies of women in capitalist societies have suffered from a common grave omission: that is, a materialist analysis of that productive activity which is largely specific to women – domestic labour – and its role in determining the relationships of women to men and to male-dominated institutions. It has been widely assumed that to the extent that they have been excluded from direct participation in the market sectors of the capitalist economy, women – as housewives and mothers – have become marginal to that economy, and have in consequence been confined to residual, largely cultural functions. This view not only contains a serious misunderstanding of the nature of women's activities in the family, but is, I believe, quite directly rooted in the central precepts of sexist ideology.

It is the neglect of the material basis of women's activities and situation in the home that has been responsible, in large measure, for the continuing dominance of the sexist paradigm in Marxist and Feminist as well as in academic social thought. This paper will show how in the case of Marxism it has led to a diminution of the urgency with which female emancipation is sought, and a virtual disregard, both in theory and in practice, of the subjection of those women who are not employed in the market sectors of the economy.

In academic sociology the view that female activity in the home is essentially cultural has often been associated with a denial of the proposition that women do in fact constitute a subordinate group at all. Such a position has, of course, been most visibly characteristic of functionalist sociology. But even more significantly, where it has been acknowledged that the relationship between male and female comprises a system of stratification, such recognition has generally been limited to a descriptive analysis of manifestations of sexual inequality, discrimination, or female subservience in apparently quite discrete fields: for instance, in employment, in personal relationships within the family, in the commercial exploitation of the female sex and so on. Unfortunately, studies of sex-based oppression in these several spheres of existence have never been satisfactorily articulated into an integrated and comprehensive theory of women's subjugation.

If academic sociology has been unable to establish the relationships between various manifestations of sex-based stratification, it has been equally deficient in analysing the structural integration[2] of women's subordination with the productive relationships of the class system, or for that matter, with any other order of stratification. These twin failings stem from an identical methodological weakness: a refusal to analyse social processes in their structural totality, preferring instead to build theory on the basis of a number of artificially isolated 'dimensions' of stratification which are initially treated as being independent of each other. Gerhard Lenski is the most unequivocal proponent of this methodological principle and his work is referred to in more detail later in the paper.

The inadequacies of academic sociology are parallelled by recent contributions to the debate from Shulasmith Firestone, Juliet Mitchell, and Kate Millett, three leading adherents to the cause of Women's Liberation. None of the three has been able to develop a coherent overall theory of women's subjugation integrally linked with a theory of class relationships, (or even to provide the necessary paradigm for such a development), while the methodological error which has the status of a cardinal principle in the work of Lenski reappears (at least in the writings of Mitchell and Millett) as the inadvertent underpinning of their theoretical constructions.

A major contention of this paper will be that this fundamental methodological weakness may only be satisfactorily avoided by a study of the role of domestic production in capitalist societies, in accordance with the principles of historical materialism.

CHARACTERISTICS OF SEXIST IDEOLOGY UNDER CAPITALISM

Building on Simone de Beauvoir's pioneering study, *The Second Sex,* feminists are beginning to undertake the considerable task of writing the history of sexist ideology in western civilization. Traditionally, these ideologies, whilst encouraging men to transcend their natural individual limitations by acting upon their physical environment, have legitimized only those female activities that were rooted in the biological functions peculiar to women. Though long predating the advent of capitalism, sexism nevertheless received powerful reinforcement and was stimulated into new forms of expression as a result of the exclusion of the wives of the bourgeoisie from the market sectors of the economy during the late seventeenth and eighteenth centuries. Simultaneously, the increasing predominance of the capitalist mode of production over other economic forms gave rise to an ideology that not only urged the untrammelled ascendancy of economic activity as such, but asserted that the free market was the *natural* form of economy, and even that its principles underlay *all* forms of economic activity. Since women, or rather bourgeois women, were now excluded from participation in the market sectors, bourgeois ideology (in incorporating the beliefs of sexism) came to the conclusion that women, in the confines of their homes, were marginal to the central processes of social life. The spheres of men and women, sundered in actuality, were held to be separate on the grounds of natural distinctions, and the life deemed appropriate for the wives of the bourgeoisie was raised to an ideal plane far removed from the vital yet mundane activities in which their husbands were engaged.[3] Moreover, since this exclusively male activity consciously embodies the principles of rationality and economic aggression, it is not surprising that the feminine character was now defined in terms of their opposites: irrationality, intuition, emotionality, empathy, passivity, etc. The dependency of women on men (which was real enough among the bourgeoisie) and the restrictions of the feminine role to wifehood and to motherhood, confirmed a situation where women invariably lived *through* other people (their husbands or their children), or more accurately through other males. In the existentialist language of de Beauvoir, women lived constantly as 'the Other'. But, as can be seen from the above, this condition had a distinct material and historical basis and was not, as de Beauvoir argues, simply the expression of a primordial and metaphysical duality: that of Self and Other.

In the present century, changing assumptions about human behaviour and its relationship to the social world (as embodied in the expanding disciplines of the social sciences) made a reformulation of sexist ideology imperative. The new improved version (Freud, Bowlby, Parsons, and Spock are key figures in this respect) has stressed the socio-psychological importance of the woman's traditional wife-mother role for other members of the family; and as I shall show it is in this variant that sexist ideology has had such a pervasive and subtle influence even on those who would discredit it.

WOMEN IN ACADEMIC THEORY

The most obvious expression of sexist ideology in modern academic sociology is to be found in the functionalist theory of the family. Let me briefly remind you of the theory's main points in its Parsonian version. Functionalism perceives a harmonious division of labour within the family (as in any small group) between instrumental and expressive functions, the former being typically performed by the male head of household, and the latter by the wife-mother. The tasks appropriate to the wife-mother are therefore those of pattern-maintenance and integration. (Zelditch even goes so far as to argue that the wife-mother may perform integrative functions even whilst engaged in instrumental activities.) But pattern-maintenance and integration prove also to be the major functions of the family as a whole, acting as a solidarity unit in the context of an always potentially non-solidaristic total society. This duplication of the wife-mother's functions *within* the family, by the family itself in the wider social system, only serves to reinforce the identification of the woman's role with that of the family.

In more familiar, but still Parsonian language, the theory states that the root functions of the family, and preeminently of the adult woman as the key personality in the internal family structure, are those of socialization and the emotional stabilization of the adult personality.

Strictly speaking, there is no theory of sex-based stratification in functionalist orthodoxy. In the analysis of the family, as elsewhere in the general theory, the crucial organizing concept of immediate relevance is that of 'structural differentiation'. But whereas the application of this concept to the division of labour in the total social system refers to a stratified hierarchy of relationships (however harmonious and stable such a hierarchy appears to be), its application to the division of labour within the family contains no such implication. The functionalist theory of structural differentiation may be the sociological heir to the nineteenth-century conservative philosophy of organic harmony, but *that* philosophy had perceived woman as an inferior and subordinate being, whereas modern functionalism manages to combine the theory of organic harmony with an ideology of familial democracy. In other words, functionalism discounts the existence of actually prevailing inequalities between the sexes which conservative philosophy had at least acknowledged – even if it had done so with approval.

Evidently, there have been sociologists who were fully aware that the relationship between the sexes was characterized by systematic inequalities. A special mention should perhaps be made of William J. Goode who has been consistently sensitive to the fact that the definition of the feminine role entailed a structural subordination of the woman to the man. But, so far as I know, Goode has never attempted to develop these scattered observations into a systematic theory of sex-based stratification.

One impediment to the emergence of a theory of this kind has surely been the fact that many sociologists regard the family, rather than the individual as the basic unit of the social system. Goode himself writes that:

'It is the *family*, not merely the individual, that is ranked in the class structure. The family is the keystone of the stratification system, the social mechanism by which it is maintained.' (Goode 1964: 80)

And in similar vein, Frank Parkin has argued that:

'Although the processes of rewarding and recruitment (within the class system – sc.) are analytically separable, they are closely intertwined in the actual operation of the stratification system. This is to a large extent to do with the prominent part played by the family in "placing" individuals at various points in the class hierarchy . . . For stratification implies not simply inequality, but a set of institutional arrangements which guarantee a fairly high degree of *social continuity* in the reward position of family units through the generations.'[4] (Parkin 1972: 13-14)

I do not wish to discuss here whether the family rather than the individual is indeed the molecular unit of the class system.[5] The point I do wish to make is that the effective, though not the logically necessary, consequence of adherence to this view has often been a concomitant devaluation of the importance of stratified relationships *within* the family and, by extrapolation, between the sexes in general. I quote Parkin again:

'The failure of some writers to recognize that the family, not the individual, is the appropriate social unit of the class system, has led to certain confusions in their analysis. Not infrequently, collectivities of individuals having particular attributes in common, such as age or sex, are designated as units of stratification. Women, for example . . . by virtue of the disabilities they suffer in comparison with men . . . are sometimes regarded as social units comparable to a subordinate class or racial minority.' (Parkin 1972: 14)

But to recognize the family as the 'appropriate social unit of the class system' should not lead us to ignore the fact that, in so far as they are engaged in domestic production, women do have a distinctive relationship to the productive system.

Parkin's immediate reaction is apparently against those occasional attempts by academic sociologists to incorporate the evidence on structured sexual inequality into a general theoretical farmework, and who have typically opted for a neo-Weberian, multi-dimensional model of social stratification. Like Parkin, I shall examine Lenski's *Power and Privilege* as a representative exposition of this approach.

It would be an exaggeration to say that Lenski has developed a theory of specifically sex-based stratification. Rather he has proposed a general theory of stratification based on the methodological principle that the overall distributive system should be regarded as a compound of a number of independent and variable dimensions of stratification, which he calls class systems. He has then simply acknowledged that among these class systems is to be found one based on sex.

Before discussing the more important issue of the limitations of his general methodology, it should perhaps be pointed out that Lenski's own analysis of the class system based on sex does not, in fact, accord with his methodological recommendations. He argues that we can no longer ignore the role of sex in the distributive process since: 'the traditional barriers which long separated the female system of stratification from the male, and kept the former dependent on the latter, are clearly crumbling' (Lenski 1966: 403).

The male and female systems of stratification are thus seen to be coalescing. Furthermore, they operate, not independently of other 'class systems' such as those based on education or occupation, but actually within the framework of these additional systems (e.g. men are recognized as having greater opportunities in education or employment, or as being more generously rewarded in the occupational sphere). Despite his claims to the contrary, it emerges that Lenski does not in fact recognize a 'class system' based on sex at all, for he denies the dependent relationship between male and female systems of stratification, and therefore misses the fact that this relationship constitutes a system of stratification in its own right. Lenski is reduced to banal conclusions of the kind that 'being male remains a resource of considerable value'. But this, after all, is the phenomenon to be explained, not the end-point of our theorizing.

The multi-dimensional approach has to be rejected primarily because it is unable to specify *within the theory itself* the exact structural relationship between stratification systems based on sex and those based on other criteria, particularly social class. Any relationship that is observed to exist between different dimensions of stratification can therefore only appear as *theoretically contingent*. This does not prevent such relationships from being patterned, of course. For example, it might be observed that the kind of discrimination against women in the industrial sphere varies systematically according to the social class of the woman concerned. Discrimination against a working-class woman might predominantly affect her rates of pay, while a professional woman might suffer more from discrimination in matters of promotion. But the explanation for any pattern so observed can only be *ad hoc*. It does not and cannot emerge from the theory itself since multi-dimensional theory refuses to treat the class system and the stratification systems based on sex as elements within a single structurally integrated process. Such 'theory' is in fact merely a systematic framework into which empirical observations and *ad hoc* explanations may be slotted. This however does nothing to further our knowledge of the field.

MARXISM AND THE OPPRESSION OF WOMEN

Marxists have traditionally accepted that the subordination of women was a serious problem for socialists. Apart from Engel's influential essay on *The Origins of the Family*, the question was actively promoted in the socialist movements of the Second International by, among others, Bebel, Kollontai, and Clara Zetkin. However, the level of theoretical discussion on this issue never matched the degree of sophistication attained by the Marxist analysis of class antagonisms.

Much of the early debate was based on Engels's suspect anthropology, but this drawback was actually much less harmful than the fact that his history of the family in recent epochs was exclusively concerned with the family systems of ruling classes. Not surprisingly, given the lack of available documentation, he had comparatively little to say about the family life of the mass of the population. But derivatively, as the unfortunate consequence of this omission, the essential materialist concept employed by early Marxist writers on the family became that of 'sexual property', a concept that may have validly expressed the social condition of many bourgeois women, but which was at best only a partial reflection of the relationship between the sexes in other social classes. Most regrettably of all, the notion of 'sexual property', used as a totalizing description of the female condition, remained caught within the domain of bourgeois-sexist ideology, in its treatment of all women as wholly passive objects of social processes, especially within the context of the family. Women were regarded as potential historical subjects only when they entered the industrial labour force – an attitude that was reflected at the organizational level, for few serious attempts were made by the socialist movement to mobilize the *wives* of proletarian workers.[6]

Classical Marxism argued that women were not an *exploited* group in the strict sense, except in so far as they became wage-labourers (i.e. it was argued that domestic labour did not produce surplus value which was then expropriated from the producer). The exact status of the marital relationship in Marx and Engels is somewhat obscure. Consider, for example, the following two brief passages from *The Origins of the Family*: first, Marx is quoted as saying that:

'the modern family contains in embryo not only slavery . . . but serfdom also' (Marx and Engels 1968: 496);

while Engels later declares that:

'in the family he is the bourgeois; the wife represents the proletariat' (*ibid*: 510).

What we are to make of such diverse and contradictory antagonisms in the one relationship is open to doubt, but it is quite clear that these inconsistencies arise because Marx and Engels did not engage in any *direct* historical examination of women's domestic labour, so that their only recourse was to an analysis by means of analogy. Furthermore, in the absence of such a history, their treatment of the condition of women could only be idealized and abstract. The point is well made by Juliet Mitchell:

'Marx . . . retained the abstraction of Fourier's conception of the position of women as an index of general social advance. This in effect makes it merely a symbol – it accords the problem a universal importance at the cost of depriving it of its specific substance. Symbols are allusions to or derivations from something else. In Marx's early writings "woman" becomes an anthropological entity, an ontological category, of a highly abstract kind.' (Mitchell 1971: 78)

When, in his later work, Marx did acknowledge the importance of historically differentiated forms of family organization, women, as such, receive no mention.

Notwithstanding the above, it is quite definitely implied that since women, as housewives and mothers, are excluded from social production for the market, their subordination is not a constituent element of the central class dynamic of capitalist societies. The conclusion of the classical Marxist view was that female emancipation must depend on the entry of women into social production.

To the extent that 'women's issues' were taken up by the early Marxian socialists, their demands were either Utopian, because not rooted in a specific analysis of women's domestic activities (for example, the slogan, 'Abolish the Family' was never supported by a detailed analysis of how it could be achieved); or, conversely, their demands were strictly reformist. When eventually the most obvious of these reformist demands were achieved through the efforts of the Suffragette Movement, the immediacy of the 'Woman Question' declined, and the struggle for full sexual equality and freedom was postponed to await the triumph of the socialist revolution. Henceforth, the further development of a materialist investigation into the specific nature of women's subjugation was abandoned. Domestic production, being a private activity as well as being privately appropriated, was dismissed as pre-capitalist – a notion reminiscent perhaps of the 'survivalist' thesis of nineteenth-century evolutionary theory, and clearly an inadequate explanation of a mode of production that has persisted into the most advanced stages of capitalist development.

Even the Marxist organizations of the post-war New Left showed little interest in the condition of women until prodded out of their complacency by the Women's Liberation Movement. The New Left's theoretical interest in the family has generally been less concerned with the way in which it might directly determine the oppression of women, than in the adverse effects the present organization of the family is likely to have on working-class consciousness, i.e. interest centres less on the family *per se* as on the family's relevance to the male-dominated class struggle being waged in the industrial sector. This represents a retreat even from the position of the Classical Marxists who were at least directly concerned with the question of women's emancipation. Emphasis is now laid on how the family functions to inhibit a direct challenge to the capitalist order by the organized working class. It does so in several ways.

First, the working-class home provides an emotionally supportive retreat for the psychologically alienated worker, thereby softening the impact of the brutality and tedium of the workplace, and making life under captialism that much more bearable as a whole. The consequence of the housewife's normal activities may also be regarded as detrimental to the possible growth in the worker's class-consciousness, for the 'good' wife is one who can make ends meet, if necessary even by going without herself, on what may be a scant income from wages or state benefits. If she succeeds, of course, her husband is under less pressure to increase his wage packet.

The second mechnism by which the family may impede the development of working-class solidarity derives from the privatized character of the typical household. At most it is orientated only towards an immediate, local community, never to the class on a national basis. Hence commitment to the family supposedly interferes with commitment to the working class as a whole. Further, given the financial dependence of wife and children on the husband, the latter's feelings of responsibility toward his family are thought likely to discourage him from engaging in militant activity, whether in the form of agitational work, or of participation in industrial – especially strike – action. The structural isolation of the family unit from the collective activities and organizations of the working class is also held to be responsible for the oft-cited political and industrial conservatism of many women. The frequent occasions on which women are known to have exerted pressure on their striking husbands to return to work is but a dramatic illustration of such conservatism.[7]

The third main means by which the family is believed to inhibit the development of a solidaristic class-consciousness concerns its ideological functions. If women are liable to be more conservative and less class-conscious than their husbands, they are also the adults given primary responsibility for the transmission of values to each new generation, so that working-class children are likely to be exposed to relatively conservative and individualistic systems of values. The values which the mother teaches and represents are – like the family as a whole – individuated and anti-solidaristic. Further, the family may act as a micrososm of the wider social system and it is the child's introduction, as a subordinate, into the authority structure of the family, with its associated emphasis on obedience and discipline, that prepares the young adult for his submissive role in the industrial enterprise.

Finally, a word should be said about the New Left's view of the family's economic activities. These are generally taken to be consumption orientated and non-productive. (We have seen that, to the extent to which they are productive, they are dismissed as pre-capitalist and not deemed worthy of further enquiry.) The consumption aspect of the family in Marxist theory has predictably taken on an increased signicance as the mass markets for consumer goods have been expanded. Female consumers have, of course, been especially subjected to the manipulative techniques of modern advertising, and this fact, as well as the manipulation of women's sexual attributes in the marketing of products, has been recognized as a central aspect of women's oppression under capitalism.

Although it paints too cosy a picture of working-class family life,[8] the above analysis is, I think, substantially accurate. My criticism is that it is insufficient. As it stands there is little in the analysis other than the the terminology it employs and the moral evaluations it passes, that would differentiate it from that suggested by Parsonian functionalism.

New Left Analysis	*Functionalist Analysis*
1 The family is isolated from the class struggle. Its values (privatized and demanding that the husband's overriding responsibility be to his family) conflict with the requirements of class solidarity.	The family is structurally isolated from the rest of the social structure, especially from the economic system. Its values are particularistic, and so are in potential conflict with the universalistic norms of the industrial system.

(The Marxist and functionalist analyses do, of course, diverge in that

Marxism stresses the need for a wider commitment to the proletarian class, whereas Parsonian functionalism focuses on commitment to the universalistic norms of the industrial enterprise. But the two analyses are comparable in immediately relevant respects, namely in their view of the significance of the family for wider social commitments, and in the manner in which it operates to inhibit such commitments).

2 The family provides an emotionally supportive retreat for the psychologically alienated worker.

One of the family's two major functions is that of tension-management. The family is the main outlet for expressive behaviour.

3 The family is the main agency for the transmission of values to new generations. These will tend to be anti-solidaristic and will encourage the acceptance of existing authority structures.

The family's second major function is pattern-maintenance, which it achieves through the process of socialization. The content of the values internalized is left vague: simply that it will be the culture of the society into which the child is born.

The Marxist analysis tends to have greater historical and empirical content (and that is a virtue), but apart from this the only major element in the Marxist analysis that is absent from Parsonian functionalism is the former's concern with the family as a consumption unit, and women's critical role in respect to this. But in a theoretical system such as Marxism, which correctly focuses on the relations of production (rather than those of distribution and consumption), this additional factor makes little difference to the status of the family in the overall analysis. The family is firmly located as an institution that functions on the level of superstructure, and women (in their capacity as housewives and mothers) are assumed to be engaged in merely cultural activities. However important such activities might be, the struggle in this sphere must be regarded as secondary to the industrial struggle, given the materialist basis of the capitalist system. Women are yet again treated largely as an appendage.

The New Left has not ignored domestic production entirely, but its comments have tended to be confined to a moralistic condemnation of the numbers of hours that many women are forced to work in the home, and of the deleterious effects that housework's routine, monotonous, and soul-destroying character are bound to have on the mind and body of the housewife. This, of course, leads straight back to the central argument of Classical Marxism: that it is necessary for women to enter fully into social production both as a means of escaping household drudgery and as a precondition of their emancipation in the wider social context.

THE FEMINIST REACTION

To quote from Juliet Mitchell's essay, *The Longest Revolution*, we have seen how: 'the liberation of women remains a normative ideal, an adjunct to socialist theory, not structurally integrated into it' (Mitchell 1966: 15).

Indeed, the widespread dissatisfaction with Marxian theory (as well as practice) on this score has inspired many sympathizers of the revolutionary left to fill the void with a *feminist* account of women's subjugation. The distinctive feature of feminist thought is its belief that *all* women, irrespective of their social class or their politics, share a common oppression and may be organized around it. In its most radical version, feminism maintains that the division between the sexes was the primordial or prototypical form of all class divisions. This is the principle message of Shulasmith Firestone's *The Dialectics of Sex*. Here, Firestone claims to present an analysis that is both materialist and dialectical, but that goes beyond the class analysis of Marxism to 'a materialist view of history based on sex'. More exactly, it is a materialist view based on the biologically imposed, but no longer immutable, exigencies of the reproductive process. Marxism is ingested in the dialectic of sex, and historical materialism receives suitable redefinition:

> 'Historical materialism is that view of the course of history which seeks the ultimate cause and the great moving power of all historic events in the dialectic of sex: the division of society into two distinct biological classes for procreative reproduction, and the struggles of these classes with one another; in the changes in the modes of marriage, reproduction, and childcare.' (Firestone 1972: 13)

An analysis grounded in the social processes of reproduction may undoubtedly be materialistic, but while these processes are taken to be the *sole* foundation, it can neither be truly historical nor dialectical. It must inevitably be ahistorical because, following the primordial 'division of society into two distinct biological classes', there have occurred no major developments in the forces of reproduction which, by coming into contradiction with the prevailing modes of reproduction, could have served as the determinant for the actual historical changes that have taken place in the relationship between the sexes, in the social organization of reproductive processes, or, for that matter, in the relationship between economic classes which now appears as part of the superstructure. History comes to a standstill, in Firestone's discourse, until the final application of empirical science to the problems of fertility control provides the preconditions for the revolutionary transcendence of sexual antagonisms.

No more is Firestone's work dialectical. Class antagonisms abound in *The Dialectic of Sex*, but the notion of contradiction is absent. We have already seen how, given the static nature of the forces of reproduction, this was necessarily the case in the history of the reproductive infrastructure; but elsewhere too the meaning of this essential concept has not been sufficiently grasped. For example, what are called the 'Sex Dialectics of Cultural History' constitute an essential ingredient of Firestone's demonstration of the prospective resolution of sexual antagonisms; but there are no indications of any contradictions at work in this process. The sexual polarity of male and female is reflected by the dualistic organization of Culture into a Technological and an Aesthetic Mode. (Firestone has in mind C. P. Snow's famous 'two cultures' distinction.) The fission within Culture is resolved by the merging of the two Modes in the creation of empirical science, which progresses, Popperian fashion, by a combination of imaginative insight and hard experiment. Finally, as we have noted, the application of empirical science to our biological constitutions makes possible the release of women from the bondage of the womb. In this analysis we find reference to an interplay between the material and cultural levels, but no treatment of a dialectical movement between them. The dual organization of Culture is held merely to *reflect* the sexual polarity (this is no more than an explanation by analogy); the cultural fission is said to be resolved by a *marriage* of the Technological and Aesthetic Modes. Again no hint of contradiction is apparent in this 'unity of opposites', which, moreover, seems to take place quite independently of the forces and relations of reproduction. Finally, although it is asserted that women must seize hold of the means of empirical science if they are to be used solely for the benefit of mankind in general, and for the emancipation of women in particular, the investigation does not proceed by an examination of how a contradiction between our capacity to control reproduction and the persisting, presumably outmoded, relationship between the sexes, might plausibly lead women to take such action.

Firestone's social universe is thus irreversibly split into two separate worlds: one material, the other cultural. An insurmountable hiatus develops between the base and superstructure, and her analysis collapses into a crude materialism and ecological determinism. As a final criticism, one must add that the primacy of the sexual dialectic as 'the great moving power of all historical events and divisions' remains no more than an assertion, and the incorporation of the class dialectic by that based on sex is simply never established.

A leading British Women's Liberationist, Juliet Mitchell, has also criticized Firestone's attempt to incorporate Marxism within a Radical Feminist framework, but nevertheless she remains a feminist because she holds that *all* women share a common existential experience (Mitchell 1971: 96). However, Mitchell advocates the search for a Marxist solution to the problems raised by feminists. She was, in fact, the first of the new wave of feminists to express dissatisfaction with the state of socialist theory on women, and, as early as 1966 was urging that we reject 'the idea that woman's condition can be deduced derivatively from the economy or equated symbolically with society. Rather it must be seen as a *specific* structure, which is a unity of different elements' (Mitchell 1966: 16).

Paradoxically, she was prevented from realizing this ambition by her adherence to the very intellectual tradition that had sensitized her to its necessity in the first place. This was the anti-monist philosophy of the Althusserian school. In this view:

> 'Dialectical materialism posits a complex (not dualistic) structure in which all elements are in contradiction to each other; at some point these contradictions can coalesce, explode and be overcome, but the new fusion will enter into contradiction with something else ...'
>
> 'Past socialist theory has failed to differentiate woman's condition into separate structures, which together form a complex – not a simple – unity ...'
>
> 'The key structures of woman's situation can be listed as follows: Production, Reproduction, Sexuality, and the Socialization of Children. The concrete combination of these produce the "complex unity" of her position; but each separate structure may have reached a different "moment" at any given historical time. Each then must be examined separately in order to see what the present unity is, and how it might be changed.' (Mitchell 1971: 90, 100, 101)

The practice recommended by Mitchell, the separate and independent analysis of structures of oppression in different areas, followed by an examination of their concrete combination in a 'complex unitity', does not differ in principle from that favoured by Lenski. In consequence, it will come as no surprise that Mitchell fails to provide an historical account of women's oppression (the selfsame charge she had levelled against Firestone), for the static quality of her analysis is determined by the methodological design. Nor, in this case, could we expect an examination of the modes of structural integration between the class-system and sex-based oppression. Here, as with all previous socialist theory, comment on women's productive activities in the home is confined to a description of the appalling number of hours worked. Mitchell accepts the thesis that women are non-productive in the home, and therefore marginal to the economy;[9] she accepts the (inherently sexist) notion that, within the family context, woman is a creature determined by her reproductive, her sexual, and her maternal roles. And since these are experiences that are open to *all* women, differences in social class affect the specific oppression of women but little. Class is considered as marginal to women's subjection in the domestic situation, as the woman is, fatalistically, deemed marginal to the class struggle (Mitchell 1971: 123 ff.). It is open for the wife of Andy Capp to link arms with Her Majesty the Queen, both to march in the solidarity of sisterhood against their shared oppression as women. Mitchell might protest against this judgement with its implicit debasement of the ideal of sisterhood, but it is the logic of her own argument that entails the divorce of the class struggle from the struggle for women's liberation.

A criticism of the methodology in Kate Millett's *Sexual Politics* may show the essential similarity between the shortcomings to be found in Firestone and Mitchell's works. Millett's theoretical edifice is founded on the concept of 'Patriarchy' – a supposedly universal system of political domination functioning within the realm of sex relationships.[10] But precisely because it predicates a pandemic set of political relationships, the concept of patriarchy lacks explanatory power for any specific historical circumstance. Instead there develops a theoretical disjuncture between the generalized notion of sexual-political domination and the sundry institutionalized relationships and behaviours that are presumed to be expressions of it. Millett's unschematic elaboration of the theory reflects this hiatus. By dehistoricizing her subject matter Millett is debarred from providing more than a disjointed enumeration of what she herself calls (in a separate context) *instances* of sexual politics. The want of a theoretical synthesis is again grievously apparent.

The devaluation of class affiliations, unintended and subterranean in Mitchell's essay, is quite explicit in *Sexual Politics*. Millett argues that the female has fewer permanent class associations than the male.

'Economic dependency . . . (as a housewife – sc.) renders her affiliations with any class a tangential, vicarious, and temporary matter . . .
Women as a group do not enjoy many of the interests and benefits
any class may offer its male members. Women therefore have less of
an investment in the class system.' (Millett 1971: 38)

Women are a dependency class, she continues, who live on surplus,
their very existence being parasitic on the men who rule them.

Once again it is women's supposed marginality to economic life that is
held to determine their consciousness (though Millett contradicts
herself on this point, for elsewhere she claims that the pre-eminent
arena of sexual revolution is within human consciousness itself). It is not
entirely clear whether Millett's perception of women's supposedly
tenuous class affiliations refers to the objective relationship of women to
the class-sytem or to their subjective identification with particular
social classes. Either way, Millett in on very dubious ground.

If it is to women's subjective identifications that Millett is referring
then there is little evidence to support her contention that women tend 'to
transcend the usual class stratifications'. The bourgeois feminist movement at the turn of the century, for example, struck few roots among
women of the working class, while most of its bourgeois leaders eventually placed loyalty to their class before that of loyalty to their sex.
Furthermore, the previously cited tendency for women to be more
conservative than men does not have the clearcut inference it is sometimes ceded. Since the phenomenon appears to hold true for all social
classes, it would seem to provide confirmatory evidence for Millett's
contention when located among proletarian women, but to have quite the
opposite implication when found among the wives of the bourgeoisie.

Millett's belief that women are a parasitic class living off surplus
reveals an astonishing lack of familiarity (or of concern) with the exigencies of working-class life. Most working-class families, for instance,
regard a second income deriving from the wife's paid employment as
virtually indispensable. Besides, the objective relationship of economic
dependency within the proletarian class,[11] such as it is, is only the
immediate and transparent form of the underlying and material relationship between husband and wife. The infrastructural and determining
relation between the sexes is based on a division of labour which will be
discussed in the last section of this paper. In its phenomenal immediacy
the relation of economic dependency corresponds to the wage-form in
the relationship between capitalist and proletarian. But, unlike the
wage-form, it is not *itself* responsible for concealing the determining

material relation; that task is performed instead by the bourgeois-sexist ideological notion that women are non-productive, (though the fact that women are denied a wage for their domestic labour, in a society whose dominant ideology would express all productive activity in a monetary form, may serve to maintain this notion). Since the relation of economic dependency is but the immediate form of the material relationship on which proletarian marriage is currently founded, it can be considered only in that immediacy. And in this respect, it hardly establishes a tangential or vicarious affiliation of the woman to the class structure. On the contrary, just as the wage-system ensnares the proletarian into sharing the *immediate* interests of the individual capitalist for whom he labours, so the relation of economic dependency between the sexes acts as an overpowering constraint on the proletarian woman, binding her inextricably to the immediate class interests of her husband. (In this context, it would be fascinating to learn Millett's exact opinions on the nature of the proletarian male's investment in the class-system, and the benefits that are deemed to accrue to him therefrom.) Whether the woman shares a more permanent affiliation to her husband's class will depend on the nature of the infrastructural relationship between them, to the examination of which we can now at last turn.[12]

A MARXIST THEORY OF DOMESTIC LABOUR

I have argued that feminist demands for an investigation into the specific oppression of women were justified by the bankruptcy of the New Left's thinking on this issue, but also that, in embracing a peculiarly feminist perspective themselves, they have encountered a number of insuperable theoretical and practical problems. Their argument has been that, just as the basis of proletarian exploitation was located in the capitalist mode of production, so the basis of women's subjection was to be found in the organization of reproductive activities within the family. Not only does this argument not escape the sexist ideology of bourgeois society which, in identifying all productive activity with that of the capitalist economy, had relegated all supposedly non-productive activity to women; it also entails an unintentional breach between the class struggle and the fight for women's liberation. Feminism, in fact, commits a sin analogous to that perpetrated by Feuerbach when he preached the message of 'anthropological humanism'. It assumes that *all women*, whatever their social class, constitute a homogeneous group defined by their common subjugation, and that all women may therefore be organized around a series of demands arising out of this experience. This last claim is, of course, quite possibly true so long as it is recognized that such demands cannot be anything but incorrigibly reformist, and will not match up to the revolutionary aims of Firestone, Mitchell, and Millett. (This is not to say that such reforms would not be beneficial in themselves.) To attain a properly revolutionary perspective, one would have to consider women not as some idealized category, but as they really are, differentiated by their objective class affiliations and experiences, which in turn determine their collective capacity for anti-capitalist and anti-sexist action.

Instead of dichotemizing the material infrastructure into separate productive and reproductive systems, one must approach both as aspects of a complex unified totality.

The Marxian analysis of the capitalist mode of production is founded on the discovery that, while labour is the only source of value, it is not actually this activity which the wage-labourers sells. Rather, he sells his capacity to labour – his labour-power. Surplus value, which is that part of the value-product that the capitalist appropriates for himself, is a product of the difference between the value of labour-power, and the value that is added to the commodity produced by the expenditure of that labour-power. The selling of labour-power in exchange for a wage is, according to Marx, an exchange of equivalents. The value of labour-power, like that of any other commodity, is determined by the quantity of labour necessary to produce it. This cost will include the labourer's means of subsistence (which incidentally, is socially variable), the means of developing his particular kind of labour-power (for example, the costs of education and learning particular skills), and finally, since labour-power – like any other means of production – depreciates over time, its value will include the cost of its replacement: the mass of necessaries required for the maintenance of the children who will perpetuate the race of labourers.

Marx neglects one major cost in the production and reproduction of labour-power; and that is the value of domestic labour, typically performed by the labourer's wife. The main functions of domestic labour in the proletarian class are first, the daily reproduction of the labour-power of those members of the family who work in the market economy, and second, the reproduction of new generations of labourers. I am not, of course, arguing that this is the conscious purpose of members of proletarian families. But whatever their motivations, the family is coerced into making the daily reproduction of the wage-labourer's labour-power its foremost concern, by its collective financial dependence on the income from his wage. That is why the continuing good health of the main wage-earner is of such desperate importance to the proletarian family; why *his* needs may often be placed first in periods of privation; why the proletarian family will sink into such poverty and distress if he is seriously incapacitated; and why state benefits to families who find themselves in such a predicament *cannot* normally be allowed to exceed the income that would otherwise accrue from the sale of his labour-power. The state welfare system is designed to ensure that the main material function of the family will be the provision of labour-power for use in the market sectors of the economy.

Domestic labour is therefore of the utmost *productive* importance to the capitalist economy. Its product, labour-power, is a commodity which, like any other, has a determinate exchange value, that can be bought and sold on the free market, and whose expenditure is the source of all surplus value. Domestic labour is therefore deeply embedded in the productive infrastructure of the capitalist mode of production, for it is a *sine qua non* of the eventual production of surplus value. Women, as domestic labourers, produce a commodity, but unlike wage-labourers do not themselves become commodities.

These two activities, domestic production and direct capitalist production, are yet further integrated into a single unified process by the fact that a large proportion of the money that the wage-labourer receives in return for his labour-power provides the raw materials and the means of production of domestic labour. The women receives a proportion of the wages her husband has earned (wages that incorporate her own past dead labour), exchanges these for material commodities (i.e. use-values), and finally labours to transform these commodities into a form suitable for the physical and mental maintenance of her family, thereby ensuring the continued reproduction of the necessary labour-power. In other words, the woman's activities traditionally conceived as directed towards consumption, are simultaneously a form of productive labour. There is, in actuality, and contrary to current interpretations, no sharp division between the processes of production and consumption. They are, as Marx himself recognized, one and the same process. The labourer's individual consumption is 'a mere incident of production' (Marx 1961: 571). Even Marx, however, mistakenly and contradictorily, conceived such productive consumption as taking place 'outside the process of production' (Marx 1961: 571).

Neither are the processes of sexual reproduction and socialization to be envisaged as separate from the total process of capitalist production. For, as we have observed, labour-power does not only have to be reproduced on a daily basis, but must also be replaced from one genera-tion to the next. This generational reproduction of labour-power con-stitutes the material underpinning of sexual reproduction and the socialization of the young of the proletarian class. It must be understood, of course, that this is a class, and not an individual phenomenon of which we are speaking.

Labour-power as the quality of a living labourer, is not an undif-ferentiated capacity. Capitalist production requires qualitatively different types of labour-power in varying proportions, and at different stages in its development. Most particularly, as the organic composition of capital increases (that is, as capital intensive industry replaces pro-duction based on simple undifferentiated labour) the demand for more skilled, informed, educated, and disciplined labour-power increases correspondingly. Attempts are then made, especially by the capitalist state, to gain some control over the process of reproducing the new generation of labourers. In the first place, the process may be partially socialized, with the state or sometimes private organizations assuming responsibility for the supervision of the education, health, and welfare of the embryonic labour-force, a process which might fancifully be called the 'socialization of socialization', but which is more generally referred to as the family's loss of functions. This development is of exceptional importance for the collective situation of women, since it usually in-volves the transfer of many of their numbers into social production – if in a restricted range of occupations. In addition, immense interest is taken in the methods of socialization still being employed in the domestic context. As Parsons has shrewdly observed, women are increasingly pressured into rationalizing their techniques of child-rearing, and in cases where they are deemed inadequate, their right to autonomous control over this process within the family may well be curtailed.

Finally we may ask what prospects this analysis holds out for the future of proletarian women in capitalistic countries. Above all, it must have become obvious that the classical socialist demands – for the entry of women into social production, and the socialization of domestic activities – are in fact being met *within* capitalist society itself. Socialists should not really find this so very remarkable, since Marx's own analysis suggested that the socialization of production (and to this we now have to add, of domestic production and reproduction) was the historic task of capitalism – not of socialism. Indeed, it is this process that creates the contradictions in a society characterized by private appropriation. The entry of women into social production and the socialization of domestic activities are indeed preconditions of female emancipation, but they are not developments that can await voluntary implementation through the conscious political programme of a successful revolutionary organization. Rather, they are developments integral to advanced capitalism, aspects indeed of capitalist planning, which should facilitate the emergence of proletarian women as collective historical subjects.

Evidently, if we accept this theory, women can no longer be regarded as marginal to the capitalist mode of production. On the contrary, their position locates them at the hub of a strategic contradiction in the capitalist dynamic: that between the social production of commodities, their private appropriation, and the collective inability of consumers to buy them. Whilst capitalist enterprise must constantly strive to expand its mass consumption markets, it must simultaneously act to deflate the rising level of wages. The reality of this contradiction seems recently to be once again percolating into the consciousness of proletarian men and women, and it is at least arguable that its consequences are most immediately evident to the women rather than the men. Notwithstanding this, however, it must be said that, despite signs of a growing militancy among working-class housewives, the problems of organizing such militancy into politically effective collective action at the national level remain as formidable as ever.

I am confident that the analysis presented in the last section of this paper will eventually supersede traditional perspectives on women in the Marxist intellectual tradition. I say this in the belief that theoretical structures impose upon us their own problematics. With Althusser I would argue that:

> 'The sighting is no longer the act of an individual subject endowed with the faculty of vision . . . the sighting is the act of its structural conditions, it is the relation of immanent reflection of the problematic and *its* objects and *its* problems.' (Althusser and Balibar 1970: 25).

It was inevitable that once the demand for an analysis of the specific oppression of women was raised and widely accepted (and this demand itself would be the product of an encounter with theory in the context of a definite and singular set of social relations), that a materialist analysis of domestic production and its relationship to the market economy would shortly follow. This inevitability is indicated by the fact that there have been, so far as I know, at least three apparently independent discoveries of this relation within the last two years.[13] But of much more significance for future prospects is the fact that this problematic has now become the focal concern for Marxists inside or associated with the Women's Liberation Movement.

An historical and materialist approach to *all* the social processes of production and reproduction, viewed as a totality, has produced a theory that meets the demand for an analysis of the material bases of those oppressions that are specific to women; that escapes from the hegemony of sexist ideology by recognizing women as historical subjects, as well as passive objects of the historical process; that structurally integrates the relationship between the sexes and that prevailing between proletarian and capitalist classes; and finally, that need not commit the fallacy of assuming that all women share essentially identical conditions of material and social existence. The theory is eminently historical because, unlike Firestone's book, it incorporates not only changes in the forces and relations of reproduction, but also those of production, social and domestic, within a unitary historical process. The structural relation of domestic production, and hence of proletarian women, to market production will therefore be seen to vary according to the historical juncture. The work that women do in the home can no longer be idly dismissed as pre-capitalist, for not only does it respond to changing demands for different kinds of labour-power, but only develops itself into a form of commodity production when labour-power becomes a commodity: that is, under capitalistic conditions.

Notes

1 The term 'academic' is admittedly an unsatisfactory epithet for such disparate theoretical approaches as funtionalism, new-Weberianism, and so on. It is used here merely as a convenient shorthand designation of that body of sociological theory that has been developed in the academies *without* ever becoming explicitly attached to any organized political movement.

2 For a discussion of the usage of 'structure', see M. Godelier (1967).

3 It is difficult to guage the extent to which this ideology was accepted by other social classes since, despite its hegemonic tendencies, its main features would have been at variance with the experience of proletarian families, where women continued to participate directly in the market economy.

4 Incidentally, the same view is implicit in Parsons' analysis of the husband-father as the key boundary-role between the family and the economy. It is the father's occupational role that is assumed to necessarily act as the source of status for the whole family of pro-

creation, and the family income is moreover largely dependent on his occupational earnings. Further to this, Parsons argues that the segregation of sex roles and the exclusion of women from the occupational system is essential for the preservation of family solidarity, since the latter would be disrupted if individual members of the family were allowed to achieve differential class status.

5 An opposing view is put forward by Juliet Mitchell:

'Of course, the ideological concept of the family embodies a paradox which reflects the contradiction between it and the dominant, capitalist method of organising production . . . When under capitalism it was made to embody as an ideal, what had been its economic function under feudalism, a chronic contradiction took place. What had hitherto been a *united* unit within the overall diversified social structure became, because of changing social conditions, a *divided* one. The peasant family works together for itself – it *is* one. The family and production are homogeneous. But the members of a working class family work separately, for different bosses in different places and, though the family interest unites them, the separation of their place and conditions of their work fragments, perforce, that unity. Part of the function of the ideology of the family under capitalism is to preserve this unity in the face of its essential break-up.' (Mitchell 1971: 156-7)

6 An additional, not altogether compatible, belief was that the proletarian family was undergoing a process of decomposition because of the extensive wage-labour of women. Compare for example Kollontai's two pamphlets: *Communism and the Family* and *Sexual Relations and the Class Struggle*.

7 A word of caution is necessary here, since the presumed conservatism of women stems from an ignorance of women's struggles in the past. Such militancy has often passed unrecorded by the history books, and the task of rediscovering it is only just begun (cf. especially the valuable research being carried out by Sheila Rowbotham).

8 There is another stream of Marxist criticism that attests to the privation and brutality of much working-class family life. But such microstudies seem to have made little impression on the New Left perspectives just outlined.

9 The structure of Production as a key element in woman's situation (cf. previous quote above) refers only to market production.

10 This is acknowledged to be 'a case of that phenomenon Weber defined as "Herrschaft",' (Kate Millett 1971: 24-5).

11 The term 'proletariat' is used here in the strict Marxian sense as that class which, being excluded from ownership of the means of production, is forced to sell its only commodity: labour-power.

12 In the final section we only have time to deal with sex-relationships in

the proletarian class. Within the capitalist class the key question to be raised would concern the extent to which women had independent ownership over means of production.

13 The other accounts are: H. Edwards (1971), P. Morton (1970), and M. Dalla Costa (1972), with an Introduction by S. James. (James, at least, is acquainted with Morton's article.)

References

ALTHUSSER, L. and BALIBAR, E. 1970. *Reading Capital* (trans. by Ben Brewster). London: New Left Books.

DALLA COSTA, M. 1972. *Women and the Subversion of the Community.* Bristol: Falling Wall Press.

EDWARDS, H. 1971. Housework and Exploitation: A Marxist Analysis. In *The First Revolution, A Journal of Female Liberation.* July.

FIRESTONE, SHULASMITH. 1972. *The Dialectice of Sex.* London: Paladin

GODELIER, M. 1967. Structure and Contradiction in *Capital. Socialist Register.*

GOODE, W. J. 1964. *The Family.* Englewood Cliffs, N J : Prentice-Hall.

LENSKI, G. 1966. *Power and Privilege.* New York: McGraw-Hill.

MARX, K. 1961. *Capital, Vol. I.* Moscow: Foreign Languages Press (English edition published by Lawrence & Wishart, London).

MARX, K. and ENGELS, F. 1968. *Selected Works.* London: Lawrence & Wishart.

MILLETT, KATE. 1971. *Sexual Politics.* London: Hart-Davis.

MITCHELL, JULIET. 1966. The Longest Revolution. *New Left Review.*
—— 1971. *Woman's Estate.* Harmondworth: Penguins.

MORTON, P. 1970. A Woman's Work is Never Done. *Leviathan* **2**(1) March.

PARKIN, F. 1972. *Class, Inequality and Political Order.* London: Paladin.

JANE MARCEAU

Education and Social Mobility in France

INTRODUCTION

This paper examines education and social mobility in France in relation to the structure of opportunity and the system of class relations. The structure of opportunity I take to be composed of a number of factors: the economic, which constitutes the effective offer of various types of occupation and the effective demand for certain types of qualification; the educational system which distributes the formal qualifications; and a set of other social institutions such as the family. These interact together to place individuals in social and economic roles. The patterned inequalities which become apparent are here taken to result from the class structure and class relations. An individual's position in the opportunity structure is his market position in a wider sense than that used by Weber as it includes the crucial years before he comes on to the labour market proper; so that in the present analysis capital will be taken to include not only economic capital but also 'cultural' capital and 'social' capital. The various factors together form the context within which persons are, or are not, socially mobile and the constraints which determine the possibility, distance and type of upward movement. Stress will be laid on the limited nature of the opportunity structure for most members of French society: the economic structure allows little upward movement for most people and the education system by its own logic, closely linked to the nature of the class system, severely limits the acquisition by the less privileged of the qualifications most important for upward social mobility, while, at the same time, it protects the most privileged from downward mobility.

The school by its verdicts on individual 'gifts' or merits, which it takes as 'natural' rather than 'social', acts both as a legitimator of social positions and as a placement agency. Its verdicts are likely to be both harsher and more crucial to success the less well endowed a person is with other forms of capital while at the same time giving less and less 'return' the further one moves away from the school system. Bourdieu and his colleagues have shown the crucial role of the education system as that of transmitting a body of cultural norms and beliefs, while its neutrality gives it a privileged place as an institution which disguises the relations of force in French society by transforming them into symbollic relations. Through the management and sanctioning of the cultural knowledge that is both virtually the *sine qua non* of a position in the upper classes and the declared justification of that position and those classes, the school explains in its own terms (the only ones generally acceptable in a society that declares itself democratic) why it has allocated people to specific occupational roles both high and low. This function is particularly important in a society with an ideology of upward social mobility through personal 'merit' and 'achievement' but one which, as will be shown in this paper, does not present many opportunities for that mobility for most members of French society.

The close links between the logic of the educational system and the class system may be seen in the extremely close 'fit' between the hierarchies of prestige of different institutions, the social origins of the pupils, and the social and economic return on investment in various types of education. Discussion of the social composition of the different types of school shows the severity and systematic nature of the educational selection process. My analysis of the educational data, and the theoretical framework of discussion of it, are based on the work of Bourdieu and his colleagues.

In the present paper I show the ways in which individuals and groups in French society accumulate advantages or disadvantages in the opportunity structure. I therefore present data on the occupational structure and the kinds of posts that are effectively available and show that, in spite of great changes in the French economy since 1945, vast numbers of jobs still require only a very low level of skill, and that the non-manual and higher white-collar jobs are still only a small proportion of the total. I then discuss the patterns found in the educational system in terms of 'who gets what'. Third, I outline the amount and kind of social mobility that occurs in France and the 'distance' travelled. The fourth section discusses the 'return on investment' accruing to various diplomas and the extent to which such diplomas are sufficient in themselves as a basis for occupational placement.

CLASS STATUS AND MOBILITY

The content and importance of the concepts 'class', 'status', 'strata', and 'social mobility' vary from analysis to analysis. Here I propose to use the term 'class' to denote a number of persons who find themselves in a basically similar position within the opportunity structure in relation to the three kinds of capital - social, economic, and cultural. On this basis three broad classes will be distinguished: the upper classes or bourgeoisie (*classes supérieures*), mainly owners and managers in industry and commerce, members of the liberal professions, senior civil servants, political leaders, and academics; the middle classes (*classes moyennes*), which comprise middle and lower supervisory staff, primary-school teachers, white-collar workers, and artisans; and the working class, (*classes populaires*), which include both farmers and farm workers and manual workers in the secondary and tertiary sectors (Bertaux 1969). It should be noted that the French terminology differs from the English, especially where the middle classes are concerned, the *classes moyennes* being lower in the scale and very heterogeneous in terms of origins, professions, and life-chances.

Status in France is very largely correlated with class position in the above sense. The relationship between professional and social mobility and status change is always problematic; social mobility involves a change in a constellation of factors, and there have been many discussion of the linkages between them (e.g. Archer and Giner 1971; intro, Parkin 1971). All aspects of a person's social position may not be congruent or may not change simultaneously but there I agree with Parkin that

'. . . . the background of the class structure, and indeed the entire reward system of modern western society, is the occupational order. Other sources of economic and symbolic advantage do coexist alongside the occupational order but for the great majority of the population, these tend to be secondary to those deriving from the division of labour . . .' (Parkin 1972: 18)

Moreover, material and symbolic rewards are so closely associated that

'. . . it is plausible to regard status honour as an emergent property generated by the class system. More concisely we can consider it as a system of social evaluation arising from the moral judgements of those who occupy dominant positions in the class structure . . . those who control the major agencies of socialisation typically occupy privileged class positions. As a consequence, their definitions of social reality and their moral judgements are far more likely to be blessed with the stamp of public legitimacy than are the social and moral constructs of those in subordinate class positions.' (Parkin 1972: 42)

Social mobility based on occupational changes implies some kind of hierarchical occupational scale. In France no large-scale studies have been carried out into how people rank occupations, but we find that there exist the same kind of patterned inequalities as in other nations and here I assume that the ranking is similar to that in other western industrial societies.

The socially mobile *par excellence* are often considered to be those who move across the manual – non-manual line as this is where the constellation of class characteristics is most acute. However this division conceals what at least in France are important movements within, and characteristics of, the non-manual sections. Thus when considering some aspects of the opportunity structure in France it seems best to use a model with the three major divisions described above and based on the following, smaller INSEE (French statistical agency) categories which largely reflect these inequalities.

Patrons de l'industrie et du commerce:
   owners (employers) in industry and commerce   *classes supérieures*
Professions libérales et cadres supérieurs;   upper classes
   liberal professions and senior executives

Cadres moyens;
   middle and lower supervisory personnel   *classes moyennes*
Employés et artisans;   middle classes
   white-collar workers and artisans

Ouvriers; qualifiés, specialisés et manoeuvres;
   manual workers; skilled, semi-skilled, unskilled
Exploitants agricoles;   *classes populaires*
   farmers   working classes
Salariés agricoles;
   farm workers

On the basis of these divisions this paper will show both considerable job mobility and much professional closure. Both are aspects of the same system and the one cannot be understood without the other. The first component of that system is the occupational structure which determines the objective possibilities open to individuals.

PART ONE: ECONOMIC AND SOCIAL TRANSFORMATIONS

Although France in the mid-to-late-nineteenth century underwent a burst of industrialization, involving considerable population transfers from agriculture to industry and country to town, the development was not sustained. The 1891 Census showed as many people living from agriculture as from all other economic activities put together and the scale of enterprises remained much as it had been in the eighteenth century (Dupeux 1964). In areas where industries (mainly textiles and iron and steel in the north and centre) became dominant, a new and powerful bourgeoisie gradually took a leading part in the affairs of state, in the *grand corps* of the administration, in Parliament, the colonies, and in the liberal professions (Lhomme 1960; Morazé 1957; Dansette 1954; Priouret 1963).

But this bourgeoisie was not on the whole an expansionist one and it was only after the crisis of the First World War that fundamental economic transformations got under way again. In the inter-war period France went through a series of booms and slumps. In spite of the introduction of new production-line techniques (and the birth of the semi-skilled worker, the *ouvrier spécialisé*) and new sources of energy, the scale of enterprises remained small and in 1936 the GNP was at its 1924 level (Dupeux 1964). In spite of the political upheavals of 1936 and after, bourgeois families largely continued to control both industry and the State. It is only since the Second World War that most of the important changes have come about and the essentials of the economic and social structure of present-day France have appeared. To many sections of the population this has meant much upheaval but some of the more important structural aspects have changed only slowly (Parodi 1971).

After the war, changed political circumstances meant that the economy could be restarted with the nationalizing of many basic industries and the planning of priorities to be given to different sectors – the whole to a great extent financed by Marshall Aid. The result of this, helped by the general post-war boom in Europe, was an enormous leap in GNP and great changes in the economic structure.

Of the changes in an economy which is industrializing fast perhaps the most striking are those involving movement of the economically active population from one sector to another. These movements can be seen in the following table:

TABLE 1

Percentage distribution of active population by sector of the economy

Economic sector	1851	1901	1921	1931	1954	1962	1968
primary	53	42	43	37	28	21	16
secondary	25	31	29	33	36	38	39
tertiary	22	27	28	30	36	41	45

Source: adapted from Dupeux 1964: 33 and 'Données essentielles sur l'industrie française', *Economie et Statistique* 1970: 14:37.

H

From these figures can be seen, especially since 1954, a rapid decline in agriculture and a great growth in industry, above all of the tertiary sector. Thus, although the French labour force until very recently stayed nearly stable, between nineteen and twenty million, its distribution changed radically.

The economic changes reflected in these data broadly show the effective demand for different types of labour and types of diploma. There is no absolute correlation – in the 1930s French writers were bemoaning the lack of jobs for doctors and lawyers then graduating from the universities (Dubois 1937) and graduate and other specialized unemployment is evident at present. The changes in economic structure have led to the decline of some occupational groups and the growth of others.

Groups in decline

The major occupational groups in decline are those in the extractive industries and agriculture. Miners lost 25 per cent of their number between 1962 and 1968. Agriculture lost 15 per cent of its labour force between 1954 and 1962 and another 25 per cent between 1962 and 1968. The early migrants were farm labourers but now include large numbers of farmers. The great majority of farm migrants went into unskilled jobs – 30 per cent became labourers, *manoeuvres*, 20 per cent went into the building trades and 14 per cent into transport. Only 7,500 out of the 80,000 leaving agriculture each year could be accommodated on government re-training schemes and there is no means whereby agricultural diplomas can be converted into equivalents useful elsewhere (de Farcy 1971: 277). Small entrepreneurs and employers in industry and commerce have also been decreasing in numbers. 'Independents' declined by 12 per cent between 1954 and 1962 and since have dropped further. They still constitute, however, about 6-7 per cent of the active population and are important both as a reference group for many workers and to some extent as a real means of upward mobility through a change of status from wage-earner to 'independent' (Andrieux and Lignon 1966; Frisch 1966).

We need also to break down the categories further to see what such changes mean for the effective opportunities open to job-seekers. In order for a person to move either up or down there must be jobs to go to, an elementary point but one not always given its due weight by sociologists. It is here that the structure of the employment market is crucial, and the expansion or contraction of the different sectors.

The expanding groups: technicians, cadres,[1] and workers

With the massive industrialization and modernization of the economic infra-structure in France since 1945, the increasing importance of the more complex automated industries and the concentration of small enterprises into big units, much sociological attention has been focused on the rise of new categories of job, and on the increase in demand for certain established ones including technicians and *cadres* of all kinds. These groups are often thought to constitute an avenue of social mobility *par excellence* – sons of the working classes moving into the lower ranks of the *classes moyennes* as technicians, and the sons of the *classes moyennes* becoming *cadres*. There has indeed been a considerable rise in their numbers. The ranks of the technicians, defined as intermediary roles between *ingénieurs* and production workers, grew by 67 per cent between 1945 and 1962 and have continued to increase since, though more slowly (d'Hugues, Peslier 1969: 267). By 1968, there were more than 500,000. Such growth is impressive but we find that the group represents *in total* only around 2-4 per cent of the active non-agricultural population over the period concerned. The capacity of the category to absorb newcomers is not, therefore, very considerable in relation to the total labour force.

Ingénieurs, too have been increasingly rapidly, by 25 per cent between 1954 and 1962, although in that year they constituted only 0.95 per cent of the active non-farm population, and this includes both those with diplomas and the self-taught (*autodidactes*), who acquired their position through length of service and proven ability.

The category office employees (*employés de bureau*) is growing fastest of all. By 1962 it involved more than one and a half million people, 10 per cent of the non-farm active population but it is largely composed of women – one in every five working women – and is well known as one with virtually no chances of promotion. Non-manual rather than manual work may be promotion for many of the girls, but office jobs will not take them far up the ladder.

The administrative hierarchy could, theoretically, be important for social mobility in the middle levels. However, although middle administrative personnel (*cadres administratifs moyens*) increased by 34 per cent between 1962 and 1968 they then only constituted 2.5 per cent of the active non-farm population. Considerable growth occurred at the high level too, to the extent that in the 1968 Census nearly one million *cadres supérieurs* could be found, but the INSEE category is very diverse and includes the liberal professions, bankers, librarians, magistrates and police officers, senior management, including *ingénieurs*, and teachers in secondary and higher education. In total, the *cadres supérieurs* are not only a very small percentage of the active population, 4.8 per cent in 1968 as against 3 per cent in 1954, but the different professions included are growing at different rates. Thus, while between 1962 and 1968 the category grew by 30 per cent, the greatest growth rate is found among the teaching and scientific professions which increased by two thirds (*Economie et Statistique* 1972: 40:53). This is particularly important for two reasons. The first is that as far as access to positions of power in organizations is concerned, the posts available grew by only 20-30 per cent. The second, which is of special interest here, is that it shows that one of the major results of the educational system is the renewal and increase of the ranks of the educators – a reproductive effect. One may see why Bourdieu has been led to conclude that the place where the diplomas given by the education system have the most value for mobility is within the education system itself. As we shall see, not only are the opportunities outside that system limited, but other factors play an important role too in placing people on the job market.

Here we must emphasize too that the working class (*ouvriers*) is also growing. Half the new jobs created are in the tertiary sector on average but many of those jobs are for *ouvriers*. Between 1962 and 1968 they increased by 9 per cent (nearly 11 per cent if men alone are counted). In absolute numbers they were 7,698,600 out of a total force (including agriculture) of 20,439,160 persons; that is about 37.7 per cent of the active population. Moreover, not only was the category increasing proportionately but it was also increasing *faster* than the total labour force, 9 per cent against 6 per cent (men alone nearly 11 per cent). A greater proportion of the population than before therefore now finds itself within the working class.

Within the working class, it was the elite, foremen (*contremaîtres*), which increased most, by 17.6 per cent. Skilled workers also increased by 14 per cent but were closely followed by the semi-skilled workers (*ouvriers spécialisés*), who grew by 13 per cent. The unskilled (*manoeuvres*) declined but only by half of one per cent (Parodi 1971: 268-9)

The 1971 INSEE survey carried out on industrial enterprises employing over ten people, showed that, of industry's salaried employees, *ouvriers* form 70 per cent and of these one half (one third male) are either *ouvriers spécialisés* or *manoeuvres*, that is, semi- or unskilled. Many of the jobs offered on the labour market must then still be unskilled or of low skill requirement. Such data suggest considerable limitations on upward movement within the working class from basically unskilled to skilled.[2]

The Regional distribution of opportunity

Regionally there are important variations in opportunity. The non-manual are expanding categories in certain areas and especially the Paris region, which in 1962 contained 18 per cent of the population but employed 49 per cent of the *ingénieurs* and 70 per cent of all industrial research personnel. Praderie (1968: 55) notes the concentration of tertiary sector jobs, the 'least manual', in towns, especially the larger ones. The wave of urbanization that took place in France after 1945 was very uneven and in 1968 one third of the population still lived in *communes* of less than 2000 people, so that many continued to be more or less isolated from the centres of non-manual employment.

Tertiary sector and 'white-coat' (*blouse blanche*) jobs are also concentrated in certain types of industry. By the late 1950s, technicians were principally in energy and chemical industries (Legoux 1959: 75) and in 1971 it was the energy sector that employed the lowest proportion of *O.S.* and *manoeuvres* (less than 10 per cent against 25 per cent *cadres*). On the other hand, in industries such as mining, textiles, and furniture, the proportion of unskilled and semi-skilled workers may be as much as half and is seldom less than 25-30 per cent (Cézard 1972: 49-51). Many of these industries have a well-known regional distribution.

It has been established too that better chances of promotion occur within the larger firms. In France in 1968 out of 350,000 industrial enterprises, 310,000 employed less than 200 people. While 21 per cent of the employed population work in enterprises of more than 5,000, these are highly concentrated by sector and region. Thus in many areas the great majority of the labour force works in small firms with few *cadres* and little room for upward promotion. Moreover these figures do not include building and 'public works', where firms are notoriously small, unstable, and unskilled, but which employ more than one person in every ten of the total work force (Données essentielles ... 1970: 46).

Conclusions

The above section has shown the structure of employment in France and the limitations of the labour market. Offers of employment tend to be for low-skilled posts in the vast majority of cases. While certain non-manual categories of job are growing fast – for instance, technician and other white-collar jobs, especially in the tertiary sector, they constitute only a tiny minority of the posts available. The objective possibilities of upward social mobility are severely limited by the constraints of the occupation structure.

PART TWO: EDUCATION: ADVANCEMENT AND ELIMINATION

The following section will demonstrate the extent of the severity and systematic nature of the selction process within the education system illustrating how it orientates young people in directions which they would very largely have followed anyway – that is, through the operation of other social institutions such as the family. The 'fit' between different 'publics' and the schools to which they go will be especially emphasized.

The selection process

Secondary education Studies throughout the 1950s and 1960s emphasized factors such as 'cultural heritage', language, parental aspirations, teacher perception, etc., each giving varying weights to the age and background of the children as determinants in the selection process (Girard 1971; Bourdieu 1966; Berger and Benjamin 1964; Grignon 1968, 1971). At each stage the elimination and the auto-elimination of certain kinds of children becomes more and more severe. The first formal selection occurs around the age of eleven years, as summarized in *Table 2* opposite.

It can be seen from these figures how closely the choice of school is linked to social origins. At the top, most prestigious level, the *lycées*, there are few children from the *classes populaires*, a high number from the *classes supérieures*, with the *classes moyennes* in the middle. When the figures are analysed by school section – classical, modern, 'transition', and technical – one finds a similar distribution. During the 1960s attempts were made by the government to make the schools more open, and now virtually all children go into some kind of *sixième* class. However, this has little altered the kind of distribution found and the choice of school and section is as crucial as before.

From the end of the second year in secondary school a series of important educational choices must be made, although theoretically not final ones, between a variety of types of class and school. Secondary schools do not all teach the same subjects nor have similarly qualified teachers, and within the schools there are 'cycles' of longer or shorter

TABLE 2

Educational choice and socio-professional group at entry to the sixième.*
1963 percentages

| | classes populaires | | class moyennes | | classes supérieures | business |
| | | | | | | |
Type of school	farmers and farm workers	manual workers	artisans com- mercial	white - collar workers	liberal pro- fessions	higher exec. civil servants
primary school	59	57	32	31	10	6
C.E.G.† ⎱6è	23⎰	29⎰	34⎰	34⎰	23⎰	19⎰
lycees ⎰	14⎰	16⎰	32⎰	33⎰	67⎰	75⎰
total in sixiéme classes	36	45	66	67	90	94

Sixièmes are the first classes in secondary schools
† *Colleges d'Enseignement Général*
Source: table adapted from A. Girard *et al.* 1963: 31.

duration which constitute roads, *filières*, leading to different academic goals and occupational possibilities; while in the C.E.G. and the new *Collèges d'Enseignement Secondaire* (C.E.S., the French 'comprehensive' equivalent), the 'transition' classes lead outwards at an early age. *Table 3* shows the probability of certain choices by socio- economic background. The probabilities are calculated using the numbers of children in *quatrième* classes, aged from twelve to sixteen years, from a given social class divided by the total number of children of that age from that social class.

Higher education The above tables show the severity and systematic nature of selection for different types of secondary schooling. The process continues in higher education with an even more accentuated 'under-selection' of students from the *classes populaires* and an increasing preponderance of those from higher social origins. Pioneering work by Bourdieu and Passeron and their colleagues throughout the 1960s showed the pattern of distribution by social origins of these students. Their results are confirmed by the Ministry of Education itself, as can be seen from *Table 4*.

Here we see not only the over-representation of students from upper-class backgrounds but also the clear class distinctions by faculty. The

TABLE 3

Probability of educational choice at the level of the quatrième* by socio-professional origins

socio-professional category	4è classics	modern 1	modern 2	practical	C.E.T.
liberal professions higher executive	0.312	0.231	0.199	0.051	0.097
cadres moyens white-collar workers	0.150	0.182	0.287	0.054	0.203
patrons, industry commerce	0.131	0.146	0.257	0.040	0.145
workers	0.050	0.090	0.202	0.079	0.259
farmers	0.049	0.064	0.199	0.032	0.103
farm workers	0.037	0.061	0.251	0.087	0.193

* *Quatrièmes* are the third year classes in secondary schools

Source: Baudelot and Establet 1971: 76.

TABLE 4

Social origins of French university students by discipline in 1960-61 and 1966-7 – by percentage

parents socio-prof. category	law a b	letters a b	sciences a b	medecine a b	phar-macy a b	all disciplines a b
patrons, ind. and commerce	18 16	17 14	18 14	17 15	24 19	18 15
lib., profs., higher exec.	28 30	26 25.5	27 27	34 41	42 43	29 29
middle exec.	16 14	24 17	18 17	12 14	13 12	18 16
white-collar employees	9 9	6 9	10 8.5	7 8	5 6	8 8.5
workers	5 7	6 12	7 13	2 5	2 3	5 10
farmers and farm workers	5 6	7 7	8 8	4 3	5 5	6 7
diverse	19 18.5	13 16	13.5 12	23 14	9 12	15 15
total nos.						
60-61:	29,700	55,300	64,000	26,800	8,000	183,000
66-67:	80,100	129,600	114,700	46,400	13,900	384,000

a = 1960-61; b = 1966-67.

Source: 'Les Étudiants en France . . .', *Notes et Etudes Documentaires* (Ministère de l'Education Nationale 1969: 3577: 13)

author of the article notes that the sons of workers are increasing in numbers every year, especially in arts and sciences. In their analysis Bourdieu and Passeron and their colleagues have underlined the 'relegation' of working-class students to those faculties whose graduates have the least good chances on the employment market. The crisis among arts graduates is not limited to France, but in France science graduates from the universities have special difficulties, as the best science-based jobs go to the *alumni* of the *Grandes Ecoles*. At the other end of the spectrum the most bourgeois faculties are pharmacy, medicine, and law, i.e., those with assured professional outlets.

This systematic selection reaches its apogee in the *Grandes Ecoles*. The following table shows the social origins not only of the students of the *Grandes Ecoles* but also of the special classes that prepare candidates for the entry examination to them; both may be compared to the faculty students.

TABLE 5

Social origins of faculty students, and candidates and students of the Grandes Ecoles

socio-professional category	fac. sci.	fac. letters	taupe	khâgne	Poly-tech.	Ulm sci.	Ulm letters
farm workers	3	3	0.5	3	0.4	2	0.6
farmers	6	5	0.5	2	2	2	–
workers	15	15	4	4	4	2.5	5
white-collar workers	9.5	10	6.5	4	5	6	8
artisans shop keepers	5	5	2	1	1	2	1
middle exec. primary school	8	9	5	3	4	3	2
teachers	5	5	3	6	6	3	5
higher exec.	9.5	11	21	30	26	21	30.5
industrialists	2	3	6	2			
engineers	8	6	15	5	20	14.5	6
liberal profs. secondary and	8.5	9	8	10	10	14	10
higher teachers	4.5	5	5	15	10	18	19

Taupe prepares for *Polytechnique: khâgne* for Ulm, Ulm is the *Ecole Normale Supérieure*

Source: Bourdieu *et al.* 1970 unpublished paper: Annexe I

Thus we find that within the general sections of the education system from the end of primary school to the highest academic institutions, children of humbler social origins are eliminated, or eliminate themselves, to a much greater extent than those higher on the social ladder.

Technical education

The *Collèges d'Enseignement Technique* (C.E.T.), the lowest-grade state technical schools, have pupils from the lowest social origins, and within the schools they vary systematically between the short and long full-time teaching cycles, leading respectively to the diploma, *Certificat d'Aptitude Professionel* (C.A.P.), and the various *brevets*. In the higher level *lycées techniques* one finds on average higher social origins. The same is true of the final rung of this part of the technical ladder, the *Instituts Universitaires de Technologie*, I.U.T. (and of course the *Grandes Ecoles* as we have seen).

Relatively little investigation has been done by French sociologists on the pupils of the technical schools (perhaps that is also part of the prestige hierarchy ?) and what follows owes much to Grignon's excellent study (Grignon 1971).

Grignon notes that although the C.E.T. are at the bottom of the academic hierarchy, and are the places to which other schools send their 'worst' products, nevertheless even they select an elite. Thus while pupils with poor academic records have little chance of entering or remaining in general education they also have little chance of entering a C.E.T. Academic criteria are dominant even over learning a manual trade and entry to a C.E.T. seems to be becoming even more competitive. Moreover, says Grignon, although the C.E.T. might seem to be the 'école du peuple' in fact the children from the least favoured social classes have less chance of entering one, and of any apprenticeship at school, than have bourgeois children of entering the high schools of the general education system. For the sons of the *classes populaires*, who represent 70 per cent of all C.E.T. pupils, entry to a C.E.T. remains less propable than entry direct to the productive system or 'on the job' apprenticeship. The probabilities only become the same for children from the higher levels of the working class and the lower levels of the *classes moyennes*. The situation seems to be constant over the generations, varying with the education of the parents – the higher the father's diploma the greater the chances.

Moreover, within the technical schools there is a hierarchy among the trades taught, a grading based by the teachers on the 'intellectuality' and cleanliness of the job and the ease with which one afterwards obtains a post. Again the academic and the social hierarchies are apparent: the students of electrical trades and mechanics are, for instance, from higher social backgrounds than their colleagues in boilermaking or the building trades. Teachers grade the pupils in the entry examination and orient the 'good' ones towards the more skilled and better paid trades (Grignon 1971: 81). Pupils coming from the *lycées* and the C.E.G., the 'failures' of the secondary schools, are oriented to the 'better' trades and never to the building ones, for example.

Adult technical education shows a similar pattern. For instance, the *Conservatoire National des Arts et Metiers*, C.N.A.M., which offers part-time courses leading to the diplomas of *ingénieur*, caters more for the sons of the *classes moyennes* and the 'failed' sons of the bourgeoisie than for working-class sons, in spite of the fact that possession of the *baccalauréat* is not required. As befits its marginal academic status and intake, the return on the very considerable investment for the few successful students is less than that to qualifications acquired in the conventional manner (Champagne and Grignon 1969, unpublished paper).

Finally, and perhaps one of the most important points to make here, there is no real parallel technical-school system. As Baudelot and Establet put it, each level leads directly out into production. Except in a few rare cases it is not possible for a child in a technical school to continue his studies further. At each stage the way is outward and not upward as each stage is dominated by the level of the general education system which leads to it (Grignon 1971: 43). Thus a person who has a C.A.P. cannot enter for a *baccalauréat:* a person with a technical *bac.* may not enter the literary faculties but must read sciences[3] (although a man who has read classics has at least until recently been able to study medicine or sciences). The *brevets* may only lead to I.U.T. which prepare students 'directly for entry to professional life in supervisory technical functions in production and services' ('Les étudiants en France . . .' 1969: 8). They do not lead on to higher university diplomas and even less to the *Grandes Ecoles*, even the most technical ones.

PART III. SOCIAL MOBILITY AND THE RETURN ON INVESTMENT

In the first two parts of this paper I have outlined the objective conditions of the economic and educational aspects of the opportunity structure in France. In this part I want to show how these aspects interact to produce what may be measured as social mobility, and this will involve a discussion of the return on investment in education. Such returns are hard to measure with precision and the data are rather scanty, but since they fit so well into the logic of the whole system a small number of crucial cases may be sufficient.

Social mobility: who moves and where to?

Three major studies on social and professional mobility have been carried out in France. The first, which supplied the much used and recently criticized data used by Rogoff and Lipset, was carried out by the Institut National des Etudes Demographique (INED) in 1948. The sample under-represented the worker (*ouvrier*) population and, as used by Rogoff, over-estimated social mobility (Bertaux 1969: 448-490). But the data are useful for a picture of social immobility for comparison with later data. The considerable degree of occupational stability can be seen in the table below:

TABLE 6

Occupational stability over three generations – percentages

occupations of persons interviewed	fathers	social origins		fathers-in-law
		paternal G-F	maternal G-F	
farmers	83	78	73	74
farm workers	37	31	30	29
workers, skilled and unskilled	48	35	35	40
small businessmen, artisans	54	36	28	36
state employees II* white-collar workers	31	11	9	30
state employees I supervisory†	17	10	5	22
industrialists and liberal professions	32	16	15	28

* *fonctionnaires*   † *cadres*

Source: Adapted from tables in Brésard 1950: 540-541

These results largely refer to the period preceeding the rapid in-dustrialization since 1945, but they are mostly confirmed by the more recent data gathered by INSEE in 1964 and covering changes in the professional situation of persons employed between 1959 and 1964.

Intra-generational mobility

The INSEE data show fairly small amounts of intra-generational social mobility, measured by professional changes, in the five-year period. The following table summarizes the movements of the categories of most interest here.

TABLE 7

Changes in socio-professional category, 1959-1964 – percentages

socio-prof. categ. men 1959	upward mobility	downward mobility
technicians	5.4	3.5
cadres moyens	7.5	2.9
white-collar workers	10.0*	5.8
foremen and skilled workers	5.8	4.4
semi- and unskilled workers	12.4	3.8†

* shop workers are more mobile than office workers
† semi-skilled only

Source: adapted from Frisch 1966: 504

The table shows mostly low rates of mobility through career promotions to a new grade and even less movement by demotion. The most mobile categories are to be found at the bottom of the scale and this is probably due to specific short-term demands for fairly low-level skills and occurs when men change firms. White-collar workers are also a group with high mobility, especially within the commercial sector, but even so only 10 per cent move and much of this movement may be due to the lengthening of certain kinds of commercial hierarchies (Frisch 1966: 505). In both industry and commerce there are also people who 'promote' themselves by leaving salaried employment and becoming 'independent', that is, artisans or small shopkeepers. Altogether between 1959 and 1964 about 24 per cent of the employed population moved occupationally but much of it was 'horizontal' movement. Of those that were socially mobile as well about equal numbers moved up and down.

Inter-generational mobility

The education system's role in relation to social mobility is usually assessed by a consideration of inter-generational movement. Not only

may a man's diplomas place him directly in a higher position than his
father but they may also place him on a career ladder that allows for
intra-generational mobility to occur. What then do the data on France
show? Again the data are from the 1964 INSEE study.

TABLE 8

Mobility of men born after 1918, active in 1959 and 1964 – percentages

fathers \ sons	2	3	4	5	6	0	1	7	8
2 owners of industry and commerce	28	9	11	9	35	1	1	2	3
3 higher management liberal professions	7	41	23	10	9	3	1	–	6
4 middle administrat.	5	17	36	11	21	2	2	–	7
5 white-collar workers	7	8	18	15	44	1	–	1	6
6 manual workers	5	2	9	8	71	1	1	0.5	3
0 farmers	5	2	3	6	33	41	7	1	3
1 farm workers	4	1	2	5	60	3	22	1	3
7 service personnel	5	6	9	18	51	–	4	2	6
8 others	6	7	13	11	46	1	–	–	16

Source: adapted from Praderie, *et al.* 1967: 11.

The over-riding impression is of considerable social immobility. In
nearly every category there is a greater tendency for sons to enter their
father's profession than any other. The major exceptions are farm
workers' sons and the sons of *patrons* of industry and commerce;
clearly due to fundamental changes in the industry in the first case and
to the heterogeneity (social and professional) of the category in the
second. However, there is some movement in all sections.

Two further highly important tendencies also stand out. First is the
tendency for the sons of all categories, with the one exception of senior
executives and liberal professions, to move down and enter the ranks of
the working class (*classe ouvrière*) when they are mobile. Not only is this
the most frequent receiving category but it is virtually always more
frequent than all the others put together. Second, where movement of
sons into other occupational groups occurs it is most likely to be into
those adjacent to those of their fathers. Thus, for example, the greatest
proportion of sons of white-collar workers are found to be themselves
white-collar workers (the same), manual workers (below) or supervisory,
cadres moyens (above). The groups *not* showing this tendency are either

isolated, not receiving any entrants, mainly agriculture, or socially heterogeneous, the owners of industry and commerce. This remains true even if the period since the Second World War is taken alone, as the following table shows:

TABLE 9

Sons' socio-professional category, those born since 1945 – percentages

	2	**3**	**4**	**5**	**6**	**0**	**1**	**7**
same category as father	20	33	40	17	74	42	35	–
next most frequent category	6.44	4.28	6.24	6.63	5.10	6.32	6.47	6.56

The bold numbers refer to the INSEE category code numbers.

Source: adapted from Praderie *et al.* 1967: 6.

As before, we see that it is the sons of the middle classes, *classes moyennes,* who are the most mobile and again we see that the most frequent movements have been into the working class, or occupational category 6, a situation we might not expect given the, by then, proportionately greater increase in the white-collar sectors. However, it should be noted that many of the sons who are going to be socially mobile are still in full-time education.

Summary

We find some mobility at all levels of the occupational structure, both during normal careers, especially in the nationalized sector, and over the generations – movement probably made possible by diplomas gained in the education system. But we also find very considerable occupational immobility, again both during careers and from generation to generation. When we distinguish between 'structural mobility', mobility due to economic changes and to differential fertility, we find that 'net mobility' is considerably less (Bertaux 1970: 43).

Moreover three very important points about the *type* of mobility found must be made. The 1964 INSEE study found that more of the persons leaving the manual category during their working lives are from non-manual origins than from manual, and of the others the great majority are skilled workers at the top of the category. This confirms the trend outlined above in the section on education. Second, we find that in both intra- and inter-generational mobility movements tend to be short: the overwhelming majority of the mobile do not move far from their point of social origin. Third, we find considerable social viscosity where certain groups are concerned, some being particularly well insulated from downward mobility, for example, the *cadres supérieurs* and the liberal professions. To such groups entry is normally by high level and specialized education – by diploma and not by intra-career promotion. Thus in spite of the great increase in the number of posts available, the education system has tended to restrict entry to limited social groups. The same INSEE study found that the liberal professions were the most hereditary group in France, with an 'index of inertia' of 34 as opposed to 1.8 for white-collar workers (Bertaux 1970; Praderie *et al* 1966, 1968).[4]

Degrees and jobs: the return on investment[5]

In France most industrial and commercial posts are the subject of *conventions collectives*, i.e., agreements in which employers and unions decide the basis of recruitment, pay, and status (e.g. *cadre*), and which to a great extent determine the theoretical prospects for promotion. A study of these has yet to be done in relation to the latter and what follows in this section therefore can only be approximate and show *grosso modo* what is involved. We will analyse the returns to some low-level qualifications but concentrate on recruitment to certain top groups, taking business and high admininstration as crucial examples.

The C.A.P. is the lowest effective discriminatory diploma in France at present. Grignon's study (1971) showed that C.A.P. holders have seven out of ten chances of remaining manual workers, but they stand a better chance of being recognized as skilled and becoming foremen (1971:57). The C.A.P., however, is not scarce on the market and jobs are by no means 'guaranteed' to its holders in the way that the holder of an engineering diploma is 'guaranteed' an appropriate post; moreover the 'title' is revocable. Such persons are more subject to unemployment than the holders of higher diplomas and for the newly created jobs the C.A.P. may be irrelevant and unrecognized. In fact, Grignon says, many small firms find it impossible to use rationally even the lowest-level C.A.P. skills, and they complain that the C.E.T. give the young workers 'airs'. Further, with the constant creation of new diplomas, people holding the older ones often find that their level in the hierarchy has dropped. Grignon also points out that employers tend to do well out of periods both of penury and over-production of certain qualifications:

during the former, those without diplomas are paid less for doing the same work, while during the latter competition for places tend to push down the value of the diploma.

The lot of persons with somewhat higher technical diplomas is often similar. Persons with a *bac. technique* or a *brevet de technician* get the appropriate technical jobs and although their diplomas contribute to their mobility they often allow no possibility of further rising. The 1964 INSEE study showed the technicians as a seldom promoted category and those who are appointed to positions as *cadres moyens* usually come from the general education system. Grignon's re-analysis of the INSEE data showed that in spite of the relative rarity of their diplomas, the holders of the technical qualifications, B.E.I. or B.E.C., had less chance of rising to 'management' positions than holders of the *brevet d'enseignement général*, reputed to have no outlets. While those who have the ordinary *bac.* have four in ten chances of having a post in the *classes supérieures*, the theoretically equivalent technical qualifications give only one or two. The same is true at the higher levels between holders of the *licence* and the higher technical diplomas.

Higher-level diplomas

We have already discussed the hierarchy of social origins by faculty and between the faculties and the *Grandes Ecoles* and now it will be useful to examine the returns to each of these kinds of diplomas by looking at the backgrounds of people in the top positions in business and the state administration.

Since 1945 recruitment to the high levels of the civil service is through a special school, the *Ecole Nationale d'Administration*, E.N.A. Of the two entry *concours* the most important one is open to students prepared in the public services section of the *Institut d'Etudes Politiques* in Paris. Studies of E.N.A. students show very little democratization and consequently very little lowering of the social origins of the *hauts fonctionnaires*, especially in the more prestigious *corps* such as the financial controllers, the *Inspection des Finances*. A recent study by Bourdieu's team showed the distribution by social origin of E.N.A. students as 3-4 per cent working class, 27 per cent *classes moyennes*, and nearly 70 per cent upper class (Bourdieu *et al.* 1970, unpublished paper). This may be compared to Bottomore's study in the period 1945-51 in which he found 65 per cent upper class, 28 per cent middle class, and nearly 7 per cent working class, including farmers (Bottomore 1952: 169). The comparison shows almost total immobility over twenty years in spite of changes in the education system. Social origins clearly play a crucial role in recruitment to the higher administration and we find there a hierarchy that is translated into a hierarchy of prestige in the Ministries:

'It is in the social ministries (14%) and Education (13.5%) that the fraction of higher officials from working class origins is highest; then in the technical (7%) and *régalien* (6%) ... it is in the Ministry of Finance (5.5%) and the services of the Prime Minister's office (2%) that they are lowest. Moreover their part varies according to the hierarchy of the *corps;* it is in the *corps* of the central administration (10%) and the *corps extérieurs* (9.5%) that their share is greatest and then in the technical and control sections and the *grands corps* (5.5%).' (Darbel and Schnapper: 1969: 95)

Through the movement of *pantouflage*, movement from high posts in the civil service to those of private and nationalized industries, becoming more and more common, the high officials of the state are linked to the chief decision-making areas of the business and commercial world, especially the most advanced industries and banking (Lalumière 1959: 85ff.). In 1960 a large-scale study found that of the senior executives and board members, *cadres dirigeants*, then active 27 per cent were themselves the sons of *cadres dirigeants:* another 30 per cent approximately were the sons of senior civil servants, political leaders (deputies, etc.), diplomats, and members of the liberal professions. Less than one in ten came from the working and farm classes (Delefortrie-Soubeyroux 1961). Later in the 1950s Girard found similarly that 70 per cent of the industrialists and businessmen appearing in the *Dictionnaire Biographique* were the sons of the upper social classes and 33 per cent were the sons of businessmen and industrialists (Girard 1961).

A far more recent study confirms the other two. Hall and de Bettignies found in 1966-7 that the social origins of *Présidents Directeurs Généraux* (PDG), of the 500 largest French companies were as shown in *Table 10.*

This shows that over 40 per cent had fathers who were themselves business leaders, that one third have married into the business *milieu* and one quarter had grandfathers who were in the same category. Only one in ten are from the working class, although nearly a third had grandfathers in that class. Other studies conclude similarly: ' ... those ruling business, the *cadres dirigeants,* are recruited from *ingénieurs* trained in the *Grandes Ecoles;* the pupils of the *Grandes Ecoles* spring from the ruling class' (Benguigi and Monjardet 1970: 101).

TABLE 10

Social origins of the leaders of French industry, 1966-7 – percentages

profession	fathers	grandfathers	fathers-in-law
heads of enterprises*	41.6	25.5	31.4
liberal professions	19.7	21.4	26.6
executives†	14.7	6.9	13.5
commerce‡	7.5	9.0	7.2
civil servants§	5.6	6.2	10.1
working classes‖	10.8	31.2	9.0

* *chefs d'entreprise*

† *cadres*, including civil servants in senior and middle-level posts

‡ *commerçants*, including both large and small

§ *fonctionnaires*, civil servants other than above.

‖ white-collar workers, manual workers, farmers, and artisans.

Source: Hall and de Bettignies 1968: 4-5.

We should also note here that geographical origins are also very concentrated: the predominance of Paris is overwhelming and indeed seems to be increasing. Hall and de Bettignies found nearly 40 per cent of the P.D.G. were born in the Paris region.

At the higher levels of industry we find in general a close correlation between positions obtained and diplomas held. All the studies showed some variation between industries, especially where promotion from the shop-floor is concerned, but a very high proportion of senior executive posts were held by men with 'university' diplomas awarded mainly by the *Grandes Ecoles*. Hall and de Bettignies found that over half the P.D.G. had such diplomas and of these one quarter were from the *Polytechnique* alone, one third had more than one diploma (including one third with a qualification from another *Grande Ecole*), and only one in ten had had no higher education at all. They show the predominance of the *ingénieurs* and technical studies; nearly all the remainder having law and economics degrees – thus demonstrating the chief educational routes to the top. All such findings concur in confirming the extent to which in France the bourgeoisie has used the education system to place its sons in top positions.

One final point in this section. Everywhere in this paper we have emphasized the hierarchial nature of educational institutions and its correlation with social origins at each level, but we must also insist here once again on the importance of hierarchies *within* each level which mean advantages turned directly into money returns. We can in fact quantify the value of different diplomas. In 1970 the '*prix des cadres*' was as follows:

TABLE 11

Initial base salaries by school: thousands of francs – 1970[6]

Schools	OOOF	Schools	OOOF	Schools	OOF
Ingenieurs		Commercial Management		University	
Polytechnique	32–39	INSEAD*	39–52	Doctor of Law	22–36
Central (Paris)	30–39	H.E.C.†	29–34	*Licence,* economics	21–26
Mines (Paris)	29–38	E.S.S.E.C.‡	27–33	*Licence,* law	17–14
Arts et Metiers	29–36	Sup. de Comm.§	26–32		
Telecom- munications	31–36	I.E.P. ‖	25–28		
Ponts et Chaussées	29–31	H.E.C. women	21–31		
Lower salaries for provincial and '*petites ecoles*'	23–34				

* Institut Européen d'Administration des Affaires
† Hautes Etudes Commerciales
‡ Ecole Supérieure des Sciences Economiques et Commerciales
§ Ecole Supérieure de Commerce
‖ Institut d'Etudes Politiques, Paris.

Source: Eggens 1970: 127.

Extra-technical advantages

To assess the role of diplomas acquired through the educational system in occupational and social placement one needs to examine also the role of 'extra-technical' factors. Such a task demands much empirical data difficult to obtain directly; so the evidence drawn upon here is necessarily indirect. It is clear that where the educational system has brought large numbers of young people identical qualifications some other means of distinguishing between applicants for posts must come into play, especially where the qualifications are not 'technical' ones. Hence, for instance, the increasing barrage of tests and the multiplication of specialist employment agencies. Even handwriting now seems to be important to judge by the number of high-level job advertisements in the French press which require candidates to make hand-written applications. There is a renewed emphasis on 'the kind of person' a man is.

Hence, too, the renewed insistence in some quarters at least on non-academic qualifications of all kinds. The most important part of what 'makes a man what he is' in France is his *culture générale* possessed in addition to technical expertise. Moreover as Bourdieu points out (1966: 338), it is not only the possession of the culture that counts but the relationship to it; it should appear to be 'aristocratic' and 'natural', a 'gift', not consciously learned. Such a relationship comes through family and environment and rarely from the school, especially where one approaches the less traditional and 'scholastic' aspects such as modern art, ballet, jazz, etc. With this goes the valorization of the 'generalist' rather than the 'narrow specialist'. Speaking of the higher civil service Bourdieu and Passeron say:

'. . . . in fact the French high civil service has perhaps never known and consecrated so totally the most 'general' and diffuse qualities . . . and never so completely subordinated specialists, experts and technicians to the "specialists of the general" trained in the most prestigious *Grandes Ecole*.' (1970: 205).

E.N.A. has, they say, peopled the administration and ministerial cabinets with *'jeunes messieurs'* accumulating the advantages of a bourgeois training and the most typically traditional education. This situation they specifically contrast with Weber's analysis of modern bureaucratic institutions and the supremacy of technical expertise.

M. Cheradame, then director of studies at *Polytechnique*, in his 1965 address to new students unconsciously agreed with Bourdieu's analysis when he reminded the students that they were not there to become narrow specialists but to have the general scientific education that the State demands and he put the accent on a 'forte culture générale (et) humaine'. He further advised them:

'You must . . . learn the social milieu of the "senior executives" of the nation, which you are going to join if your families are not already there . . . This is indispensible to finding yourself at ease tomorrow . . . Do not neglect any aspect . . . of its usages and savoir-faire. I even dare to add, hurry and acquaint yourself with this milieu before you choose your wife . . . for you will both suffer in the future

if she should be ill at ease and not do you justice.' (Quoted in Bon and
Burnier 1966: 166.)

Bon and Burnier themselves emphasize the same factors for the civil
service and business as also does the business review *Entreprise*.

For many such young men there already exist family connections of
the first importance in the form of family businesses and available
economic capital. Many too have 'social' capital and are recruited to
other businesses through a network of relationships which mean that
some candidates for a post are known socially while others are not.
Given both the closure of many of the top groups in French society
through professional heredity and marriage (Girard 1964) and the
concentration on Paris this seems inevitable. We may conclude then:

> 'That the economy can no longer be run without specialised skills
> is one thing, that the ruling class renews itself from among those
> who hold such skills is another, just as clear. But as long as the ruling
> class controls access to such skills it renews itself from its own breast.
> That birth is no longer sufficient by no means implies that skill alone
> is sufficient but merely implies the necessity of adding skill to birth
> and the *Grandes Ecoles* are there for that . . .' (Benguigi and Monjardet
> 1970: 102)

CONCLUSION

We have shown in this paper how certain classes and certain areas in
French society accumulate both advantages and disadvantages in the
opportunity structure. An upper-class son in the Paris region is virtually
sure of educational and occupational success and of maintaining the
position in society held by his family of origin. He will acquire the right
diplomas, the right connections, the right capital, and the right position
despite the massive economic changes of the last twenty-five years. At
the other end of the scale, the son of a farmer or of a small provincial
town manual worker will be virtually sure of maintaining his. The
economic changes have barely altered the latter's position in the
opportunity structure, if not actually increasing his disadvantage. He
lacks cultural, social, and economic capital and the meagre school
institutions at his disposal will seldom allow him to acquire diplomas
facilitating movement away fron his *milieu* of origin. Any social mobility
he does achieve will seem to be by 'luck'. In France as elsewhere there is
most movement in the middle levels – it is these strata which have
benefitted most from the basic economic transformations and whose

members are able to use the school system to some extent to acquire 'cultural capital' in the form of diplomas. On the whole, however, they also acquire middle-range qualifications which do not allow long-distance movements. Where they manage to acquire high-level qualifications, their occupational position remains less sure than that of those 'born to it'. They owe everything to the school and find that on the job market their diplomas only have full value within the school system. Outside that system they are a necessary but not a sufficient condition of access to the posts theoretically 'guaranteed' by the possession of the diplomas. The degrees remain embedded in a social context which gives them a symbolic as well as a technical significance; they 'assume' the existence of other assets necesary for their full theoretical value. When one has 'done' Polytechnique one is assumed to be 'more' than an engineer, and indeed the social origins of the students almost always confirm the expectation.

The different assets continue to be linked together and continually reinforce each other. The class structure has not changed, nor has the nature of the education system in spite of the expansion in numbers. As Bourdieu points out, the 'culture' transmitted by the school and presented as 'school' culture can in reality only be fully assimilated by those whose culture it already is; in this as in other spheres 'capital' attracts 'capital' and the school has only to treat its pupils equally, has only to fulfil the mission with which it is outwardly entrusted, for their inherent inequalities to be given full rein (Bourdieu 1966). It becomes clear then that this paper is less concerned with social mobility than with social immobility; that whether one considers its manifest or latent functions, the primordial role of the education system is the reproduction of the social order and hence the maintenance of a certain class and hence opportunity structure which we outlined above. Thus we many agree with Bourdieu and Passeron that by delegating to the school system the power of selection to occupational and social roles, the privileged can appear to abdicate their own power to a neutral institution and so appear to renounce the more arbitrary privileges of hereditary transmission. By its verdicts on different individuals which, as we have seen, virtually never work to the disadvantage of the privileged classes, the school system contributes powerfully to the reproduction of the established order (1970: 205-206). The mobility of individuals that does occur through education only legitimizes the system; the very 'autonomy' of the educational system and the dedication of its teachers to the dissemination of a body of general knowledge only indirectly related to economic opportunity, contributes to the illusion. At the same time as it helps to prepare the sons of the upper classes for their position in life by the acquisition of diplomas, it also allows them to justify that position and their privileged relationship to the culture which is at least nominally valued by the whole society. It allows its possessors to claim not only privileges in relation to the rewards of society but also moral worth. To a very considerable extent the school system upholds the choice of criteria defined as relevant for status-ranking by the dominant strata and encourages the excluded to accept the system which places them both symbolically and materially in a subordinate position. The schools provide in this way the cultural capital which can be allied to economic and social capital at the highest levels but whose lack constitutes a final judgement on those less well-endowed.

The school system, conclude Bourdieu and Passeron, is to bourgeois society in its present phase what other forms of legitimation of the social order and other forms of the hereditary transmission of privileges were to other social forms; and as the

'. . . privileged instrument of bourgeois society (sociodicée) which confers on the privileged the supreme privilege of not appearing privileged (the school) can the more easily convince the disinherited that they owe their scholastic and social destiny to their own lack of gifts and merits that in cultural matters absolute dispossession excludes consciousness of that dispossession.' (Bourdieu and Passeron 1970: 252)

Since most are unaware of their exclusion they do not feel relatively deprived. The ideology of social mobility, of rising through one's gifts and one's merits, in short one's desserts, can thus be maintained and even strengthened in spite of the fact that, as has been constantly shown in this paper, opportunities for most people are in reality extremely limited. The economy has changed, most people's lot has improved but it is the same lot as before; the structure of opportunity has changed relatively little.

Notes

1 *Cadre* has no single English equivalent. *Cadres* share a broad 'status' reflected in a national pension fund and a trade union, but are much divided. They may be described as representing management in some capacity, but vary from the high level *cadres supérieurs* (senior

executives), through the *cadres moyens* (middle supervisory staff), down to plant foremen who are often but not always included. The term *cadres supérieurs* is also used in a wider sense to refer to the elite of the nation.

A similar translation problem arises also for the important *ingénieurs*. 'Engineers' is both too wide and too narrow to render *ingénieurs* who acquire their title from the diplomas obtained from one of the technical *Grandes Ecoles* (another translation problem: elite specialist school) and it means broadly that they have specialized in a technical subject at a very high level. As well as a qualification, the term *ingénieur* also denotes a status or title which in certain firms may be acquired through promotion. In this paper both the terms *cadre* and *ingénieur* will be left in the original where appropriate.

All translations of quotations which appear in the paper are my own.

2 Changes of job which involve better working conditions or higher salary may be experienced as upward mobility but do not appear in the statistics and do not usually involve stratum changes (Frisch 1966: 503). Rogoff and Lipset included movement from farm to urban working class as upward movement but there is evidence that it is not experienced as such by many farm migrants (Karpik 1965).

3 This is beginning to change. This year, 1973, the technical *baccalauréat* will become the full equivalent of the *baccalauréat* proper and will for the first time give equal access to the universities.

4 Since writing in 1973 a second INSEE study carried out in 1970 has appeared. It shows no great changes in mobility.

5 Until recently a major part of the population entered the labour market without diplomas. In 1968 30 per cent of young employed persons between 14 and 25 years of age, had no diplomas, either of the general or technical education systems (*Economie et Statistique* 1971: 20:48).

6 INSEAD graduates enter the labour market several years later than others and mostly hold at least one other high-level qualification.

References

ANDRIEUX, A., and LIGNON, J. 1966. *L'Ouvrier Aujourd'hui*. Paris: Gonthier.

ARCHER, M. S., and GINER, S. 1971. *Contemporary Europe: Class Status and Power*. London: Weidenfeld and Nicolson.

BAUDELOT, C., and ESTABET, R. 1971. *L'Ecole Capitaliste en France*. Paris: Maspéro.

BENGUIGI, G., and MONJARDET, D. 1970. *Etre un Cadre en France?* Paris: Dunod.

BERGER, I., and BENJAMIN, R. 1964. *L'Univers des Instituteurs.* Paris: Editions de Minuit.

BERTAUX, D. 1969. Sur l'Analyse des Tables de Mobilité. *Revue Française de Sociologie* **10**: 448-490.

—— 1970. 'L'Hérédite Sociale en France'. *Economie et Statistique* **9**: 37-47.

BON, F., and BURNIER, M. A. 1966. *Les Nouveaux Intellectuels.* Paris: Cujas.

BOTTOMORE, T. 1952. 'La Mobilité Sociale dans la Haute Administration Française,' *Cahiers Internationaux de Sociologie* **13**: 167-178.

BOURDIEU, P. 1966. 'L'Ecole Conservatrice . . .', *Revue Française de Sociologie* **7**: 325-347.

—— 1971. Réproduction Cuturelle et Réproduction Sociale. *Inform. Sciences Sociales* **10**(2): 45-79.

BOURDIEU, P., and PASSERON, J. C. 1964. *Les Héritiers,* Paris: Editions de Minuit.

—— 1970. *La Réproduction: Eléments pour une Théorie du Système d'Enseignement.* Paris: Editions de Minuit.

BOURDIEU, P., 1970. *Les Fonctions du Systeme d'Enseignement: Classes Préparatoires et Facultés.* Unpublished.

BRESARD, M. 1950. Mobilité Sociale et Dimension de la Famille. *Population* **3**: 533-566.

CEZARD, M. 1972. 'O.S. et Manoeuvres forment un Tiers des Salariés de l'Industrie'. *Economie et Stratistique* **38**: 49-51.

CHAMPAGNE, P. and GRIGNON, C. 1969. *Rapport d'Enquête sur le Public du Conservatoire National des Arts et Métiers.* Unpublished.

DANSETTE, J. L. 1954. *Quelques Familles du Patronat Textile de Lille-Armentières, 1789-1914.* Lille: E. Raoust.

DARBEL, A. 1967. Inégalités régionales ou Inégalités Sociales?. *Revue Française de Sociologie.* Special no.: 140-166.

DARBEL, A., and SCHNAPPER, D. 1969. *Les Agents du Système Administratif,* Paris: La Haye Mouton.

DELEFORTRIE-SOUBEYROUX, N. 1961. *Les Dirigeants de L'Industrie Française.* Paris: A. Colin.

DUBOIS, N. 1937. *Que deviennent les Etudiants?* Paris: Sirey.

DUPEUX, G. 1964. *La Société Française, 1789-1960.* Paris: A. Colin.

INSEE. 1970. Document. Données Essentielles sur l'Industrie Française. *Economie et Statistique* **14**: 33-50.

—— 1971. Un Million de Cadres Supérieurs Dénombrés au Recensement de 1968. *Economie et Statistique.* **40**: 51-54.

EGGENS, J. B. 1970. Le Prix des Cadres 1970, *Expansion* **31**: 125-137.

FARCY, H. de 1971. La Réconversion des Agriculteurs, *Etudes* fév.: 225-235.

FRISCH, J. 1966. Les Comportements ouvriers de Mobilité. *Année Sociologique* **17**: 499-532.

—— 1971. L'Importance des Diplomes pour la Promotion, *Economie et Statistique* **21:** 33-44.

GIRARD, A. 1961. *La Réussite Sociale en France.* Paris: Presses Universitaires de France.

—— 1964. *Le Choix du Conjoint.* Paris: Presses Universitaires de France.

—— 1971. *'Population' et l'Enseignement.* Paris: Presses Universitaires de France. (The book reprints the articles on educational selection and stratification based on studies by INED and published in *Population* in the 1960s.)

GIRARD, A. et. al. 1963. Enquête Nationale sur L'Entrée en Sixième de La Democratisation de l'Enseignement. *Population* **18:** 9-48.

GRIGNON, C. 1968. L'Orientation Scolaire des Elèves d'une Ecole Rurale. *Révue Française de Sociologie* **9** (no. spécial): 218-226.

—— 1971. *L'Ordre des Choses: les Fonctions Sociales de l'Enseignement Technique.* Paris: Editions de Minuit.

HALL, D., and BETTIGNIES, H- C. de 1968. The French Business Elite. *European Business* **19:** 1-10.

HORDLEY, I., and LEE, D. 1970. The Alternative Route – Social Change and Opportunity in Technical Education. *Sociology* **4** (1) 23-50.

d'HUGUES, P. and PESLIER, M. 1969. *Les Professions en France.* Paris: Presses Universitaires de France (Cahier de l'INED no. 51).

KARPIK, L. 1965. Trois Concepts Sociologiques: Le Projet de Référence, Le Statut Social et le Bilan Individual. *Archives Européennes de Sociologie* **6** (2): 191-222.

LALUMIÈRE, P. 1959. *L'Inspection des Finances.* Paris: Presses Universitaires de France.

LEGOUX, Y. 1959. Les Techniciens de la Chimie. In Floud, J. et. al. (eds.) *Ecole et Société.* Paris: M. Rivière.

LHOMME, J., 1960. *La Grande Bourgeoisie au Pouvoir* (1830-1880). Paris: Presses Universitaires de France.

MINISTÈRE DE L'EDUCATION NATIONALE. 1969. Les Etudiants en France . . . . *Notes et Etudes Documentaires* No. 3577.

MORAZÉ, C. 1957. *Les Bourgeois Conquérants.* Paris: A. Colin.

PARKIN, F., 1971. *Class Inequality and Political Order.* London: Macgibbon & Kee.

PARODI, M. 1971. *L'Economie et la Société Française de 1945-1970.* Paris: A. Colin.

PRADERIE, M. 1968. *Ni Ouvriers ni Paysans.* Paris: Editions du Seuil.

PRADERIE, M., and PASSAGEZ, M. 1966. La Mobilité Professionnelle en France entre 1959 et 1964. *Etudes et Conjoncture* **21** (10): 1-166.

PRADERIE, M. et al. 1967. Une Enquête sur la Formation et la Qualification des Français. *Etudes et Conjoncture* **22** (1): 3-109.

PRIOURET, R. 1963. *Origines du Patronat Français.* Paris: Grasset.

GAVIN MACKENZIE

The 'Affluent Worker' Study: An Evaluation and Critique

My concerns in this paper are twofold. First, I examine in some detail the theoretical perspectives utilized by Goldthorpe, Lockwood, Bechhofer, and Platt in the Luton study. Second, and in the light of the Cambridge team's findings, I discuss briefly some of the changes that might be occurring in the structure and composition of the British working class. In this section my concern is more with what the *Affluent Worker* study has *not* told us, rather than with the authors' detailed analysis of the class situation (and perhaps revolutionary potential) of the affluent worker *per se*. This means that I do not intend to review existing criticisms or evaluations of the study.[1] Such a course of action could be repetitive and tedious, and would contribute little of orginal value. Rather, I prefer to concentrate upon a number of theoretical and empirical issues which have received too little attention in recent discussion – issues which must be at the centre of continuing debate on changes in the middle levels of the class structure.

I

As is well known, the dialectic between theory and empirical findings, an integral feature of the research process, has in the case of the *Affluent Worker* study led to the emergence (or more accurately re-emergence) of a social action perspective for the explanation of industrial behaviour. Indeed, examination of the Luton study as, in Hammond's phrase, a 'chronicle of social research' provides a far more exciting and revealing insight into the *process* of sociological investigation than any of the studies outlined in *Sociologists at Work* (Hammond 1964). However, concentration upon this social action approach has attracted attention away from the theory of social class. The analysis of changes in class structure therefore, the prime focus of the project, is neither as complete nor as powerful as might have been expected. In the paragraphs that follow I attempt to trace, and account for, the research team's move away from its earlier and explicit approach to the analysis of social class.

In their theoretical writings prior to the actual fieldwork, the two senior researchers, John Goldthorpe and David Lockwood, adhered to a clear and unambiguous view of the nature of social class and class structure – a view evident in, and generated from, research they had carried out independently in the 1950s (Lockwood 1958; Goldthorpe 1959). According to this perspective, for the majority of any population, i.e. those not owning productive wealth, position in the division of labour is seen as being the crucial determinant of class situation, while community and family structure are accorded secondary importance. In so far as the occupancy of a particular position in the division of labour gives rise to a particular market situation *and* work situation, then the relationship between work and social class is demonstrated. Market situation means simply the life-chances and access to economic resources enjoyed by virtue of occupational role; the possession of differing degrees of skill gives groups (classes) differing degrees of power in the market. It includes therefore not only source and size of income, but also level of job security, sickness and pension rights, and opportunities for career mobility. Work situation, on the other hand, has to do with the fact that in occupying given roles in the division of labour, individuals are involved in distinct socio-technical environments which, in turn, are seen as 'creating and sustaining' the 'basic social imagery which is prevalent among the members of a class, and around which their characteristic attitudes and values cluster . . .' (Lockwood and Goldthorpe 1962: 9). This means that 'without doubt in modern society the most important social conditions shaping the psychology of the individual are those arising out of the organisation of production, administration and distribution. In other words, the "work situation" ' (Lockwood 1958: 205). In *The Blackcoated Worker*, Lockwood was concerned mainly with the way in which the work situation engendered distinct patterns of *social relationships*, thus affording possibilities of identification with certain co-workers (e.g. other manual employees) and isolation from others (e.g. managers and supervisors). Two years later however, he stressed the importance of other components of role in the division of labour in explaining class differentials in value and normative patterns.

'The size of the factory, the organization of the work group, its relation to supervisors and management, the degree to which the worker has control over his work process, the extent to which the job facilitates or prevents communication between workers, the rigidity of the distinction between staff and workers, security of tenure, the progressiveness of earnings, and job discipline; these represent some of the points of reference for a construction of a typology of work relationships, without which no clear appreciation of class identification can be obtained.' (Lockwood 1960: 256-257)

In a later paper, written this time in collaboration with Goldthorpe, attention is focused upon two features of the industrial organization which are claimed to have particular influence on many of the features of the work situation detailed in the quotation above. These are plant or unit size and type of production system (Lockwood and Goldthorpe 1962: 11-17). The size of the industrial organization is important in so far as it affects the nature of the relationship between management and workers. The small plant facilitates relaxed personal relationships between the members of the two groups. Workers are thereby easily persuaded to identify with management and indeed with the enterprise in general. In contrast, the bureaucratic organization of the large firm engenders remote and impersonal relations between workers and management. The worker finds himself one of a large and distinct mass and is thus in a situation highly conducive to the development of a 'working class social imagery', that is, imagery which views society essentially in dichotomous terms.

In discussing some of the differences generated in work situations, and therefore in social imagery and value patterns, by alternative types of production technology, Lockwood and Goldthorpe make the conventional distinction between unit or small-batch production, large-batch or mass production, and process production. Following Blauner and Woodward they argue that the 'social and psychological implications' of these differing types of production technology vary widely. In particular, they are at pains to point out that the work situations engendered by mass production are far more likely to give rise to class consciousness and class conflict than are those associated with unit and process forms of manufacture. The fragmentation and standardization of work task, the absence of any significant degree of differentiation within the work force, and the necessity of strict supervision all combine to inculcate in the manual labour force a dichotomous social imagery and a sense of isolation and separation from management. The assembly-line manufacture of motor cars is, of course, the classic example of such a situation. In contrast, the operation of process forms of production requires frequent and close contact between managers and workers, while the nature of work tasks provides the employee with a relatively large degree of autonomy and freedom of movement. This is also true of small-batch production, where workers, often highly skilled, are *using* machines rather than being dominated by them. Correspondingly, in both instances, class consciousness and notions of 'them and us' will be little developed.

As already mentioned, while Lockwood and Goldthorpe regarded position in the division of labour as *the* crucial determinant of class situation, attention was also focused on the way in which the social structure of the community may reinforce (or perhaps diminish) the influence of work situation. In particular, importance was attributed to the fact that the tightly-knit and homogeneous working-class community or neighbourhood exercises a significant influence on the maintenance of a traditional working-class life-style and pattern of values. It follows that the gradual breaking up of such working-class enclaves, and the concomitant urban re-development programmes, raise the possibility of large numbers of workers becoming exposed to 'new' value patterns and life-styles at the same time as the 'control' exercised by the old neighbourhood is removed. To the extent, therefore, that neighbourhoods are *homogeneous* and *stable*, then the influence of the community will reinforce pressures emanating from the work situation. In instances where these conditions do not hold, an important factor contributing to the maintenance of class differentials has been removed. In this regard Lockwood and Goldthorpe place special emphasis on the extended family, which they see as strengthening the solidarity and cohesion of the working-class community. 'In the traditional working class community the family acts as a mechanism for perpetuating the existing social system not only through biological reproduction, but also through providing, in its more extended form, a matrix of closely-knit relationships in which traditional class norms are firmly embedded' (Lockwood and Goldthorpe 1962: 24). However, the break up of many traditional working-class communities and the movement to new projects or estates has been associated with a large scale disruption of these family patterns – the nuclear rather than the extended family becoming the norm. A feature of working-class life, which, in the past, has strengthened the influence of certain types of work situation is therefore being considerably weakened.[2]

This then was the theoretical approach to the analysis of social class adhered to by the two senior investigators at the outset of the research project. Fundamentally, class structure was seen as being rooted in the division of labour, although significance was also attached to the influence of community and family structure. In my view this conceptualization of social class is most useful, especially if the central concern is with an analysis of changes in the middle levels of class structure.

However, as is well known 'a more or less unforeseen by-product' (the Cambridge team's term) of this study of changes in the British class structure was their conversion to, and subsequent advocacy of, a social action perspective for the analysis of *industrial behaviour*.[3] Indeed the first publications based upon data gathered in Luton were concerned not with the position of the affluent worker in the class structure, but with the industrial attitudes and behaviour of small- and large-batch process and production-line workers. Analysis of these data on behaviour in the work situation led the research team to express serious reservations about the adequacy of current theorizing in the realm of industrial sociology – theorizing which previously had been incorporated into their own writings on class and class structure. And, as already suggested, these reservations are a product of the interplay between theory and data that must exist in any empirical piece of sociological investigation. In Goldthorpe's own words:

'1. Certain data are produced which on examination, are found not to fit well with the existing body of theoretical ideas – i.e. are not capable of being adequately explained and understood in terms of these ideas;
2. an attempt is then made – as an exercise in informed conjecture – to modify and renovate existing theory so that the range of empirical findings can be better accommodated and accounted for.' (Goldthorpe 1970: 199)

In this particular case, the Luton findings suggested that both the 'human relations' and the 'technological implications' approaches to the analysis of behaviour at work were inadequate, and needed therefore to be supplemented by an action frame of reference. This latter perspective makes explicit recognition of the prior orientations that actors (workers) bring with them to the work place, and which therefore influence their choice of job, the meaning they assign to it, and hence their reaction to it.

' . . . we believe that in industrial sociology what may be termed an action frame of reference could, with advantage, be more widely adopted; that is to say, a frame of reference within which actors' own definitions of the situations in which they are engaged are taken as

J

an initial basis for the explanation of their social behaviour and relationships.' (*I.A.B.*: 184, my italics)[4]

This does not mean, of course, that the influence of work situation
was rejected completely. For example, the researchers show clearly the
ways in which type of production technology was a major factor in
determining levels of job satisfaction, of work deprivation, the presence
or absence of solidary work groups, the extent of contact between
supervisors and workers, and so on. But, it is now argued, workers'
responses to these situations will not be automatic or reflex but will
depend on their prior expectations or orientations. And in the case of
the instrumental Luton workers, so the argument goes, many of these
deprivations will be expected and accepted because of the compensation
of high and relatively secure wages – wages that are defined by those
workers as more desirable than job satisfaction or having good work
mates or positive relationships with supervisors. In other words, as far
as industrial behaviour is concerned, features of the work situation are
now seen 'not so much as positive determinants of socially significant
behaviour, but rather as constraining and limiting factors' (Goldthorpe
1965: 19).

It is not my concern here to evaluate the merits or demerits of the
action approach within industrial sociology. The extent to which the
Cambridge team are guilty of 'over-interpreting' their data, the degree
of inconsistency in their findings, the questionable validity of their
measures, or the extent to which features of the work situation *can* indeed explain their subjects' industrial behaviour and attitudes, are all
issues which have been debated elsewhere. What does need to be
emphasized, however, is that the adoption of an action perspective in
connection with a 'by product' of a study of changes in class structure
entails a serious dilution of the authors' earlier conceptualization of class
and class structure. For whatever the merits of focusing on 'prior
orientations' in the examination of industrial behaviour, the analysis of
the class structure of capitalist society requires an examination of structured inequality and life-chances – which as Lockwood and Goldthorpe
argued earlier, typically depend upon position in the division of labour.
To be sure, these writers also emphasized that community and family
structure potentially reinforce various forms of social consciousness
generated within differing types of work situation. And certainly, one
might look to community and kin relationships as a potential source of
'prior orientations' to work. *But the crucial fact remains that community
and family structure are shaped by the industrial and therefore the occupa-*

tional structure of a particular area or region. In the analysis of industrial behaviour it may indeed be useful artificially to separate work and non-work influences; for a study of changes in class structure, this procedure can only be described as regrettable.[5] For while it would be stupid to describe this study as atheoretical – as some critics have suggested – it has strayed away from a central theory of social class.[6] To be sure the analysis contains explanation as well as description; and these explanations are original, persuasive and, above all, sociological. But they are also piecemeal; the interplay between the division of labour and community and family structure, explicit in the two senior authors' earlier theoretical formulations, is lacking. For example, much of the analysis of the political behaviour and attitudes of the Luton workers consists of a detailed and meticulous demonstration of their continuing attachment to the Labour party, albeit an attachment of an essentially instrumental nature. Furthermore, the authors demonstrate convincingly that commitment to the Labour party is highest among trade-union members. Three possible reasons are suggested for this relationship. First, that the union acts as some kind of agency of socialization – if not in changing political views, at least in activating the indifferent. Second, that a process of self selection goes on: Labour party identifiers are more likely to join unions. Third, that both trade-union membership and Labour party loyalties may be linked to some third factor, for example plant size, and that this lies behind the perceived link between union membership and the Labour vote. Unfortunately the data do not allow the authors to test these various hypotheses, but they do give some indication that 'increasing exposure to trade unionism leads to a higher level of Labour support' (*P.A.B.:* 66). The question that then arises, given the fact that unions appear to be maintaining traditional working-class voting patterns and political loyalties, concerns the nature of the relationship between the trade-union movement and the working class, and the *bases* of that relationship. And here the two senior authors' earlier theoretical formulations are highly pertinent, as they themselves recognize.

'. . . the more routinised and disciplined nature of work in large plants, the physical and symbolic segregation of manual from non-manual employees, the collective pressure of workmate opinion, and the probability that unsatisfying jobs make the extrinsic rewards of pay and conditions very prominent in the worker's mind are all factors which predispose workers in large plants to join trade unions.'

(*P.A.B.:* 51)

Yet although the Luton sample did all work in large plants, and although this provides an opportunity clearly to link position in the division of labour with political behaviour, plant size is referred to only in a single early paragraph, following which the discussion assumes a more psephological nature, centering on the relationship between union membership *per se* and Labour party support.[7]

This is not to say that market and work situations are never used to explain certain of the behavioural and value patterns of affluent workers. For example, in discussing the absence of an active and middle-class social life on the part of their respondents, the research team refer to deprivations experienced by these workers in the performance of their jobs:

'. . . we have seen that in the plants in which these men were employed overtime working was the normal practice, and that the majority were required to work according to some form of shift system. Consequently, leisure hours were frequently curtailed and occured at unusual and often varying times of day; in addition, energy and what could perhaps be termed 'social vitality' were likely to be unduly sapped. In these ways, therefore, obstacles must inevitably have been created not only to the acceptance of distinctively middle class styles of sociability – such as, say, evening parties or extensive participation in clubs and societies – but indeed to *any* kind of frequent and regular association with persons outside the immediate family group.'
(*A.W.C.S.*: 97).

Prima facie this is a plausible and theoretically persuasive argument.

Yet two points should be made. First, as I have said, explanation couched in terms of position in the division of labour is sporadic and piecemeal. Second, where it does occur it appears often, as in the above case, in somewhat simple and elementary terms. However, as Lockwood earlier remarked, the potentiality exists for the construction of a much more detailed typology of work situations which would focus on a large number of components of work situation, and which would therefore provide an explanation of a large number of aspects of class situation. Regrettably, this potentiality is not realized in the Luton study.

In fact, it is only in those cases where a number of affluent workers exhibit certain facets of 'middle-class' behaviour and value patterns that attention is directed toward occupational role in any consistent manner. In a number of instances, but primarily in the account of political attitudes and behaviour and of 'style of sociability', there is often painstaking analysis of the way in which the white-collar affiliations of manual workers may expose members of this group to a middle-class milieu, which in turn may be associated with the adoption of certain aspects of life-style not usually found amongst blue-collar workers. In fact within the sample, 20 per cent of the manual workers had come from white-collar homes, while 24 per cent had white-collar fathers-in-law. Futhermore, 45 per cent had wives who were, or who had been, engaged in non-manual work themselves. 'Bridges' to the middle class therefore existed in a significant proportion of cases. And it was amongst those manual families where the 'bridges' were strongest that there was evidence of, for example, a relatively high non-Labour vote or the entertaining at home of friends who were not relatives (*P.A.B.*: ch. 4; *A.W.C.S.*: ch. 4).

Nonetheless, as I have said, in the third volume of the *Affluent Worker* study, references to the occupational structure or to certain features of the division of labour in explaining class situation and class differences appear to be essentially of an *ad hoc* or fragmentary nature; they stand alongside discussion couched in terms of 'prior orientations' (without necessarily explaining the origin of such orientations),[8] or references to the influence of trade unions or community structure, without relating these aspects back to the material base. Why should this be so? I would suggest that the answer to this question lies in the choice of Luton as the locale for the research project – a locale which is by no means as suitable as the authors claim for an empirical study of changes in the structure and composition of the working class.

Luton, it will be remembered, was seen by the researchers very much as a critical case; if it could be shown that *embourgeoisement* was not occurring in this community, then substantial grounds existed for arguing that it was not happening anywhere else in British society. Luton itself was a new town whose population had increased dramatically in the post-war period, many of the newcomers living in private developments. Economically, the whole area was prosperous, expanding rapidly, and relatively isolated from the traditional industrial regions of the North and Midlands. The actual sample was drawn from three large firms known for their 'progressive' employment policies, high wages, and level of job security. Two of the firms were involved in large-batch or mass production; one manufactured chemicals using process techniques. 229 manual workers were interviewed as well as fifty-four routine white-collar employees. The large majority of the former group were non-skilled. The authors' rationale of their choice of Luton is unambiguous: 'in deciding upon the place and population for our research we were guided as closely as possible by the way in which the *embourgeoisement thesis was actually formulated and argued for in the existing literature*' (*A.W.C.S.*: 161, original italics). Given this limited brief (to which I shall return) there can be little doubt that they were successful. The question that must now be raised, however, is whether their group of affluent, primarily non-skilled workers is in fact prototypical of the British working class, as the authors would have us believe. There are two reasons which lead me to suspect that it is not.

First, as Banks has pointed out (1969) the very high levels of geographical and social mobility experienced by the sample means that it must be regarded as an exceptional and extreme case. Only 30 per cent of the workers interviewed had been brought up in the Luton area, while a similar proportion (59 per cent in the case of the sub-sample of machinists) had been inter-generationally downwardly mobile (*I.A.B.*: 150-159). This means, as the authors readily admit, that the 'sample was in some degree "self-selected" for a high level of motivation towards material advancement; that is to say, it was one which comprised a high proportion of men who were found together in Luton *because* of a decision on their part to leave a former area of residence in quest of improvement, in one way or another, in their living standards' (*I.A.B.*: 154).

Second, it is important to stress the fact that the majority of individuals in the sample were non-skilled and were employed in large-scale enterprises using mass-production techniques. Again, however, the research team was aware of problems created by the use of such a sample. Indeed, the two senior authors had previously commented:

> 'So far as work relations are concerned, then, we would doubt that favourable social conditions for *embourgeoisement* exist where workers are employed in large scale plants using large batch or mass production systems. The immediate experience of their working lives would seem to stand opposed to the social perspectives, attitudes and values which we have regarded as "middle class".' (Lockwood and Goldthorpe 1962: 17)

In this particular case, however, the use of respondents working in large-batch and mass production plants is justified first on the grounds that 'arguments relating to the influence of technological developments were relatively little emphasized in specifically British versions of the *embourgeoisement* thesis' (*A.W.C.S.*: 40). Second, their own data show technology and work situation to be less important than prior orientations to work. And yet, as we have seen, one plausible explanation of these data is that the sample was largely 'self-selected' for just these orientations. The fact that on certain issues, although by no means all, there were similarities between mass-production and process workers cannot really be taken as an indication of the lack of importance of work situation.[9] This is especially the case since two crucially influential aspects of work role were not considered in the Luton sample; namely, plant size and level of skill. All three plants studied in Luton were large, while three quarters of the sample were non-skilled employees. To be sure there were craftsmen in the sample, but they cannot be regarded as typical, and certainly bear little resemblance to the superb 'ideal type of craftsmanship' put forward in one of the early papers by the two senior authors.[10] Rather, in the Luton study, 'as in large-scale plants generally, even skilled work is subjected to the logic of specialization and control, and in this way the autonomy of craftsmen and their opportunities for applying their skills are inevitably curtailed' (*A.W.C.S.*: 58-59).

The atypical nature of the production and process workers interviewed, the absence of a sub-sample of skilled craftsmen working in more normal craft surroundings, and the lack of comparison between workers in small and large-scale enterprises all contributed to make the Luton sample less than ideal. In particular I suggest that these features of the sample were directly linked with the emergence of an action frame of reference as the major theoretical perspective, together with the demise of the theoretical approach to the analysis of social class enunciated in the early stages of the project. The result is a meticulous, and in many ways excellent, portrayal of the class situation of a particular group of affluent workers. But in the last analysis, it is not a portrayal that is grounded, as any study of class structure must be, in the material base, or division of labour, of the community or society concerned.

II

Focusing upon the sample used in the *Affluent Worker* study provides a convenient bridge to the second set of issues raised in this paper. In this section I would like to move from a theoretical to a more empirical discussion. In particular I intend to argue that the Cambridge team's analysis of changes that may be occurring in the middle levels of British class structure is strikingly narrow. Not only does the study limit itself to a test of the *embourgeoisement* thesis; it focuses upon the most simple and sociologically unlikely version of that thesis. Once again the authors are fully aware of this. The research project 'arose out of the debate on the working class in the particular form in which this was being carried on in one industrial country, Great Britain, at one period of time, the late 1950s and early 1960s' (*A.W.C.S.*: 21). There is no doubt that ten years ago a number of pollsters and politicians, political scientists, journalists, and indeed a few sociologists *were* suggesting that post-war affluence was leading to the breakdown of class lines. But other writers, predominantly sociologists, in this country and elsewhere had put forward alternative hypotheses regarding the nature of structural changes affecting the western working class. And many of these hypotheses were, and are, a good deal more sophisticated sociologically than the version of the *embourgeoisement* thesis alighted upon by the Cambridge team. Why much of this literature should be neglected and attention focussed on a narrow and – in the light of the two senior authors' superb earlier theoretical formulations – unconvincing hypothesis is therefore puzzling. We have been presented with a study which is technically excellent and admirably presented, but which tells us far more about what is not happening than about what is actually taking place. In my view, discussion of changes in the structure and composition of the working class must take explicit account of the class situation of two key groups of workers: skilled craftsmen and routine white-collar employees. This the Cambridge team did not do in any systematic or satisfactory manner.

Recognition of the unique situation of the aristocracy of labour has been central to the analysis of the western working class at least since the middle of the nineteenth century. Hobsbawm has claimed that the period 1840-1890 'may be regarded as the classical period of the nineteenth-century labour aristocracy'; 'skilled labour aristocrats being, if anything, superior in social status to many white collar workers'; 'An "artisan" or "craftsman" was not under any circumstances to be confused with a "labourer" ' (Hobsbawm 1967: 321; 323; 324). This upper stratum of the working class had to be regarded as distinct from the remainder of the manual work force on virtually every measure of life-chances. And this superiority was reflected in an emphasis upon respectability and political 'moderation', and upon a life-style that had far more in common with business and white-collar groupings than with that enjoyed by the remainder of the working class. It is generally claimed that the privileged position of the craftsman in nineteenth-century Britain rested upon his ability artificially to restrict entry to his craft, thereby increasing the scarcity value of skilled labour. This has led to the assertion that with increasing mechanization and the rise of a class of semi-skilled machine operators, the market power, and therefore privileged position, of the aristocracy of labour has been increasingly eaten away. Hobsbawm in fact argues that this has been happening in this country since the First World War so that 'Step by step the labour aristocrat found himself forced into the ranks of the working class' (Hobsbawm 1967: 381).

Whether the line separating skilled and non-skilled workers has become blurred, or even disappeared, during this century we are not in a position to say. Certainly not all writers have taken the view espoused by Hobsbawm. Michels, writing in 1915, argued that with the passage of time differentials between craftsmen and the mass of non-skilled workers were becoming 'transformed into veritable class distinction' which meant that the working class 'will become severed into two unequal parts, subject to perpetual fluctuations in their respective size' (Michels 1962: 273; 276). In opposition to Hobsbawm then, Michels suggested that as capitalism progressed we might expect the '*formation* of sharply distinguished working class aristocracies' rather than their demise (Michels 1962: 275). And certainly Lenin, in his well-known castigation of labour aristocracies, saw these formations very much as a part of British, and indeed western, society of the 1920s.

'Present day (twentieth century) imperialism has given a few advanced countries an exceptionally privileged position which . . . has produced a certain type of traitor, opportunist, and social-chauvinist leaders, who champion the interests of their own craft, their own section of the labour aristocracy.' [They have thus] 'become separated from the "masses", i.e. from the broadest strata of the working people.' (Lenin 1969: 533)

Recent research suggests that this situation might remain, albeit in less extreme form. The current work of Brown and Brannen on Tyneside shipbuilding workers, for example, shows the existence of highly structured differentials between skilled and non-skilled workers (and indeed in some cases between various groups of skilled employees). In general the skilled craftsmen adopt a paternalistic attitude towards non-skilled men, while at the same time taking care to maintain their own privileged position. 'The craft group (which comprises two thirds of the work force in their study) then can be seen both as a moral community and as an interest group. The members of a craft group have a sense of exclusive competence in the use of certain tools and techniques and a belief in their right to protect this area against the encroachments of other groups' (i.e. semi-skilled and non-skilled workers) (Brown and Brannen 1970: 200). Similarly Wedderburn and Crompton recently found 'sharp contrasts between the attitudes and behaviour between the skilled craftsmen and the semi-skilled or general workers . . .'. 'This constellation of attitudes can be termed "craft consciousness". It was this craft consciousness which supplied the tradesmen with a sense of self-worth, which was significantly lacking among the general workers' (Wedderburn and Crompton 1972: 134: 143).

Both the studies mentioned immediately above indicate the importance of distinguishing between skilled and non-skilled members of the working class; however they are primarily oriented towards industrial behaviour. In the United States, on the other hand, the _embourgeoisement_ thesis has often focused explicitly upon the changing class situation not of affluent workers _in toto_, but of affluent skilled craftsmen.[11] And my own research conducted in America would suggest that there were good reasons for doing so. For while that research led to the rejection of the thesis of _embourgeoisement_ in its simple form, I did feel able to claim that there now exists in the middle ranges of the American class structure an aristocracy of labour isolated both from the remainder of the working class _and_ from the lower reaches of the established middle class (Mackenzie 1973). While the class structure of the United States is, in many ways, very different from that of Britain, there are good theoretical reasons why one might at least expect my findings to be replicated in this country. It must be stressed that I am _not_ claiming this to be the case, but suggesting it as a possibility. It could well be that the distinction between the skilled and non-skilled worker is irrelevant to any discussion of changes in the structure of the British working class. Regrettably, however, the Luton study is able to contribute little to this particular aspect of the discussion.

As the authors of the Luton study have been quick to point out, the theme of the 'worker turning bourgeois' is not new. Neither is that of the proletarianization of the clerical or blackcoated worker. While accepting that the growth of clerical labour was an inherent feature of the development of the large scale enterprise, Marx also argued that, with the advance of capitalism, 'the commercial labourers' . . . wages have a tendency to fall, even in proportion to the average labour' (Marx 1946: 237). This Marx attributed largely to a decline in the market power of clerical workers brought by the spread of popular education and the increasing fragmentation of office work. And as in the case of the _embourgeoisement_ thesis there has been no shortage of debate revolving around the notion of the proletarianization of the routine white-collar worker.

Writing in the 1930s, both Klingender in this country and Speier in Germany put forward similar views regarding the changing class situation of the clerical employee (Klingender 1935; Speier 1952).

Klingender assigned particular significance to the twin processes of office rationalization and office mechanization. The latter especially he saw as undermining the class situation of the black-coated worker – replacing clerks with 'machine tenders' and opening up the office to large numbers of women prepared to accept lower wages than those expected by men. Similarly, Speier placed a good deal of emphasis on the impact of the rationalization of clerical tasks coupled with the introduction of more and more office machinery. In addition, he saw the extent to which clerical workers were increasingly being recruited from working-class homes as contributing to the breakdown of class differentials and, more particularly, to a process of 'decreasing social esteem' of routine clerical labour (Speier 1952: 76).

More recently, a number of writers have suggested that this process of the proletarianization of the office worker is likely to be reinforced and accelerated 'as the traditional compensation of routine clerical work disappears: that of a reasonable chance of promotion' (Westergaard 1965: 95). To take one example, Mills has argued that the opportunities for mobility inherent in routine white-collar jobs have been drastically reduced since the First World War. Two reasons are offered to account for this process. The emphasis on technical expertise and formal qualifications as requirements for upper-level positions has increased; and the concentration of office work into larger and larger units has led to a substantial reduction in the ratio of managerial to clerical posts (Mills 1951: 272-278).

Writing seven years after Mills, Lockwood argued that similar processes of bureaucratization and administrative rationalization were occurring in this country, going on to suggest that in varying degrees this was leading to the 'isolation of a separate clerical class' (Lockwood 1958: 142). This hypothesis is in direct accord with the findings of my own study previously referred to. Indeed, many of my data suggest that routine white-collar workers have, in past decades, experienced more significant and far-reaching changes in their class situation than have affluent skilled craftsmen (Mackenzie 1973).

As in the case of my discussion of the aristocracy of labour, however, I must stress that I am not arguing that clerical workers are being absorbed into the working class in Britain or that they are becoming increasingly dissociated from the established middle class.[12] But I am suggesting that, *in the light of the existing literature,* any study of changes in the class situation of affluent workers must also focus upon the position of routine clerical employees. This, surprisingly, the Cambridge team did not do in any systematic manner. To be sure, there is a sub-sample of fifty-four clerical workers 'To facilitate detailed comparisons between our affluent manual workers and men in lower level non-manual occupations' (*A.W.C.S.*: 52). And such comparisons, when they are made, are important and suggestive, especially, for example, those relating to family structure and the socialization of children. However, because 'in view of the very restricted nature of the white collar sample, we have not attempted to give any great weight to the findings it produced . . .' (*A.W.C.S.*: 53), the analysis of the class situation of routine white-collar workers is by no means as complete as one might have wished.

One final, and hopefully unnecessary point should be made. I have discussed above what I see as a number of weaknesses in the Luton study as an examination of changes in the middle levels of the British class structure. Nevertheless, the fact remains that it has contributed immeasurably to the analysis of class and class structure in this country. In the introduction to the third volume, the authors remark: '. . . our ultimate aim is certainly not the vain one of bringing controversy to an end. It might more accurately be defined as that of providing controversy with more and better material on which to feed' (*A.W.C.S.*: 1). There can be no doubt they have been successful in that aim. And that is a considerable and enviable achievement.

Notes

1 Perhaps the two most important critiques are those of Westergaard and Daniel. Westergaard has been concerned to show the fragility and therefore conflict proneness of the 'cash nexus' binding the Luton workers to their work situation. See Westergaard (1970) and also Blackburn (1967). See also the debate between Goldthorpe and Daniel on the validity of the action approach in industrial sociology: Daniel (1969, 1971); Goldthorpe (1970).

2 Lockwood has also been at pains to stress the importance of 'family bridges' that may span the line separating adjacent social classes. Such bridges may lead to a breakdown of class differentials by exposing members of a working-class family for example, to middle-class standards and values. Obvious instances might be where the wife of a manual worker is herself employed in a non-manual capacity, or where a woman of middle-class origins becomes downwardly mobile through marriage. See Lockwood 1960: 255-256; 1966: 263, footnote 4.

3 It could, I suppose, be argued that references to the 'conversion' of the *Affluent Worker* team to an action perspective is illusory, in that there

are signs of such an approach in the earlier theoretical writings of the two senior authors. It might, for example, be suggested that Lockwood's celebrated dictum 'a washing machine is a washing machine is a washing machine' is an indication of this writer's recognition of the importance of motives or orientations. I would not be impressed by such an argument. To be sure both Lockwood and Goldthorpe focussed on differing value and normative patterns prior to entering the field, but such differences were seen to be grounded firmly in positions in the division of labour.

4 The three volumes resulting from the Luton study will be referred to in abreviated form. *The Affluent Worker: Industrial Attitudes and Behaviour* (I.A.B.); *The Affluent Worker: Political Attitudes and Behaviour* (P.A.B.); *The Affluent Worker in the Class Structure* (A.W.C.S.).

5 It should perhaps be pointed out that not all 'action theorists' have implied that work and non-work influences are distinct. In the words of one recent writer:

> 'Variations in the value attached to non-economic aspects of industrial work are likely to be the result of prior work experience of different kinds of jobs during which time the worker's priorities concerning non-economic rewards are developed.' (Ingham 1970: 137)

6 Nevertheless it is interesting to note that in the third volume the authors do preface discussion on their findings with the following comment:

> '. . . a *straightforward description* of the social lives of our affluent workers and their families, set against the available comparative material from studies of white collar groups, can provide an appropriate and cogent test of the *embourgeoisement* thesis in the form in which this has generally been advanced. *Such a description* constitutes the main context of the chapters that follow.'
> (*A.W.C.S.*: 52, my italics)

7 Again contrast this approach with that of Ingham, who is concerned to demonstrate the *interaction* of 'salient work situation factors' and 'the out-plant determinants of workers' social and political consciousness' (Ingham 1969: 240). In fact this writer demonstrates that large plants foster 'left-wing' attitudes and commitment to the trade union movement, *regardless* of party affiliation.

8 An example might be the author's discussion of 'normative conversion' between 'advanced' manual and routine white-collar workers. Although a valid sociological explanation is provided for the departure of affluent workers from traditional working-class patterns of behaviour (by reference to 'family bridges') why *clerks* should be

behaving in ways distinct from those of the established middle class is not explained. See the discussion of the move to 'family-centredness' on the part of both affluent workers and lower-level white-collar workers (*A.W.C.S.*: 106-115).

9 See, for example, the differences between skilled and non-skilled workers with regard to preferred method of payment (*A.W.C.S.*: 69).

10 'The following might be put forward as an "ideal" type of craftsmanship. The craftsman works with tools which, if not his own property, are his at least in a psychological sense; over a lengthy period of apprenticeship he has mastered their use and made them extensions of his hands, and even, one might say, of his personality. The craftsman's task is either one which is complete in itself, such as the making of a specific article – a gun, a shoe, a wheel – or, if not, forms part of a collective task – say, the building of a ship – in which the relationship of his contribution to the whole can be clearly seen. In carrying out his work the craftsman is able to proceed largely according to his own pace and plan. He requires no external assistance nor external supervision; he is his own taskmaster. The craftsman thus in various ways derives gratification directly from his work activity – from the initial devising of his task, from the continual joining of design and action and from the ultimate creative achievement. His work is his chief form of self expression, the mainspring of his entire way of life. His leisure, for example, is not a refuge from his work but an adjunct to it, a time of recreation in the full sense of the word.' (Lockwood and Goldthorpe 1962: footnote 19)

11 See, amongst others, Mayer (1955: 41-42); Lenski (1963: 48-49).

12 For example 83 per cent of the Luton white-collar sub-sample considered that a 'worker of ability' could be promoted at least to the level of 'middle-management' within their own place of employment.

References

BANKS, J. A. 1969. Review of: *The Affluent Worker: Industrial Attitudes and Behaviour*. *British Journal of Sociology* **20** (1) March.

BLACKBURN, R. 1967. The Unequal Society. In Blackburn, R. and Cockburn, A. (eds). *The Incompatibles*. Harmondsworth: Penguin.

BLAUNER, R. 1964. *Alienation and Freedom*. Chicago: University of Chicago Press.

BROWN, R. and BRANNEN, P. 1970. Social Relations and Social Perspectives amongst Shipbuilding Workers – A Preliminary Statement. Part I: *Sociology* **4** (1) January; Part II *Sociology* **4** (2) May.

DANIEL, W. W. 1969. Industrial Behaviour and Orientation to Work – A Critique. *The Journal of Management Studies* **6** (3) October.

—— 1971. Productivity Bargaining and Orientation to Work – A Rejoinder to Goldthorpe. *The Journal of Management Studies* **8** (3) October.

GOLDTHORPE, J. H. 1959. Technical Organisation as a Factor in Supervisory-Worker Conflict. *British Journal of Sociology* **10** (3) September.

—— 1965. Orientation to Work and Industrial Behaviour Among Assembly-Line Operatives: A Contribution Towards an Action Approach in Industrial Sociology. Paper presented to the Sociology Teachers Section of the British Sociological Association.

—— 1970. The Social Action Approach to Industrial Sociology: A Reply to Daniel. *The Journal of Management Studies* **7** (2) May.

GOLDTHORPE, J. H., LOCKWOOD, D., BECHHOFER, F., PLATT, J. 1968. *The Affluent Worker: Industrial Attitudes and Behaviour*. Cambridge: Cambridge University Press.

—— 1968. *The Affluent Worker: Political Attitudes and Behaviour*. Cambridge: Cambridge University Press.

—— 1969. *The Affluent Worker in the Class Structure*. Cambridge: Cambridge University Press.

HAMMOND, P. E. (ed.) 1964. *Sociologists at Work*. New York: Basic Books, Inc.

HOBSBAWM, E. J. 1967. *Labouring Man*. New York: Anchor Books.

INGHAM, G. K. 1969. Plant Size: Political Attitudes and Behaviour. *The Sociological Review* **17** (2) July.

—— 1970. *Size of Industrial Organisation and Worker Behaviour*. Cambridge: Cambridge University Press.

KLINGENDER, F. D. 1935. *The Condition of Clerical Labour in Britain* London: Martin Lawrence Ltd.

LENIN, V. L. 1969. *Selected Works*. London: Lawrence and Wishart.

LENSKI, G. 1963. *The Religious Factor*. New York: Anchor Books.

LOCKWOOD, D. 1958. *The Blackcoated Worker: A Study in Class Consciousness*. London: George Allen and Unwin Ltd.

—— 1960. The 'New Working Class'. *European Journal of Sociology* **1** (2).

—— 1966. Sources of Variation in Working Class Images of Society. *The Sociological Review* **14** (4) November.

LOCKWOOD, D. and GOLDTHORPE, J. H. 1962. The Manual Worker: Affluence, Aspirations and Assimilation. Paper presented to the Annual Conference of the British Sociological Association.

MACKENZIE, G. 1970. The Class Situation of Manual Workers: The United States and Britain. *British Journal of Sociology* **21** (3) September.

———— 1973. *The Aristocracy of Labour: The Position of Skilled Craftsmen in the American Class Structure.* Cambridge: Cambridge University Press.

MARX, K. 1946. *Capital* Vol. III. Calcutta: Saraswaty Library.

MAYER, K. B. 1955. *Class and Society.* New York: Random House.

MICHELS, R. 1962. *Political Parties.* New York: Collier Books.

MILLS, C. WRIGHT. 1951. *White Collar.* New York: Oxford University Press.

SPEIER, H. 1952. The Salaried Employee in Modern Society. In Speier, H. (ed.) *Social Order and the Risks of War.* New York: George W. Stewart, Inc.

WEDDERBURN, D. and CROMPTON, R. 1972. *Workers' Attitudes and Technology.* Cambridge: Cambridge University Press.

WESTERGAARD, J. H. 1965. The Withering Away of Class. In Anderson, P. and Blackburn, R. (eds.), *Towards Socialism.* London: Collins.

———— 1970. The Rediscovery of the Cash Nexus. In Miliband, R. and Saville, J. (eds)., *The Socialist Register* 1970. London: The Merlin Press.

WOODWARD, J. 1958. *Management and Technology.* London: H.M.S.O.

———— 1965. *Industrial Organization – Theory and Practice.* London: Oxford University Press.

LESLIE BENSON

Market Socialism and Class Structure: Manual Workers and Managerial Power in the Yugoslav Enterprise

This paper takes as its theme the high degree of power wielded by management in the Yugoslav enterprise and deals with the way in which that power is established and sustained. The progressive strengthening of the workers' councils over the past decade, particularly over questions critical for class relations appeared to hold out to the working-class strong hopes for extensive control over their work situation, so blurring the social rift between office and works employees characteristic of capitalist society, which stems from the experience on the shop floor of 'the impersonal and standardized relationships of the factory bureaucracy' (Lockwood 1958: 71). In practice, there is a structural discrepancy between the system of institutionalized authority and the factual distribution of social power.[1]

INFLUENCE WITHIN THE COLLECTIVE

All empirical studies indicate that the influence of workers on their representative organs is low. The workers' sense of separation from these bodies is expressed in the fact that they attribute to them a degree of influence well above that which they consider themselves to have in enterprise decision-making. Further, despite the legal status of the councils as the sole source of legitimate authority on all major questions within the enterprise, the influence of top management personnel is invariably evaluated as greater than that of the self-management organs themselves (Zupanov 1969: 174-5; Siber 1966, passim). In short, no research findings have yet come up with the conclusion that the introduction of workers' self-management in the economy has resulted in a democratic distribution of influence within the enterprise. This is true even if we take into account the fact that, as we might expect, in the struggle over certain key issues various competing groups within the collective are highly motivated to mobilize support. This does indeed happen, as one analysis of certain specific areas of decision-making has demonstrated. But the increased influence of manual workers is matched by other groups, and in twelve of the thirteen fields scrutinized managers continued to have the greatest say, including over such crucial matters as income distribution, hiring and firing, and disciplinary procedures (Zupanov 1969: 177).

TABLE I

Influence of socio-economic groups on the work and decisions of the workers' council in three Zagreb enterprise, A, B, and C.

Group	influence		
	A	B	C
top management	4.66	4.40	4.49
staff specialists	4.02	3.85	3.81
heads of economic units	3.36	3.25	3.46
party and T.U. officials	3.55	3.60	3.64
supervisory staff	2.72	2.92	3.08
white collar	2.85	3.04	2.87
highly skilled and skilled workers	2.85	2.76	2.94
Semi- and un-skilled workers	2.52	2.39	2.30

Source: Zupanov 1969: 221, table 3. A five-point scale was used, so that $1 =$ no influence, $5 =$ very strong influence.

Work situation as itself conditioning participation in decision-making has been the subject of one study in a Slovenian enterprise. The investigation is of particular interest because it covered a high proportion of skilled men, who tend to be relatively active in self-management affairs. The study set out to elicit the conditions conducive to such activity and concluded that the key lay in the process of communication which went on within the work-group. Thus, 'of workers who rarely communicated fully, two-thirds never participate, while only 20 per cent of those who communicate frequently do *not* participate' (Rus 1966a; 99). Given the importance of communication in opinion formation, it followed that workers participated most often in matters about which they had personal experience and knowledge, even those who habitually participated a great deal.

This finding is in itself trivial, and could have been predicted. However, it provides an explanation for two generally observed facts.

First, relative intensity and frequency of communication as factors
conditioning participation tells us why skilled workers are differentiated
from their unskilled colleagues with respect to influence. The author
notes that highly skilled men and those with long service communicate
best. The point to observe, however, is that job-classified skills, not
educational attainment, is here in question. The job-related skill
classification is largely a function of on-the-floor training, and so constitutes a rough index both of length of service and of integration within
the work group. The inference is, therefore, that we cannot expect any
major improvement in workers' influence as the manual labour force
becomes increasingly urbanized and schooled. The second conclusion of
the study is related to this point and is of much greater weight. The
work situation of *all* manual workers, the investigation points out,
severs them from the structure of influence within the enterprise. The
types of discussion in which the men felt at home and could participate
freely were of a formless and spontaneous kind, without influence on the
self-management organs, because the workers could not successfully
channel opinion so as to take effect within the institutional framework of
decision-making. Thus, although they discussed income questions
rather infrequently, the workers felt they had most influence over these
questions because their voice had to some degree been institutionalized
through the establishment of clear and publicly known pay schedules
(Rus 1966a: 108). This degree of institutionalization was confirmed by a
survey carried out by a weekly journal in eleven Serbian enterprises,
which produced the rather surprising finding that manual workers
participated most often concerning issues of general business and investment decisions, not incomes. The reason given to account for this
was that income questions had already become routinized.[2] Under
conditions of normal profitability, where the enterprise receipts are
sufficient to cover all the claims made on the pool of incomes, the
workers do not need actively to mobilize in defence of their rights. It is
of considerable interest, incidentally, that the political authorities have
always interfered (at least until the mid-sixties) in the formulation of
pay schedules to quite a marked degree. It points to the conclusion,
which will emerge during the course of this discussion, that the successful inclusion of manual workers in decision-making processes needs
the operation of countervailing power on their behalf, *vis-à-vis* management, to ensure that all important questions are resolved with respect
to rules that are clear, and which can be routinized.

In fact, workers are constantly at a disadvantage because they are
very often unable to perceive and correct disabling abrogations of their

authority vested in the workers' councils. Even in highly industrialized Slovenia, where the working class appears to be generally sensitive of its rights, we find some extraordinary omissions in the framing of enterprise rules, which leave them open to the possibility of exploitation and manipulation. Of 100 enterprises surveyed in one study, in no less than 92 per cent of cases the firms' statutes failed to specify the procedure by which labour norms were to be approved. In a third of them it was not even clear which body had the final say over income distribution (Kavcic 1972: 39). A more detailed analysis of enterprise statutes carried out in 1966 indicated that they are typically framed in such a way as to leave organizational rules unclear, or to result in the transference of important decision-making powers to smaller organs, sometimes even to individuals. The statutes commonly take the form of parrotted versions of the federal laws on self-management, virtually being a paraphrase of the preambles to such legislation. As a consequence, while stating as a principle the inalienable right of the workers' council to the final say in all matters affecting the collective, the statutes in practice work on quite other lines. It is usually the case, for example, that the management board is invested with full rights to decide on questions where workers lodge complaints with a view to securing restitution of labour rights which have been infringed. Sometimes management personnel are actually exempted from the disciplinary procedures which cover the rest of the collective. The net outcome of all this is that the workers self-management body tends to become an ancillary committee for deciding questions of relatively small importance.

Two examples from the sensitive area of income distribution illustrate how ignorance or carelessness on the part of workers at strategic moments in the establishment of pay schedules later led to conflicts in which they found they had no legal rights of redress. The 'Partizanka' knitwear factory in Belgrade operated a pay schedule incorporating a basic wage and an incentive bonus scheme. Those working in production received a bonus if they fulfilled their norms by 80 per cent or more; if production fell below the norm they got only a percentage of their basic pay. In 1964 this latter situation occurred. At the same time, the office administration was eight days late with the accounts. The workers accepted their loss of income without fuss, but demanded that the accounts personnel should also have their pay reduced by 25 per cent, eight days expressed as a proportion of a calendar month. In fact, these employees got their full basic pay *plus* a 100 per cent incentive bonus! The workers' protests were met with an instruction to consult the rules more closely, which on inspection were shown to contain a clause exempting the white-collar administration entirely from the operation of norms. A similar situation cropped up at the Zenica steelworks, in Bosnia. There, the pay schedule worked on a points system and included a clause stating that the number of points allocated to management personnel could not fall below a fixed minimum. When the income pool proved insufficient to cover all the points earned in a month, the amounts allotted to management were subtracted from the pool, and the points amassed by the other grades were paid out at a reduced value per point. In this case, the collective had apparently acquiesced in the offending clause under the impression it would never have to be invoked (Jovanov *et al.*: 1967: 124).

TABLE 2

Estimates of Group A (subordinates) and group B (managerial personnel) of the distribution of influence in the Zagreb economy.

group/organ	influence (5-point scale)			
	enterprise level		economic unit level[3]	
	A	B	A	B
workers' council	3.33	3.64	3.07	3.25
management board	3.45	3.61	3.15	3.21
top management	4.77	4.56	4.68	4.26
EU heads	3.66	3.27	4.93	3.91
supervisory staff	3.01	2.64	3.45	3.26
subordinates	1.86	2.08	2.18	2.55
no. of respondents	68–70	85–90	68–71	84–87

Source: Zupanov 1969: 186.

The situations just described explain at least in part the contents of *Table 2*. Irrespective of place in production, all respondents agreed that top managerial figures have a greater influence on decision-making than the organs formally constituted for that purpose. However, managements do not wield this high degree of influence simply by default, or because the workers are not adept at operating the system in their own favour. They have it because of their crucial position within the enterprise, which confers on them a monopoly of the information necessary to the effective functioning of the enterprise. The fact that managers appear at meetings of the workers' council wearing their 'self-management' hats in no way erases the power they have to withold or make public all the possible options open to the collective. Only they can offer the voters real choices based on a clear statement of the issues involved and presented with a minimum of mystification. From the point of view of workers' influence it would seem to be of little moment whether the management takes the trouble to carry the workers' council with it or not, since the power of managements *over* the councils can just as well be interpreted as power *within* them. The cooperation of management personnel is thus critical in making self-management rights more than a formality, since without a sustained flow of information from them to the worker there is no alternative source of knowledge which can aid the workers' councils in the formulation of their views.[4]

Management influence is greatly augmented by the fact that much of the day-to-day routine, and the preparation and execution of policy, must of necessity fall to organs smaller than the workers' council, and where manual workers are in a minority of two to one. The presence of top management and specialists in large numbers on the executive organs would seem to be unavoidable if business is to be carried on at all. They play an indispensable part not only within the organization itself, but as mediators with the world outside. An early study of self-management in small enterprises (employing less than thirty people) showed that collectives in small firms were disadvantaged in decision-making because of the 'various legal regulations concerning labour and business operation, the recommendations of the local authorities, chambers of commerce and technical institutions. It was found that there are many enterprises where the collective is unacquainted with these legal regulations, which are studied and applied by the specialists in the enterprise' (Matic 1960: 125). The point about these small firms is that all decision-making is made on a collective basis, without intermediary organs, so that in them, if anywhere, workers' influence ought to be a real possibility. Under the circumstances, it is not really surprising that the blue-collar respondents ascribed more influence to the management boards than to the workers' councils, a judgement from which the managerial group barely dissented.

Supposing that an issue comes to the full workers' council in such a form as to provoke conflict, there are still great difficulties in the way of a decision in favour of manual workers, because the latter make up only a bare majority on the councils. This is a fact which has only recently come to light, and a short digression is needed to explain it. Earlier statistics were organized on the principle of formal skills only, as shown in the first part of *Table 3*. Presented in this way, the composition of workers' councils has always looked fairly heavily biased in favour of manual groups, though even by this classification the number of 'workers' has been falling over time. However, formal skills are an unreliable guide to position in production. The maverick groupings are 'highly skilled' and (to a lesser extent) 'skilled' workers. During the rapid industrial expansion of the 'fifties and early 'sixties, the schooling system lagged in its capacity to produce trained technical personnel. Many enterprises had to make shift to use skilled labour, particularly those with *formal* qualifications (applying to the man, not the job), so that many were upwardly mobile into the first ranks of line management and middle-grade technical positions. In addition, after the war political priorities persisted long enough to produce a large influx of workers into top managerial positions, as the figures on directors' qualifications in 1966 clearly show.[5] Both these trends have combined seriously to exaggerate the extent of manual representation on the workers' councils when possession of formal skills, rather than occupational status, is used as the criterion of social composition.

TABLE 3

Composition of the self-management organs of Yugoslav enterprises, 1970, according to (i) formal skills and (ii) position in production.

Group/organ				
(i)			*manual*	*non-manual*
workers' councils			67.6	32.4
management boards, commissions			44.2	55.8
(ii)	*top management*	*manual*	*routine non-manual*	*technical staff*
workers' councils	6.1	54.9	15.2	23.8
managements boards, commissions	23.3	32.0	14.2	30.5

Source: *Statisticki Bilten* no. 658, tables 1-4, 1-5, 1-8, and 1-9.

All the indications are that the lines of conflict follow the classic western division between manual and non-manual groups. This is dramatically borne out by the incidence of industrial action. Strikes are increasingly figuring as a working-class response to their distinctive isolation within the political system of the enterprise. By the mid-sixties, strikes were averaging well over two hundred a year, and unofficial estimates put the number considerably higher than this (Popov 1969: 610). Significantly, well over 80 per cent of strikes analysed in a survey covering this period occurred in the three most highly developed republics, and skilled men appear to have taken over as the leaders in strike activity (Jovanov 1972: table 8, 116; Jovanov 1967: 135). In other words, self-management institutions are being manipulated against those workers who are most articulate and sensitive about their rights. At the same time, strike action is almost entirely confined to the manual working class. In four-fifths of all cases recorded manual workers alone were involved. Even in those cases where non-manual personnel joined them, they usually did so because they formed an integral part of the work unit in question and not as an independent force with specific white-collar grievances. The intensification of the socialist market and the move to enterprise autonomy has thus sharpened the social divisions between manual and non-manual personnel. The instability and uncertainty arising from economic reform threw great strain on self-management mechanisms, which has erupted into a struggle within enterprises. In this struggle the workers have learned that management has the whip hand, and the classic weapon of the strike is more effective in combatting managerial power than is the workers' council. It has, in fact, been suggested that the workers increasingly see the self-management structure as a sort of talking shop, ideally suited to the tendency of managements to compromise and procrastinate in their own favour, which actually detracts from the power of the working class to take direct action.

> 'By striking, workers often achieve what they were unable to bring about by normal means. Sometimes workers get negative answers to their demands, with the explanation that these demands cannot be met because circumstances do not permit it. But when they down tools everything is immediately put right, money is found for rises, a way is found of transferring the foreman who doesn't fit, and so on ... The strike is shown up as an efficient way of resolving problems, at least as far as the workers are concerned.' (Kavcic 1966: 203-4)

Another feature of industrial organization suggests that working-class influence is likely to diminish rather than increase in the future. The process of amalgamation into larger industrial units is accelerating. Between 1965 and 1967 alone, 202 enterprises were absorbed, nearly a third of them employing 250 to 1000 people. Even small firms frequently have second levels of self-management – that is, decision-making organs representing the firm as a whole *and* self-management organs in the parts. In the large firms, second and even third levels of self-management are quite usual.[6] The problem of exercising influence through the self-management structure is thus becoming enormously complicated by the intricacies arising from the relationships between self-management hierarchies. The constitution of economic units in enterprises, a progressive aspect of the self-management system which aimed to get real influence down to the shop-floor is in this way undermined in its effect. The following evidence of a skilled worker to a trade-union enquiry team shows very clearly how decisively the shop-floor worker is affected in his control of the work environment by the quality and kind of administrative arrangements made for deciding issues. The evidence is particularly valuable because it is not simply a grouse, but a reasoned criticism of self-management practice from the point of view of a collective whose members are clearly strongly motivated to participate. It serves very well as a summary of the analysis so far.

'Things don't happen as we are told they should in theory. What's the use of us wasting time working out rules for management and distribution when in practice we don't stick to them? We workers know how much we turn out on the job. We have a concrete operation to carry out, and we even know how much we should get for it, but we don't know about the working and operation of our economic unit, because the administrative services, the accounts department and so on, are not yet in a position to determine the income of our work unit, and in particular we know very little about the working of the whole collective. But, as well as these weaknesses, we see to it that there are possibilities for real management and better distribution. In the economic unit, at meetings of all the workpeople, we decide who to take on to the collective and who to fire. At these meetings, we also discuss other matters connected with the better functioning of our work unit. That's good, and the workers willingly discuss problems. It has been proved that we are well able to discuss a concrete job, or something that needs to be done in the work programme, but as far as economic results are concerned, that we don't know about. So we are often surprised by the outcome at the end of the month, when we get our personal incomes. This puts us in a situation where we're not certain whether we shall get our wages, our personal incomes as they call it.[7] For this reason there is a lot of irritation among us.' (Jovanov *et al.* 1967:21)

There is, then, no way in which manual workers can challenge the influence of top management over decision-making, as the system now stands. In a situation where they have far-reaching legal rights, the workers find themselves heavily dependent on the *goodwill* of the administration, and particularly of the director, for the chance of a real say in the running of the enterprise. The director has important powers of control assigned to him by federal law which make him the lynchpin of managerial power within the collective. He is the only individual to whom the law allows a permanent self-management function, as an *ex officio* member of the management board. It is his responsibility to ensure the efficient running of the enterprise, and to implement the decisions of the workers' council, which he is also empowered to suspend if he believes them to contravene state regulations. It is the director's job to see that the self-management organs get material and proposals on the basis of which to exercise their decision-making functions, and to represent the firm as a legal person in all dealings with third parties. Even this short catalogue makes it clear that he is not just another management figure. The way in which the director elects to discharge his functions can make or mar the activity of the workers' council, despite his theoretical subordination to it.

Managements do not, therefore, have to do anything to maintain their influence. It is already maintained by law and organizational logic, and managements can simply withold the cooperation the workers need if they are to activate their formal powers. The most important question for the functioning of the system is thus how management personnel are to be subjected to sanctions when they fail to seek and take account of the aspirations of shop-floor men. We have a link here between the concepts of influence and power touched on at the beginning of the paper. In practice, the line between the two is very hard to draw. Once decisions are taken in the worker's council they are legally binding on the collective, and workers can be subjected to disciplinary action if they break the rules. The rules can, of course, be changed. But the limitations on workers' influence operate as fully in the second case as in the first. Actions against arbitrary managements can therefore never take the form of a competition for influence, which of its nature implies compromise and exchange. Where workers fail to get their voice heard through the channels of self-management representation they have to face the problem of mobilizing countervailing power.

COUNTERVAILING POWER

The Party underlines the weakness of the self-management system because it will not divide its authority by making class conflict respectable, to borrow Geiger's phrase (1969: 96). Although the managerial stratum no longer constitutes an integral part of a state bureaucratic machine, as in the immediate post-war period, the Party continues to see to it that leading *cadres* in the economy are recruited on the basis of political activism, so that there is a close connection between managerial personnel and local political elites. (A survey of 245 top managers showed that every single respondent was a functionary in one organization or another outside the enterprise (Zupanov 1969: 247).) In the Yugoslav system of economic organization, because patterns of authority at the workplace are not stabilized by the organized political power of the working class, there are no structural constraints on the abuse of managerial power by outside agencies. Indeed, the close association of managements with local elites means that it is they who are able to mobilize power from that source in order further to strengthen their position within the enterprise. The mechanisms of mobility by which the Party authority is united with the professional apex of the occupational order becomes in turn a mechanism by which managements can tighten their grip on recalcitrant workers' councils.

It is not very surprising to learn that the pattern of association between organizational function and political office is duplicated within the firm itself. One large-scale survey of seventy enterprises showed that nearly 70 per cent of managerial personnel were also officials of the Party and trade-union organizations, and *more than a third* of them occupied the key post of Party secretary. Nearly two-thirds of them were members of the self-management organs, and they supplied an extremely high proportion of the presidents both of the workers' councils and of the management boards (Dzinic 1961: 357-8). Although central government policy has been to discourage multiple office-holding in enterprises, figures for the mid-sixties show that it continues to occur with great frequency.[8]

The predictable effects of this fusion between party and management are indicated in a recent study of the Slovenian workforce. Manual workers in this investigation were outnumbered in even the trade-union posts by management personnel (Kavcic 1969: 122). Union activity under these conditions becomes essentially low key, dominated by quasi-social work such as organizing funds for distressed individuals, arranging works' outings, and New Year celebrations, and the like. When asked what their union branch had done for them during the previous year, only 23 per cent of respondents mentioned the settlement of grievances, and this activity was listed thirteenth in a total of eighteen fields of operation (Kavcic 1969: 99). This confirms the point that major decisions continue to be taken within management enclaves, although of course the formal rites of union consulation are always observed. Perhaps the best comment on the relationship of the trade unions to working-class aspirations and needs is expressed by the fact that the only strikes that have been union-led have been those staged by teachers (Zupanov 1971: 441).

The worker is equally disadvantaged by the institutional arrangements flowing from the self-management philosophy with respect to grievance procedures. Self-management theory does not acknowledge the principle of class conflict and treats all disputes as soluble through the formal channels. There is no specifically working-class organization that enables the shop-floor man to seek the redress of grievances beyond the enterprise. He is expected to assert his rights through those very mechanisms which infringed them in the first place. While the management can initiate disciplinary action against the workers, there is no device by which workers can effectively move against managements. The only resort is to the courts which are slow, uncertain, and expensive; and in the meantime the worker remains exposed to managerial reprisals at the workplace.[9]

Consideration of the evidence lends superficial credibility to the view that the whole edifice of self-management is an elaborate sham behind which stands the reality of authoritarian political control. This view is not very convincing because it requires us to explain why the Party should devote its energies to subverting by covert activity the very institution which it has itself promoted through legislation designed to extend workers' rights; although it is common practice for directors to include in their management teams party functionaries and key members of the self-management organs, so creating an 'informal enterprise management, by means of which the director can secure *de facto* those decisions over which the regulations give him no authority' (Zupanov 1969: 251). However, this association by no means indicates that the director relies on Party support to carry out his policies. It is simply a device of convenience, which enables the director to substitute for the complex process of carrying the collective with him a less arduous 'rule by activists'. The erroneous assumption on which the 'conspiracy theory' of self-management rests is that the Party organs within the enterprise constitute a unified source of independent power controlled from Party headquarters outside. But in fact the contrary is the case; the dominant position of managerial personnel within the Party hierarchy means that they are able to block the Party's influence as a potential source of countervailing power. It is not authoritarian *political* control which is at the root of manual workers' problems, but lack of it.

As one Party leader has expressed it, 'The worker does not condemn the Party for its *usurpation* but because of its *lack of struggle* against usurpation; he does not condemn it because it because it interferes in self-management practice but because it is *missing* from it, because it makes no real effort to develop that practice' (Vasilev 1967: 360). The problem for the workers is that increasingly the communist in the enterprise is also a superior in the division of labour, and the bureaucratization of the self-management system is a problem inseparable from the increasing coincidence of political and organizational authority. This problem is itself connected with a weakening of centralized political control which has followed a major devolution of authority to the communes over the last twenty years. This devolution has led to the increased autonomy of local political elites, which are able to defy the policy directives emanating from the Party's central leadership.

This comes out most clearly in the case of arbitrary and unpopular managements which, having succeeded in uniting their workers against them to the pitch where an approach has to be made to the federal agancies, contrive to escape the consequences of their abuse of power through the use of political connections. This is always a likelihood when power is exercised through informal structures with a pronounced degree of decentralization. When managements act in this way, the dislocation of power must first be detected, which may be difficult in itself, and then dealt with by action from the Party's upper echelons directed at dismantling and reconstituting the very elite structures on which the integrity of the political chain of command rests. Ironically, this cannot be achieved without reactivating methods of bureaucratic supervision of managements which decentralization was designed to supplant. In practice control by the federal government simply remains weak, because '. . . politic and managerial groups are intimately linked to form a more or less homogeneous social stratum, wielding considerable social power which even the courts can do nothing to curb' (Rus: 1966b: 1094).

It is not, of course, suggested that the central Party leadership has lost the capacity ultimately to compel obedience through the threat of force. However, it is unwilling arbitrarily to dislodge the full-time officials at local level, around which elites form, because their loyalty to the Party (though not always to its policy principles) is a safeguard against the usurpation of political command roles by the professional middle classes, and the consequent secularization of the Party itself. By the same token, however, these political stalwarts are apt to conform only with difficulty to the liberalization of social and economic life, and they have plenty of scope for the creation of local satrapies in the absence both of democratic criticism and control from below and of detailed administrative directives from above. The central Party leadership is becoming greatly concerned by the check these communists present to an alliance of Party power with the skills and prestige of the newer communists, and there has been a brisk ideological campaign 'to take away from the "upper" stratum of communists all possibility of usurpation' (Vasilev: 1967: 360-1). (Observe the studied use of 'upper'.) However, there is no sign that moves towards the democratization of political life will be allowed to reinforce the rhetoric. Since the Party desires the untrammelled power of the political machine, it must tolerate its abuse and temper it where it can. In this sense, the failure of workers' self-mangement can be seen as an unintended consequence of the wish to maintain a Party monopoly of political power combined with a move to market mechanisms which have given enterprises and their managements greater independence. The authorities recognize the dilemma they have created for themselves, and have already made one symbolic concession to the situation. Strikes, while not acknowledged in constitutional theory, are in practice accepted as a legitimate means of securing the restitution of workers' rights. Here, again, the Party does not want to see the political initiative slip away from it, and there is now talk of the trade union heading 'justified' strikes, which may be understood as an attempt to revive the Party's mediating role between the working class and management – a role which was previously exercised through the fusion of economic and political power. However, this cannot lead to any major redistribution of power within the enterprise so long as the union itself is so closely intertwined with the dominant political structure *and* with managerial functions.

CONCLUSION

'Market socialism' embodies two principles of stratification which overlay the increasing deprivation of the working class[10] with a collective experience of the authority structure of the enterprise which compares unfavourably with that of their western counterparts. The system of workers' councils in the economy has had no major effect on social relations within the enterprise, and the line of social cleavage between workers and managements is as salient in Yugoslavia as elsewhere. Work situation and factors arising from the dual role of managements as businessmen and local elite members combine to create a setting where the existence of an informal enterprise administration is the rule, not the exception. Clearly, it is only a short step from here to exploitative and repressive relationships in the firm, and the evidence suggests there is already enough of this to constitute a political problem. This problem can be traced back to the fact that decentralization has distanced the working class from Party power, while at the same time the emergence of independent working-class safeguards, like all forms of pluralism, is politically unacceptable.

Notes

1 Following Zupanov, whose research forms the empirical basis of much of this paper, social power is conceived of as the latent possibility of introducing coercion into the social situation. See R. Bierstedt (1950). Influence can best be thought of as the chances that any group or person will affect in a given degree the outcome of events in the enterprise, within the area of decision-making that the law assigns to the self-management organs. This definition is derived from A. Tannenbaum (1962). The use of these distinctions will emerge in the course of discussion.

2 *NIN* (Belgrade weekly journal) 9 May, 1971, p. 32.

3 Despite its name, an economic unit is one which has decision-making rights, although the scope of these rights can vary greatly, as can the size of the unit. Its defining feature (hence the name) is that it is a separate entity in the accounting and income distribution process.

4 *Politika Ekspres* (Belgrade daily evening paper) 12 January 1972 p. 4.

What happens when the flow of information breaks down is illustrated by the remarks of a skilled worker in the Serbian electrical industry: 'We get material in a rush, hardly anybody reads it. For instance, we voted for the rules on incentive payments in a hurry, and only found out later that they didn't suit us. Communications are not good. Our four-page newsletter comes out twice a month, but it only carries stuff which is of no interest to us.'

5 54 per cent of retiring directors in 1966 had manual formal skill ratings. See *Statisticki Bilten* no. 447, tables 3-2 and 4-2

6 Of 6356 enterprises employing more than 70 people in 1979, 4898 had economic units which functioned as separate collectives for some decision-making functions. *Statisticki Bilten* no. 658, table 1-2.

7 The slip of the tongue is an interesting sidelight on the opaqueness of the administrative system from the horizon of the workbench. 'Pay' is what a man takes home, what he understands, and is the word used in everyday speech (*plata*). 'Personal income' is a part of Marxist jargon handed down to him with the administrative system. There

is no exact equivalent in translation, unless it is the medieval phrase of the 'just price' as applied to labour and surplus value.

8 *Jugoslavia izmedju VIII i IX Kongresa SKJ*, Savezni Zavod za Statistiku, Beograd, 1969, table 8: 20.

9 In Croatia, in 1970, 40-50 000 cases were recorded of persons seeking help and advice from the Zagreb trade-union advice bureau. This is between 5 per cent and 6 per cent of the total workforce of the republic. They are the braver ones, who come to find help which the union is mostly unable to give. Commenting on the work of his bureaux the chief observes:

'There is reason to suspect that a large number of aggrieved people do not come because they are afraid of dismissal and the carryings-on which would ensue. Even those who do come ask us to keep it a secret from their managements . . . A worker can be got at not only if he constantly receives the most difficult jobs . . . but also when he gets the easiest, or none at all. In that case, if he asks my advice, I tell him straight out, get out of that place as fast as you can.' (Zupanov 1971: 445)

10 The effect on the working class of a decisive shift to market controls after 1965 has been catastrophic, even more so than for other social groups. A recent issue of *Politica* carried a joke which speaks volumes: 'Nowadays the priests don't ask you if you've fasted, they ask you if you are a worker. If you are, they give you absolution at once.' The period has been notable for its high rate of manual workers' defections from Party ranks. They made over 60 per cent of the total in 1965, but only formed about one third of the total Party membership.

References

BIERSTEDT, R. 1950. An Analysis of Social Power. *American Sociological Review* **15.**

DZINIC, F. 1961. Politicki i Strucni Profili Rukovodilca u Preduzecima. *Nasa Stvarnost* **10.**

GEIGER, T. 1969. Class Society in the Melting-Pot. In Celia S. Heller (ed.) *Structured Social Inequality.* London: Collier MacMillan Ltd.

JOVANOV, N. *et al.* 1967. *Obustave Rada.* Beograd: Centar za Politicke Studije i Obrazovanje.

JOVANOV, N. 1972. O Strajkovima u SFRJ. In *Drustveni Konflikti i Socijalisticki Razvoj Jugoslavije.* Ljubljana: Jugoslovensko Udruzenje za Sociologiju.

KAVCIC, B. 1966. O Protestnim Obustavama Rada. *Gledista* **2.**

—— 1969. The Employees Estimates, Opinions and Attitudes Concerning Labour Unions. *International Review of Sociology* Series II, 5 (2).

—— 1972. Drustveni Sistem i Konflikti u Radnim Organizacijama. In *Drustveni Konflikti i Socijalisticki Razvoj Jugoslavije* op. cit.

LOCKWOOD, D. 1958. *The Blackcoated Worker*. London: Unwin University Books.

MATIC S. 1960. Tri Ankete o Funkcioniranju Radnickog Samoupravljanja. *Sociologija* 1.

MOZINA, S. 1971. Izvori Konflikata u Radnim Organizacijama. *Sociologija* 3.

POPOV, N. 1969. Strajkovi u Jugoslovenskom Drustvu. *Sociologija* 4.

RUS, V. 1966a, Socijalni Procesi i Struktura Moci u Radnoj Organizaciji *Sociologija* 4.

—— 1966b. Klike u Radnim Organizacijama. *Gledista* 8-9.

SIBER, I. *et al.* 1966. Percepcija Distribucije Utjecaja u Radnoj Organizaciji. *Politicka Misao* 4.

TANNENBAUM, A. 1962. Control in Organizations. *Administrative Science Quaterly* 7 September: 239.

TAVCAR, J. 1967. Normativna Delatnost Radnih Organizacija na Podrucju Radnih Odnosa. In Blagojevic T. (ed.) *Mesto i Uloga Normativne Delatnosti Radnih Organizacija u Pravnom Sistemu SFRJ*. Beograd: Pravni Fakultet.

VASILEV, M. HADZI 1967. Dva Prilaza Reorganizaciji Saveza Komunista. In Nikolic M. (ed.) *SKJ u Uslovima Samoupravljanja*. Beograd: Kulruta.

ZUPANOV, J. 1969. *Samoupravljanje i Drustvena Moc*. Zagreb: Biblioteka Nasih Tema.

—— 1971a. Contribution to a colloquium in Drustvena Pokretljivost i Razvojne Perspektive Jugoslovenskog Drustva. *Gledista* 11-12.

—— 1971b Upravljanje Industrijskim Konfliktom u Radnim Organizacijama. *Sociologija* 3.

K

J. M. COUSINS and R. L. DAVIS

'Working Class Incorporation'—A Historical Approach with Reference to the Mining Communities of S.E. Northumberland 1840-1890

THE INCORPORATION THESIS AND EXPLANATION OF WORKING-CLASS POLITICAL ACTION

It is at first sight surprising that a decade which has seen several studies that have appeared to confirm the continued integrity of the working class should have ended on a note of despair or resignation about the political effectiveness of that class.

> 'It seems rather unlikely that the proletariat carries *in itself* the power to be a class *for itself*.' (Mann 1973: 73)
> 'To the particularism of the working class there had logically to correspond a whole web of particularisms, the weird heterogeneity and pluralism of society as a whole in England. The English social world *had* to become a world of the inexplicably concrete, the bizarre, the eccentric individual thing and person defying analysis. Is this not the true historical sense of the quiet madness of England?' (Nairn 1972: 202)
> 'A question mark is put against the continuation of radical perceptions in Britain and other countries where the mass working-class party has virtually ceased to disseminate an oppositional view on the reward system.' (Parkin 1972: 10)

Two main types of argument have been used to explain the alleged or apparent political ineffectiveness of the working class. The older argument is essentially derived from the lack of homogeneity within the working class caused by either a 'labour aristocracy' or categories of 'new' or 'affluent' workers who in crucial respects are unlike (or even opposed to) other workers in their status, level of rewards, degree of organization, or social aspirations. The labour aristocracy argument in its classical form, of course, argues for the existence only of a small privileged minority (Hobsbawm 1964). The typifications devised by Lockwood for different types of worker (Lockwood 1966) are not limited in that way, although if the affluent worker is merely 'proto-typical' (Goldthorpe *et al.* 1968) he must be assumed to be, if only at present, a minority not too dissimilar from the earlier conception of the labour aristocracy. Nonetheless the 1966 typifications, like that of the labour aristocracy, point to the lack of homogeneity of the working class as an explanation of political ineffectiveness. The architects of the *Affluent Worker* clearly admit this possibility though trying to contest it (Goldthorpe *et al.* 1969). We have elsewhere tried to point out (Davis and Cousins 1972) that the difficulty in employing this argument is that while it is easy to argue for the existence of differences, or sectionalism, in the working class it is less easy to compose these differences into rival or alternative types of enduring importance and internal coherence; even if differences *do* take such a form in some respect they may often be overlaid by other factors making for a wider unity (e.g. Brown *et al.* 1972). The arguments that Pelling adduces against the concept of a labour aristocracy (Pelling 1968) can equally well be mounted against the elegant typifications of 1966. Historically, lack of homogeneity results in the changing position of working-class groups as much as the mere existence of these groups: 'new' workers therefore become 'old'; situationally, workers are faced with competing allegiances or definitions of self in the situation, sometimes of an extremely complex kind. Patterns of working-class identification, even if heterogeneous, are not necessarily *fixed*. The argument arising out of lack of homogeneity can-not then distract from, and may indeed in a sense actually support, the view that the fundamental reality of the working-class situation is that labour is a commodity. That is, that the uncertainties of working-class identification and the irregularities of working-class experience might be held to result from the uncertainties accompanying labour's com-modity status.

But recently another argument has been advanced, derived in one version from the New Left out of Gramsci, and in another version seemingly influenced by phenomenological sociology: the working class is ineffective because it has been 'incorporated'. It is this argument to which we intend to address ourselves here. The second argument is quite unlike the first since it openly admits and indeed depends upon the unity of the working class at some (unspecified) cultural level. The working class has been 'incorporated' but swallowed whole and perfectly intact. The culture of the workers, though all-pervasive for workers, and limited only to them, is a subordinate culture. It is 'hermetic' in the sense that it encloses the working class; yet it is also 'permeated' by non working-class norms and institutional forms and behaviour so that this enclosure ensures subordination rather than, as the labour aristocracy argument tended to assume about working-class homogeneity, 'dominance', or 'hegemony'.

Naturally this summary does not adequately represent the arguments involved; and as will appear later there are important alternative glosses in the structure of the overall argument. Nonetheless this does represent a general theme of analysis first inaugurated by Anderson's influential essay, 'Origins of the Present Crisis'.

'The working class fought passionately and unaided against the advent of industrial capitalism, its extreme exhaustion after successive defeats was the measure of its efforts. Henceforward it evolved, separate but subordinate, within the apparently unshakeable structure of British capitalism, unable, despite its great numerical superiority, to transform the fundamental nature of British society . . . the power structure of English society today can be most accurately described as an immensely elastic and all-embracing hegemonic order . . . This imperative order not merely sets external limits to the actions and aims of the subordinated bloc, it structures its intimate vision of itself and the world imposing contingent historical facts as the necessary co-ordinates of social life itself. The hegemonic class is the primary determinant of consciousness, character and customs throughout society.' (Anderson 1965: 29-30)

Again:

'The English working class has since the mid nineteenth century been essentially characterised by an extreme disjunction between an intense consciousness of separate identity and a permanent failure to set and impose goals for society as a whole. In this disjunction lies the secret of the specific nature of the working-class movement in England. *The very intensity of its corporate class consciousness, realized in and through a distinct hermetic culture has blocked the emergence of a universal ideology in the English working class.* It has not been lack of class consciousness but – in one sense – excess of it which has been the obstacle to the commitment of the working class to socialism.' (Anderson 1965: 34 – original italics)

A series of arguments analogous to this in their general formulation have subsequently been presented. Thus, Nairn has written that the English working class '. . . after the 1840s . . . quickly turned into an apparently docile class. It embraced one species of moderate reformism after another, became a consciously subordinate part of bourgeois society, and has remained wedded to the narrowest and gravest of bourgeois ideologies in its principle movements' (Nairn 1972: 198).

Similarly Young has argued that the 'popular egalitarian-collectivism' of the working class is '. . . in part traditional, in part articulated in opposition to the other major normative deviation from the paternalist traditionalism – bourgeois individualism, utilitarianism and political economy'. The major expression of this collectivism was '. . . the creation of a set of, what became eventually largely defensive, institutional bulwarks which protected and insulated normative alternatives . . . Thus it is concluded that the hermetic culture whilst preserving class identity, has by way of introverting consciousness kept the class and its ideals, subordinate' (Young 1967: 2-3).

From a different route, the phenomenological concern with normative structures and meaning-systems, sociologists were advancing towards analogous positions. Parkin's 'two-cultures' theory of political loyalties was the first sign of this (Parkin 1967). The same type of explanation was taken up by Mann in 1970.

'Cohesion is therefore affected by the relative success of society's insulation processes as well as by the nature of the values themselves . . . where insulation processes operate cohesion results precisely because there is no common commitment to core values . . . Thus the most common form of manipulative socialization by the liberal democratic state does not seek to change values, but rather to perpetuate values that do not aid the working-class to interpret the reality it actually experiences . . . For the reason why most working-class people do not "accept" (in whatever sense) their lot and do not have consistent deviant ideologies we must look back to the historical incorporation of working-class political and industrial movements in the nineteenth and twentieth centuries within existing structures.' (Mann 1970: 424, 437).

In this counterpointing of 'deviant' and 'dominant' values and the linkage of this to incorporation and insulated cultures of inadequate interpretation, Mann's argument is very close to Anderson's and apparently arrived at independently.[1]

Parkin has outlined not different levels of consciousness but different modal types of consciousness in society – the dominant value system, the subordinate value system, and the radical or oppositional value system (Parkin 1971). Empirical variations in consciousness are seen as dependent partly on access to these 'meaning systems' in a way that echoes Mann's references to insulation. The subordinate value system is identified with the working class:

> 'the generating milieu of this value system is the local working class community . . . the subordinate value system could be said to be essentially accommodative; that is to say its representation of the class structure and inequality emphasizes various modes of adaptation, rather than either full endorsement of, or opposition to, the status quo . . . it would be misleading to construe the subordinate value system as an example or normative opposition to the dominant order, least of all perhaps should it be understood as exemplifying class-consciousness or political radicalism . . . Nor is the pervasive sense of communal solidarity which is typically found in the underclass milieu to be equated with a class outlook on politics and society.' (Parkin 197: 88-9).

The insulation process works in such a way that it operates inside men's consciousness – 'the answer will depend on the level of generality at which the inquiry is pitched'. For abstract questions the worker refers to dominant values; situationally or concretely he is more likely to use class values. That is to say, Parkin is referring to something akin to Mann's vicious circle of levels of consciousness; and to Nairn and Anderson's parallel concept of a hermetic but permeated culture.

But despite these apparent similarities it can be seen that this newer theme of conceptualization about the working-class is quite different from the earlier arguments from lack of homogeneity. It is constructed around generally agreed key words: culture, subordination, incorporation. An examination of the argument more closely reveals considerable variegation about what factors compose these three elements and how they are related. These matters are critical. It will be seen that some of this group of writers see the line of development running from culture to incorporation leaving culture as the initial cause. This seems a little un-Marxist, particularly as the periods of culture formation (post 1840s) and the periods of incorporation (post 1880s) are so far apart. And what exactly is this culture anyway? A second group of writers while concentrating on culture see incorporation as being the root cause. But Mann, while referring us to incorporation and traditions of compromised economism, does not offer much of an explanation either as to how incorporation occurred at the outset or how incorporation was transmitted in such a way as to produce the results he describes. This seems necessary if we are to accept this longterm impossibilism. Parkin, while firmly rejecting many of the secondary cultural explanations discussed by Mann, places the main weight of his argument on 'de-radicalization' of the working-class mass parties. The explanation of this however takes a mere six pages (Parkin 1971: 130-6) and is focused on the familiar themes of bourgeoisification of leadership, the need for middle-class electoral support, and the compromising effects of working an alien system.

(1) The argument from culture

For Anderson and Nairn the culture of the English working class is not merely subordinate, it is a specific culture of subordination and incorporation. It is a culture of defeat formed in the 'profound caesura' that followed the collapse of Chartism. In this 'caesura' exactly what happened to English culture? Anderson only tells us that Marxism (which had 'for simple technical-educational reasons to be the work of non-working class intellectuals' (Anderson 1965:21)) was missed. 'In England . . . Marxism came too late: the Communist Manifesto was written just two months before the collapse of Chartism' (Anderson 1965: 21). But Marxism also came too early as well. 'It was not until the 1880s that the working class really began to recover from the traumatic defeat of the 1840s. By then the world had moved on. In consciousness and combativity, the English working class had been overtaken by almost all its continental opposites. Marxism had missed it' (Anderson 1965: 25). In truth, the only defeat really examined by Anderson and Nairn in English working-class culture is its failure to be dominated by socialist intellectuals (see esp. Nairn 1972: 204-6). Anderson stresses the failure of the intellectuals to lead the working class. Nairn stresses the need for 'consciousness, theory, an intellectual grasp of social reality '. . . 'the working class had to become . . . a class dominated by reason' (Nairn 1972: 200). Clearly Anderson and Nairn have a rather special understanding of culture; and attribute to it a rather special importance. For in a later article Anderson goes so far as to say 'there was never *any chance* of there being a hegemonic strategy available to the Left in Britain' (Anderson 1966: 23 – original italics).

From the failure of Marxism to secure intellectual mastery of English working-class culture a number of secondary failures are derived such as the survival of a myth of a pre-industrial golden age and the hope of its restoration in the working class; the failure to resist the influence of

Fabianism; the failure to challenge social imperialism; the failure of the leadership to resist implication in social relations with pseudo-feudal significance; the failure above all to clean up anti-intellectual English bourgeois thought with its 'thick pall of philistinism and mystagogy'.

(2) The argument from incorporation

Young and Mann seem to take up this position. Young's position is more explicit in asserting that the working class did develop 'a nascent counter-culture' (Young 1967). In this he is not merely taking up a different position from Anderson and Nairn he also uses culture in a less particular way and traces the connection between culture and 'counter-institutional formation'. Quoting 'industrial groups, friendly societies, village life' he says an 'implicit rival societal frame' *was* created. Again, unlike Anderson and Nairn, he sees the myth of the pre-industrial golden age as supporting an anti-capitalist communalism which later underpinned 'myriads of characteristic defensive class institutions' (Young 1967: 13, 15). Thus Young's argument is dependent on incorporation. 'Having been defined as deviant these institutions ['of proletarian collectivism'] were at first repressed, then accommodated and finally incorporated into the structure of the nation-state'. Young is also sceptical of the importance of secondary sources of subordination such as religion and imperialism. 'The crucial nexus of civic and national incorporation' is identified as 'the Labour Party in Parliament' (Young 1967:3). Even the unions Young regards as potential agents of transformation but for 'three factors which enabled the gap to be bridged and the unions incorporated. First the lack of any hegemonic ideology based on industrial actions; second, industrial collaboration; and third, *by far the most important* the incorporative parliamentarianism involved in the Labour Party' (Young 1967: 22 – our italics). It is unclear from Young's argument whether he regards the aim of getting into Parliament or the consequences of participation in it once arrived as being the main cause of incorporation. Either or both of these factors clearly have to carry the main strain of his argument. But can they? It is not clear why incorporation should have occured so successfully particularly as he also conceives the native culture of the workers as continuing unaffected. Thus his argument, at first sight likely to be more structurally grounded than Anderson and Nairn's, ends on a note of collusion and betrayal by a small number of Parliamentary leaders. We are not told what mechanics of transmission ensured the dominance of the incorporation strategy nor why Parliamentary methods were resorted to in the first place, or why once resorted to, had such calamitous effects.

Mann's 1970 articles concentrates mainly on outlining the 'pragmatic' subordination of the working class. Like Parkin he sees the working class as having a duality of allegiance, though rather in terms of levels of consciousness than in types of situation (e.g. 'a conflict between dominant and deviant values taking place within the individual' (Mann 1970: 437)). Hence the working class has neither normative values of its own nor does it accept the normative values of society. But the pragmatism of the workers seems to extend to Mann's arguments. It seems that 'only those actually sharing in societal power need develop consistent societal values'. The failure to develop societal values amongst workers is therefore part of the workers' failure to control society; and vice versa. Neither can therefore be used to explain the other. Mann refers to socialization through the educational system, though admits 'that the most common form of manipulative socialization by the liberal democratic state does not seek to change values, but rather to perpetuate values that do not aid the working-class to interpret the reality it actually experiences'. Mann thus points out the insufficiency of this argument; he does the same for 'voluntray deference, nationalism . . .' and 'false consciousness' as well. The impressive fact of pragmatic role acceptance is then referred briefly to the 'historical incoporation' of the working class. Thus, as in the case of Young, plausible secondary explanations of subordination are mentioned only to be rejected in favour of the primacy of a rather weakly-stated case for incorporation.[2]

(3) The argument from subordination

Parkin seems to reject as full explanations both arguments based on culture and arguments based on incoporation. The mass party he sees not as the locus of incorporation but of the radical, oppositional value system, able to change and radicalize the subordinate consciousness of workers (Parkin 1971). This is a marked contrast with both Mann and Young. Parkin does, though, agree with Mann on trade-union economism. 'Collective bargaining and its attendant strategies imply a general acceptance of the rules governing distribution. Organised labour directs its main efforts toward winning a greater share of resources for its members – not by challenging the existing framework of rules but by working within this framework' (Parkin 1971: 91). This unusual separation of union and Party suggests that Parkin is taking up a position similar to Anderson and Nairn's stress on the role of political theory and socialist intellectuals. Parkin sees the mass Party still as an important source of 'the moral content' and 'class basis' of politics; and he sees de-radicalization resulting as much from the empirical failure of social-democratic governments to master social forces opposed to them as to any necessary process in incorporation itself. It is a series of political defeats as much as a process of absorption that results in merito-cratic socialism. On the other hand he maintains a commitment to more traditional variants of incorporation – the routinization of the working-class organization, the acculturation of working-class leaders, and the entrance of bourgeois recruits. Even in the midst of this, however, an equal place is seen for electoral exigency – the Party cannot mobilize its full class support or must mobilize non-worker groups in order to win power. Thus Parkin's argument, at the least, puts an equal stress on the pre-given fact of subordination resulting in political defeat at the polls, or in power, as on incorporation itself.

How then does Parkin account for this subordination? While he does not see subordination as being overcome except by a radical value-system from *outside* the local working-class culture, nor does he see working-class culture as being inherently subordinate. It can be modi-fied; and in working-class experience there are ready made points of entry for the radical value-system. Though permeated by dominant values it can be permeated by radical ones as well. Parkin then finds the cause of subordination not in working-class culture but in specific sets of constraints which keep the working-class subordinate and obstruct the growth of radical value-systems; and also cause the lowering of working-class expectations. It looks as though Parkin is going to offer a structural explanation of working-class action that depends neither on an intrinsic cultural defect nor on a narrowly based and ill-defined incorporation. And of course it is just such an explanation that is needed not merely from the standpoint of socialist analysis, but from the standpoint of sociology. For the defect of other arguments discussed here is that they seem to be rather vaguely stated; and purpose-built to explain things that did not happen rather than things that did.

But unfortunately Parkin does not offer such an explanation. He makes reference to the role of education in reinforcing allegiance to market principles; to the influence of socialization; to the role of the socially mobile in class permeation; to the reduction of ambition by the lower class, its sense of failure induced by examinations and the content of the educational system. But Parkin himself regards such explanations as partial; he is openly sceptical about the role of religion in this process. And in the last analysis Parkin offers not a structural but a mystical explanation. 'It is this tendency for the underclass to throw up symbolic systems which explain their life situation in secular, non-political terms which is perhaps the most important of the safety-valves we have discussed in this chapter' (Parkin 1972: 77). Thus the 'underclass' are resigned and acceptant – because they are resigned and acceptant.

Parkin's analysis, like the others, seeks to explain working-class political action by perceptions and not by resources. And the admitted inadequacy of the explanations of the perceptive failures leads to one of two conclusions: either some very strong tide is running somehow, somewhere, that it is and will be impossible to resist; or alternatively, that the whole problem is a fictional one; that the working-class is a sociologically 'analytic' or a-prioristic category that would be better dispensed with. Mann's statement that class in itself and class for itself are likely always to be separate seems indeed to point to both of these conclusions.

WORKING-CLASS CONSCIOUSNESS AND COMMODITY PRODUCTION

Our intention here is not to 'test' any or all of these ideas built around culture, subordination, and incorporation. Indeed, given the variegated nature of the explanations, any test is probably impossible to devise. It is merely to suggest that what is needed is a much closer grounding of the argument in the industrial and economic situation of the working class. Mann argues that the four levels of working-class consciousness that he postulates (Mann 1973) are not reducible to the conflict of capital and labour; and that therefore the non-work sector of life is an autonomous source of consciousness. Mann does not tell us what these forms of consciousness might be other than by saying that they favour economism. But even this implies that there may be dominant types of consciousness among workers that are not reducible to the category of specifically working-class types of consciousness. This is a critical argument for by it not merely is work divided from non-work, but consciousness and perception are separated from economic determinants. Mann's economism can be thus not merely the preference for certain forms of economic action over others; it presents theoretically the possibility of the subordination of consciousness derived from economic action to other forms of consciousness with different origins.

We would suggest: (1) that the conflict of capital and labour, though implicit in the economic situation of the working-classes, is not the essential feature of this situation; and (2) that the concept of commodity may lead to a much better understanding of it. The non-work aspects of working-class life are readily relatable to, but are not reducible to, the economic situation of workers (construed less narrowly than the conflict of capital and labour); this constitutes in our view not the cause of working-class political ineffectiveness, but rather one of the proofs of its success. The claim that sectors of life should or do systematically operate on the basis of personal or use-value criteria rather than market or surplus-value criteria – as qualities or services rather than commodities – may be a challenge to the dominant value-system rather than a sign of insulation, and pragmatic acceptance of capitalist hegemony (Mann 1973).

The existence of commodity-production follows from the social division of labour. Labour is concentrated in great masses thus potentially becoming aware of its great strength; it is also specialized in separate tasks and this diversity of tasks appears in an institutionalized and reified form as separate occupations and industries with competing claims over tasks and rewards, and as different labour markets. In short, both concentration and homogeneity *and* division and fragmentation result. Simultaneously, the worker's labour is identified as the source of all production, yet it becomes dependent on a co-ordinated system of production on which his job, and the supply of goods he no longer provides for himself by his specialized labour, both depend. In short, while labour is abstractly 'the source of all value', the specific quanta of labour represented by jobs and occupations are dependent on the system of commodity production as a whole. As markets become international, and the lines of financial co-ordination and physical distribution become longer, this dependency increases. Thus the worker appears not merely to have separate interests as producer and consumer; but producers and consumers are themselves physically and organizationally separated. Both in their necessary opposition of interests as producers and consumers, and in their necessary and mutually sustaining connections they are dependent on the co-ordination of the market (Mc Clellan 1971). Subordination, 'hermetic' privatization of working-class culture, incorporation, are thus not cultural or political products. They are a necessary and logical feature of the system of commodity-production. But so also is the potential for their opposites. The 'dualistic consciousness' to which Mann refers (Mann 1973) is undoubtedly a result but cannot be mapped onto simple dualities of work and non-work; or economism or control.

Three strategies are open to workers in this situation. They can, first, assert their independence and self-control (their personal or human status as opposed to their commodity status) by pursuing individualistic strategies of mobility. But this only ends by emphasizing their commodity status. Or, second, they can isolate certain sectors of life (as described before) as services and not commodities, and so free them from the market. Or, finally they can replace co-ordination by the capitalist or the market by planning and social control. We hope to show eventually that in the case of the Northumberland miners there was a slow evolution towards this third strategy, at least up to 1945. But all we attempt here is a description of how the commodity situation of the Northumberland miner, with all its contradictions, resulted in social and organizational contradictions in the critical early years of permanent unionization.

COMMODITY PRODUCTION AND 'CONSERVATIVE' TRADE UNIONISM

The earlier discussion of class incorporation revealed considerable vagueness about the period and the mechanisms of incorporation. The period after 1880, and the development of trade unions and working class participation in Parliament seem, though, to provide the setting for most of these discussions. The Northumberland coalfield during this period saw the development of both a permanent union, which early on developed the character of being one of the more 'conservative' miners' organizations, and also some of the first involvements of workers in politics – Thomas Burt, the secretary of the union, being elected a miner M.P. for Morpeth in 1874; and Fenwick, another miners' leader, being elected for Wansbeck in 1885. An account of the 'progress' or 'development' of the local and regional institutions of south-east Northumberland (specifically, of Seaton Valley) from the 1840s to the 1880s can easily be made to portray a gradual evolution of institutions of a certain type and political character (in the widest sense), which by their very nature incorporate their constituents or clients into society. However, what one loses in such an account is an idea of the basic nature and position of those constituents or clients. This, and the contradictions inherent in it, can only be seen in the light of external constraints imposed upon the Northumberland coal industry.

Briefly, combinations of workmen had existed prior to the nineteenth century, but unions as such only began to develop in Northumberland along with the expansion of the industry, the direction of resources put into it, and the use by entrepreneurs of labour as a commodity. Chronologically, the story is usually one of formation, defeat, and dissolution – until the 1860s. Hepburn's union of 1825 (usually called 'the first', and known as 'The Colliers of the United Association of Northumberland and Durham') struck in 1831 for more wages, shorter hours, and a lessening of the owners' powers (such as 'Tommy' shops, for instance). This strike was partially successful, but victimization of union men subsequently took place; another strike was called, only to be broken by blacklegs and evictions, and the union was beaten and fragmented. In 1842-3 the 'second union' formed itself – the Miners Association of Great Britain and Ireland – a *national* union to which Northumberland belonged. It is this organization that Challinor (1968) refers to as 'a union in the age of Chartists'. Its aims were 'to lessen hours, get fair wages, agitate for government interference, and for inspectors to enforce the law'. At the end of the 'bond' in 1844 it struck – for 'a fair day's pay for a fair day's work'. The strike lasted sixteen weeks, during which time the union made a great attempt to ensure their members 'kept the peace'. The strike failed, the owners won by importing black-leg labour, and at the end were able to impose a new system of bonding based on a monthly period instead of a yearly one (Fynes 1873; Welbourne 1923). Following this, Fynes says, unionism died; Welbourne contends that the *idea* lived on. Certainly, a formal union did not appear again until 1862; it followed the Hartley mining disaster, and concerned itself largely with safety, having as one of its objects 'the better protection of the labours of the members'. In the same year, the Miners' Permanent Relief Fund had come to exist. In 1864, the Northumberland men seceded from the organization and called themselves the Northumberland Miners' Mutual Confidence Association. In 1865 Thomas Burt was elected secretary and agent (in the middle of another long strike for an advance of wages at Cramlington). This union survived all further troubles, though with difficulty, and came to be *the* union of the Northumberland miners. This union was noted both then and now for its defensive and accommodative strategies.

Although coal mining in Northumberland has a history traceable to Roman times (Archer 1897), the real 'opening-up' of a Northumberland coal-*field* did not take place until the nineteenth century. Technological developments such as improved mining techniques and railways (Atkinson 1966); demand from industrial and domestic centres for good quality coal; the dissolution of restrictive practices like the 'Vend' (owners' agreed restriction of output in a near monopoly situation so as to raise prices); and competition from other coalfields previously unable to exploit their reserves because of transport problems; all this combined to produce the rapid development of the deeper reserves of Northumberland. Northumberland and especially south-east Northumberland, became a coal producing area of a specialist kind, with a high proportion of its population engaged in mining or associated activities. The price of this process was to produce, on the part of the actors caught up in it, a much greater dependence on external forces (especially markets outside the region and abroad) than had previously been the case when some diversity of activity had existed.

In south-east Northumberland, for instance, coal was mined near Blyth in the seventeenth and eighteenth centuries both for export and use in local manufacturing industries (Sullivan 1971). At Bedlington, iron-works began operations in 1736 and briefly prospered in the early nineteenth century when a method of utilizing coal for smelting was implemented. On the coast, Seaton Sluice exported coal from the Hartley pits and manufactured glass and salt (Burgess 1972). The inland area now known as Seaton Valley supported a few landsale pits (small works getting at coal near the surface) while being mainly agricultural (Parsons and White, 1828).[3]

These 'local economies' seem to have suffered a decline alongside the intensive exploitation of the coalfield and diversion of resources into greater coal production, exemplified by the demise of Hartley, the problems faced by the Bedlington iron works until its collapse in 1865, and more spectacularly by the virtual elimination of the Northumberland pig-iron manufacturing industry in the second half of the nineteenth century. Accompanying all this, the new pits in the Seaton Valley area began to be sunk, beginning with Backworth in 1818 and continuing with Cramlington (2), Earsdon and Seghill (in the 1820s) and Seaton Delaval, West and East Holywell and New Hartley (by the 1840s).

Such activities, aided by imported capital and undertaken largely by new entrepreneurs and speculators, led to wholesale movements of population within and into the area and a subsequent increase in the production of steam coal. Local control, however, over the conditions of that production, had been undermined with the dissolution of the 'Vend'. The new colliery proprietors were not large-scale capitalists, but the heads of at best medium-sized companies with responsibilities to subscribers in the national investment markets (Leifchild 1856). (Mergers did begin to take place towards the later part of the century.) They had to compete, also, with other developing British coal-fields for home markets. Foreign exports, though long a feature of the trading situation, came to assume a much larger and regular importance. Thus, just as the working community of the coal-field came to be dependent upon an entrepreneurial class for its existence, this class was itself strategically in a position of dependency upon external forces, over which it had little control. Coal owners and the colliers were both to an extent partners in dependence on the commodity system.

That this mutual dependency was in part recognized by the working population we can only suppose; but the mining population was in many respects a migratory one. In Seaton Valley, for instance, the labour force was comprised of men and their families who, on the decline of the Tyneside and neighbouring pits, had moved northwards. Such population shifts corresponding to the exhaustion of flooding of colleries were a common feature of the industry. Not until the coming of deep-mining and adequate pumping was mining a continuous and settled source of employment.[4] Being a miner meant moving, and the mining population was familiar with this fact of life. Their livelihoods were dominated by their status as a commodity. Upon this depended their provision of basic human necessities, like housing, since the provider of these was in nearly every case the employer, the house going with the job. (Eviction was held as the major threat in any prolonged industrial dispute.) Welfare of some sorts was also his responsibility, like the decision whether to compensate for loss of work through accident by the customary payment of 'Smart money'. Thus, the functions of employer, landlord, and general provider were incumbent upon the employing class. The latter's own dependency upon market forces was all to clear.[5] In fact, the basic economic position of the Northumberland coal-field was its dependence on export markets outside its own control.[6] To an extent therefore, the owners and the miners had logical grounds for common action; and the industrial relations strategy of the miners' union cannot therefore be regarded as simply accommodative. The patterns of relations of subordination and dependence in a commodity-system are more complex than is allowed for in the simple theories of class incorporation we have described.

Thus the subordination of the Northumberland miner was inherent in his economic situation; the factors which composed this subordination were central to his experience and widely understood. The Northumberland coal trade, particularly that part of it which produced steam coal, was dependent on extra-regional export markets. The coal-owners were not in control of their markets. The miner was therefore not merely dependent upon the coalowners for employment and housing but dependent with him on the fate of the industry. In north Durham, Cumberland, and Northumberland employment rose by 80 per cent in the boom period of the early 1870s. Employment then fell by 25 per cent in Northumberland during the middle 1880s and slowly rose again to its previous levels. These facts conditioned the industrial relations

L

strategy of the miners' union. Variations in the claimed membership of the miners' union were much sharper than in employment as a whole. Between 1874 and 1879 the miners' union lost over half its members, the density of union membership in the labour force went down from about 80 per cent to between 45-46 per cent. Ironically it is just this period which ends in the adoption of a sliding wage-scale that might be seen as the victory of economism and incorporation. It is likely that the sliding scale in fact preserved the union from collapse. And with the adoption of the sliding scale membership immediately began to recover, though the level of employment was continuing to fall. A considerable penalty was incurred for the attempt at resistance of the economic constraints. After the strike of 1887 union funds per member declined from 42s. 7½d to 5s. 7½d; and the steady recovery of membership was (briefly) halted. Union action was limited by necessity not choice. The potential price of failure was the existence of the union organization itself. Yet in fact policies of resistance and opposition continued to be urged despite the difficulties.

Isolated strike action in the economic circumstances of the coal-field, where pits were not directly linked to ironworks and factories, was in fact likely to be ruinous to the organization that attempted to support such a strike; Burt in fact became secretary of the union during the near-disastrous Cramlington strike of 1865. The union rules forbade strike action except by consent of the Executive and a two-thirds majority ballot vote. New pits joining the union were examined carefully for the likelihood of strike action there.[7]

Much of the effort of the union was devoted to securing unity within the organization. Hewers, who composed about half the mining labour force, were pieceworkers.[8] It was also faced by pressure groups within its organization for banksmen, stonemen, mechanics, and others. The system of 'county average rates' inaugurated in 1872 was designed to preserve the internal unity of the organization. No case for increases at a particular colliery was submitted by the union unless the rate concerned produced earnings 5 per cent less than the county average. Similarly the owners prevented their members applying for a reduction unless the rate concerned was more than 5 per cent over the county average rate. In 1879 the first of a series of sliding scales, based on coal prices, was adopted at the union's request as the basis of the county average to produce more frequent and smaller adjustments. The system of continuous adjustment is thus by no means simply either economism or incorporation or the acceptance of market evaluations. It helped to produce unity in the labour force and much less abrupt variations in wages and earnings. It was the union which first pressed for the adoption of a sliding scale, and the seventeen-week strike of 1887 was a strike against a reduction, which though warranted by market conditions of the scale, was far more abrupt, than any adjustment for ten years. From November 1878 to May 1887 fourteen adjustments had occurred, six up and eight down, but none of more than $2\frac{1}{2}$ per cent. Thus the sliding scale represented as much an attempt to achieve a stable level of earnings as it did an acceptance of the market.

SOCIAL AND POLITICAL ORGANIZATION IN THE MINING COMMUNITIES

The same structural difficulties that we have noted in the case of the union can be seen in the wider social and political life of the mining communities. The same difficulties of interpretation are presented. But once again we would argue that the ambiguities are structured; i.e., strategies of independence, opposition, and 'incorporation' are all present; and all are related directly to the economic situation of the miner. The period after 1860 does certainly seem to be a period of organizational growth and organizational participation by the people of the mining villages. Yet the signs of this do not point unambiguously either to accommodation, opposition, or group self-assertion. Alongside the foundation of the union had come the formation of the Co-ops at West Cramlington in 1861. In 1862 a Co-op was started 'in the pantry of a colliery house' in Seaton Delaval; and this was followed in 1864 by a similar store in the Blyth mining suburb of New Delaval. Fynes in 1873 named at least nine village Co-ops in the coalfield areas.

Miners also became active in local politics, though somewhat later. Northumberland County Council was set up in 1889, and miners' candidates were first elected in 1898. Twelve miners' candidates were elected out of the fourteen places on the Holywell Parish Council in 1894, defeating the colliery manager and clerk; miners' candidates also took five of thirteen places on Seaton Delaval Parish Council the same year. Both these elections were hotly contested not merely by miners but by organized 'slates' of miner candidates. Elected local district councils were also formed during this same period at Cramlington in 1865, Seghill in 1895, and Earsdon in 1897.

Quite apart from the miners' participation in union politics there was a very high degree of voluntary organization in the mining villages. Records compiled from the *Blyth News* 1894-1897 (which are likely to be highly incomplete) show ten voluntary organizations in Seaton

Delaval, four in Seghill, three in a small district of Holywell called
Bates Cottages, seven at Cramlington, and five at New Hartley. These
organizations cover a wide range from mechanics institutes, church and
chapel organizations, to leek clubs, associations campaigning against
Armenian atrocities, and the Irish National League. Many of these
voluntary organizations might also be regarded as 'accommodative'
since they involved the joint participation of both miners and agents of
the coalowners as well as the local middle class, such as it was.

Typical of this was the management of the schools. Seghill Colliery
School, for example, was founded in 1861; it was run as 'an institution
of the colliery and shall not be dissolved except by the unanimous consent of owners and workmen'. The school was financed by miners'
levies; it was run by a committee on which the owner nominated
president, treasurer, and three committeemen; and the contributors
elected a vice-president and seven committeemen. Quarterly meetings
of contributors were to be held at which complaints would be heard.

CONCLUSIONS

To read the signs of the Northumberland miners' union with regard to
working-class incorporation is not a simple matter. The apparent
strategy of adaptation to market forces has a quite different motive: the
achievement of stable earnings. Large reductions produced crises
either within the union organization or between it and the coalowners.
Similarly while the union structured and limited working-class activity
it also served to make the miners a more homogeneous group of men, as
well as providing the organizational basis of the miners' involvement in
politics. Indeed the objects of the union were as much 'political' as
economistic in character being to 'obtain laws for the more efficient
management of mines; to procure an eight hour day for boys in mines;
to secure the wages contracted for and the true weight of material at the
pit-banks; to prevent illegal stoppages of wages; to support members
out of work through disputes, bad trade etc.; and to assist other societies
with similar objects'. Apparently, then, the miners' union knew very
well that it could not hope for control over the irregularities of economic
life except by 'political' or legislative means. No doubt this is the reason
for its very early participation in formal politics. This suggests that
economism and political incorporation are *different* rather than *identical*
strategies; and it also suggests that much of the evidence for incorporation can legitimately be interpreted in quite different ways. The union
provided the basis of the miners' participation in politics. And in

politics, as in industrial relations, the strategies of seeking representation to share and seeking representation to oppose are both present.

A study of the Northumberland miners' union then does not obviously confirm the simplistic versions of the incorporation thesis; nor the simplistic, but nonetheless contradictory notions of economism, culture, and subordination upon which the thesis relies. The structual subordination of workers to the commodity-system is a necessary, inherent, and well understood feature of advanced capitalist market societies. In its utter and immediate dependence on extra-regional and international trade the Northumberland coal-field of the 1870s was in this sense a 'modern' context for working-class action. This action and the organizations it produced are shot through with contradictions of the working-class situation. Outright oppositional policies risk the collapse of the organizational means of opposition so painstakingly built up; outright integrative policies mean the acceptance of unacceptably large cuts in pay which it is one of the main purposes of the organization to resist. Economism implies the attempt to regulate and socially control market forces; the coal coalowners both attempt to 'incorporate' and 'dis-incorporate' the union according to their own economic exigencies. To the extent that the proponents of the incorporation thesis do seize upon real historical events – such as the development of unions or working-class institutions they fail to see the double-meanings inherent in their growth – the means of resistance are themselves dependent; and the means of dependence are not unconditional and can generate opposition.

Nonetheless the logical object of working-class action as the proponents of incorporation see it – a revolutionary socialist transformation – has not occurred.[9] But the resulting impasse is a result of the theory not of the reality it purports to describe. The incorporation thesis ends by producing what it sets out to explain – the political isolation of the intellectuals. Perhaps the resulting combination of high ideals and low commitments can, like the contradictions implicit in an analysis of working-class action, be related to the structural exigences of their situation.

Notes

1 More recently Mann has conceived of four escalting levels of working-class consciousness: identity – opposition – totality – the conception of an alternative society (Mann 1973).

'Among manual workers in traditional industries a realistic appraisal
of alternative structures is lacking even among the most class conscious workers in the most explosive situations. Whatever the
objective possibility that they might be the bearers of a new principle of social structure – collectivism – they themselves either do not
perceive this or do not know how to translate it into action. Collectivism more often means for them collective identity. The explosion
of consciousness is trapped in a vicious circle (from identity to
opponent to totality and then back to identity) and so does not make
a revolution.' (Mann 1973: 69).

Yet while this is conceptually a better description of the failure to
break out of the vicious circle of subordination it does not provide a
better explanation apart from the compromising economism of the
working-class organizations.

2 It is true that Mann's latest work (1973) though it does not go further
into the whole argument for incorporation, does stress one particular
aspect of it: the economism of the trade unions. Mann sees the non-
work area of life as maintaining its autonomy of the work area. Indeed
the non-work area of life by favouring economism in trade unions
asserts its dominance over work. Mann also sees the duality of work
and non-work resulting in another duality: the split between strategies
of economism and job control at work. The dominance of work over
working-class consciousness is only conceivable in the first shock of
industrialization. From then on economism at work and outside work
gradually triumph by the institutionalization of conflict; the creation
of shop-floor links between employer and worker. This economism
accepts the hegemony of capitalism even when for tactical reasons (as
in factory occupations) it seems not to.

3 Local landowners often entered these activities: the Delaval family
(Knights but later aristocrats) developed Hartley commercially
(Burgess 1972), and the Ridleys (merchants, then landowners, then
aristocrats) did likewise with the Blyth area (Sullivan 1971).

4 For example, the deep mines of Wallsend, which gave their name to
the high grade housecoal of Tyneside, were sunk about 1800, flooded
in the 1850s and not re-opened until the late 1890s. This served to
underline the commodity-dependence status of the mining community.
Perhaps Thomas Burt's family was not untypical: his father was a
hewer from Hebburn, south of the Tyne, his mother from Cowpen,
and he was born in Backworth in 1837.

'From Murton Row, my parents moved to Whitley. After a year or
two an explosion occurred in the Whitely pit which compelled them
to seek a fresh home at Seghill Colliery, three or four miles northwards. This was the beginning of a wandering, gypsy life which

continued until I was fifteen years of age. Within that short period my father worked at some seven or eight collieries in Durham and Northumberland, and I can count no fewer than 18 houses in which we lived.'

This experience of mobility can be replicated, though in less detail, by case studies of the birth-places of mining households drawn from the census Enumeration books of 1851 and 1861.

5 In a memorandum to the Royal Commission on Labour of 1892 is the statement, by the Northumberland Miners Mutual Confidence Association, that 'as a large quantity of the coal produced in this country is exported to the Baltic, and as the Baltic ports are closed in winter, the pits usually work about 20 per cent less time from the end of October to the end of March than they do during the rest of the year'.

6 The divisions among the coalowners who organized into three different bodies with different functions and spreads of membership to some extent reflect this. The chief coalowners' association in Northumberland, the Steam Collieries Defence Association, was by no means solely aimed at the wages question. Strong complaints were also made by the coalowners on the question of royalties and wayleaves to landowners; and against the landowners who tried to prevent their colliery lessees from adopting the Limited Liability Acts (see evidence of R. Watson Cooper to the Royal Commission on Mine Royalties. C 6979. 1893: 27-45).

7 'They are working at peace with their employers; and there is no sign of anything else at the colliery' (report on the application of Longhirst colliery – NMMCA Delegate meeting 27 January, 1872). Interestingly, the rules of the owners' association imposed similar tests and restrictions.

8 Their pay varied considerably from colliery to colliery. In reports by the NMMCA from its lodges the variations were up to 40 per cent (NMMCA Council 15.5.1873 – 27 collieries: highest 10s 1d per shift, lowest 6s 3d; 27.9.1873 – 34 collieries: highest 10s 1d, lowest 7s 1½d).

9 As Mann himself appears to realize, such a transformation *without* the aid of mass unions or political parties is likely to be impossible or ugly (Mann 1973).

References

ANDERSON, P. 1965. Origins of the Present Crisis. In P. Anderson and R. Blackburn (eds). *Towards Socialism*. London: Fontana.
—— 1966. The Myths of Edward Thompson. *New Left Review* **35.**

ARCHER, M. 1897. *Sketch of the History of the Coal Trade of Northumberland and Durham*. London: King, Sell & Railton.

ATKINSON, F. 1966. *The Great Northern Coalfield 1700-1900*. Durham: Durham Co. Local History Society.

BAUMAN, Z. 1972. *Between Class and Elite*. Manchester: Manchester University Press.

BROWN, R. K. *et al*. 1972. The Contours of Solidarity. *British Journal of Industrial Relations* 10.

BURGESS, R. 1972. *Those Delavals*. Newcastle: Oriel Press.

BURT T. 1924. *Thomas Burt, pitman and privy councillor: an Autobiography*. London: Unwin.

CHALLINOR, R. and RIPLEY, B. 1968. *The Miners' Association: A Trade Union in the age of the Chartists*. London: Lawrence & Wishart.

COATES, K. and TOPHAM, T. 1968. *Industrial Democracy in Great Britain*. London: Macgibbon & Kee.

CRAMLINGTON DISTRICT CO-OPERATIVE SOC. LTD. 1912. *Jubilee Souvenir, 1861-1911*, Manchester: C.W.S. Press.

DAVIS, R. L. and COUSINS J. M. 1972. The 'New Working Class' and the Old. In *Proceedings* of the S.S.R.C. Conference, *The Occupational Community of the Traditional Worker*. Durham (limited circulation). (To be published by Routledge & Keegan Paul in 1974, edited by M.I.A Bulmer.)

FYNES, R. 1873. *The Miners of Northumberland and Durham: a History of their Social and Political Progress*.

GOLDTHORPE, J. H., LOCKWOOD, D., BECHHOFER, F. and PLATT, J. 1968. *The Affluent Worker: Industrial Attitudes and Behaviour*. Cambridge: Cambridge University Press.

—— 1969. *The Affluent Worker in the Class Structure*. Cambridge: Cambridge University Press.

GOLDTHORPE, J. H. 1972. Class, Status & Party in Modern Britain. *European Journal of Sociology* 12: 342-372.

HOBSBAWM, E. 1964. The Labour Aristocracy. In *Labouring Men*. London: Weidenfeld & Nicholson.

JEVONS, H. S. 1915. *The British Coal Trade*. London: Kegan Paul.

LEIFCHILD, J. 1856. *Our Coal and Our Coal Pits*. Newcastle: Oriel Press (2nd ed.).

LOCKWOOD, D. 1966. Sources of Variation in Working Class Images of Society. *Sociological Review* 14 (3).

MCCLELLAN D. 1971. *Marx's Grundrisse*. London: MacMillan.

MANN, M. 1970. The Social Cohesion of Liberal Democracy. *American Sociological Review* 35.

—— 1973. *Consciousness and Action among the Western Working Class*. London: MacMillan.

NAIRN, T. 1972. The English Working Class. In R. Blackburn (ed.) London: *Ideology and Social Science*. London: Fontana.

NORTHUMBERLAND COUNTY HISTORY COMMITTEE 1909. *History of Northumberland*, Vol. IX. Newcastle: Reid.

PARSONS and WHITE 1828. *Directory of Northumberland*. Newcastle: White.

PARKIN, F. 1967. Working Class Conservatism. *British Journal of Sociology*. **17**.

—— 1971. *Class, Inequality and Political Order*. London: MacGibbon & Kee.

PELLING, H. 1968. *Popular Politics and Society in Late Victorian Britain*. London: MacMillan.

SULLIVAN, W. R. 1971. *Blyth in the 18th Century*. Newcastle: Oriel Press.

STORM CLARK C. 1971. The Miners 1870-1970. *Victorian Studies* **14** September.

TAYLOR, H. A. 1963. *Historical Survey of Cramlington*. Unpublished paper: Northumberland County Record Office.

WELBOURNE, E. 1923. *The Miners Unions of Northumberland and Durham*. Cambridge: Cambridge University Press.

YOUNG, N. 1967 Prometheans or Troglodytes?. *Berkeley Journal of Sociology* **10** Summer.

OTHER SOURCES

Blyth News

Bulmer: *Directory of Northumberland*, 1887

Census Enumeration Books, 1851 and 1861 (microfilm, Northumberland County Records Office)

R. Hunt: *Mineral Statistics of G.B. and Ireland* (annual 1854-1881)

Mineral Statistics (annual 1881-1894)

Mines Inspectors Reports 1864

Northumberland Miners' Mutual Confidence Association (NMMCA) – Minutes and Records

Northumberland County Council – Minutes

Royal Commission on Labour 1892 *et seq*.

Royal Commission on Mining Royalties, 1895

Select Committee on Darness of Coal, 1873

Whellan: *Directory of Northumberland*, 1855

Name index

Name index

Name index

Subject index

Subject index